Legal
CORRECTIONS

Harvey Wallace, J.D.
Califronia State University, Fresno

Cliff Roberson, LL.M., Ph. D.
Washburn University

Australia • Brazil • Japan • Korea • Mexico • Singapore • Spain • United Kingdom • United States

Legal Aspects of Corrections
Harvey Wallace, J.D.,
Cliff Roberson

© 2000 Wadsworth, Cengage Learning

ALL RIGHTS RESERVED. No part of this work covered by the copyright herein may be reproduced, transmitted, stored or used in any form or by any means graphic, electronic, or mechanical, including but not limited to photocopying, recording, scanning, digitizing, taping, Web distribution, information networks, or information storage and retrieval systems, except as permitted under Section 107 or 108 of the 1976 United States Copyright Act, without the prior written permission of the publisher.

> For product information and technology assistance, contact us at **Cengage Learning Customer & Sales Support, 1-800-354-9706**
>
> For permission to use material from this text or product, submit all requests online at **www.cengage.com/permissions**
> Further permissions questions can be emailed to **permissionrequest@cengage.com**

Library of Congress Control Number: 99-91520

ISBN-13: 978-0-942728-92-7

ISBN-10: 0-942728-92-0

Wadsworth
20 Davis Drive
Belmont, CA 94002
USA

Cengage Learning is a leading provider of customized learning solutions with office locations around the globe, including Singapore, the United Kingdom, Australia, Mexico, Brazil, and Japan. Locate your local office at **www.cengage.com/global**

Cengage Learning products are represented in Canada by Nelson Education, Ltd.

To learn more about Wadsworth, visit
www.cengage.com/wadsworth

Purchase any of our products at your local college store or at our preferred online store **www.cengagebrain.com**

Printed in the United States of America
2 3 4 5 6 7 14 13 12 11 10

DEDICATION

To Tim Leonard and Laura Moss for their understanding, support and love.

Harvey Wallace

To Lynne

Cliff Roberson

PREFACE

As the discipline of corrections is maturing within academe, it has become apparent to the authors that a book devoted to the undergraduate level of study covering legal aspects of corrections was overdue. Thus, to this end, *Legal Aspects of Corrections* was written.

The authors bring to this topic a combination of over forty years of experience in the legal profession ranging from prosecution to prisoner advocacy and death penalty appeals. With these unique backgrounds, they provide a wealth of knowledge that is conveyed to the reader.

Legal Aspects of Corrections is designed to provide the reader with a general overview. Included are significant case decisions. A portion of the book is devoted to a discussion of prisoners' rights and the mechanics of litigating §1983 issues, in order to form a more complete understanding of our contemporary corrections legal scenario.

Correctional law is constantly evolving. The key legal issues discussed herein will be kept up-to-date within the instructor's manual and through timely revisions. It is our intention to keep this text and the instructional support material as current as possible.

Your comments and suggestions will be greatly appreciated and can be directed to the authors at *crimlawy@aol.com*.

Harvey Wallace
Cliff Roberson

TABLE OF CONTENTS

PREFACE .... *v*
TABLE OF CASES .... *xv*

Chapter 1

THE CORRECTIONAL PROCESS 1

PUNISHMENT 1
    Beginning of Legal Punishments 2
    Early Codes 3
    Middle Ages 4
PHILOSOPHY OF PUNISHMENT 5
    Purposes of Criminal Sanctions 5
        Retribution 6
        Deterrence 8
        Incapacitation 8
        Rehabilitation 9
    Social Purposes of Punishment 10
CHANGES TO THE "JUSTICE" PHILOSOPHY 10
    Sentencing Guidelines 12
    Presumptive Sentences 14
JUDICIAL PROCESS FOR MISDEMEANANTS 14
JUDICIAL PROCESS FOR FELONS 15
ALTERNATIVE SENTENCING AND DIVERSION 15
PRISON DISCIPLINE 16
    Disciplinary Hearing Procedures 16
    Grievances 18
    Rules of Conduct 20
RELEASE FROM CONFINEMENT 21

INTENSIVE SUPERVISION	22
SEX OFFENDER REGISTRATION LAWS	22
PRISONERS' RIGHTS	25
Areas of Involvement	27
Due Process Rights	27
Torts	27
Conditions of Confinement	28
Habeas Corpus	28
Prison Litigation Reform Act	30
BACK TO THE BASICS	30
CASE SUMMARIES	43
SUMMARY	45
DISCUSSION QUESTIONS	47
ENDNOTES	48

Chapter 2

THE COURT SYSTEM 51

COURT STRUCTURE	51
Introduction	51
The State System	53
Trial Courts	53
Courts of Appeals	55
Supreme Courts	55
The Federal System	55
Federal District Courts	56
Federal Circuit Courts	56
U.S. Supreme Court	56
THE PARTIES	57
The Victim	57
The Defendant	58
Law Enforcement	58
The Prosecutor	59

    The Defense Attorney 63
    The Judge 69
        Judge Selection 71
        Terms 72
        Federal Magistrates 73
    The Jury 74
PRETRIAL 76
    Decision to Prosecute 76
    Bail 77
    Pretrial Hearings 79
TRIAL 82
    Jury Selection 82
    Opening Statements 83
    Case in Chief 84
    Closing Arguments 84
    The Verdict 84
CASE SUMMARIES 85
SUMMARY 86
DISCUSSION QUESTIONS 87
ENDNOTES 88

Chapter 3

SENTENCING AND PLEA BARGAINING 89

PLEAS 89
PLEA BARGAINS 89
    Negotiated Pleas 91
    Due Process Requirements 92
    Statutory and Rule Requirements 94
    Right to Plead Guilty 100
BREACHES OF PLEA BARGAINS 103
RIGHTS DURING SENTENCING 104
SUMMARY 118

DISCUSSION QUESTIONS 119
ENDNOTES 120

Chapter 4

FREEDOM OF ASSOCIATION 121

INTRODUCTION 121
UNION MEMBERSHIP 122
NEWS MEDIA CONTACT 123
VISITATION 125
    Pretrial Detainees 129
    Conjugal Visits 130
    Exclusion of Certain Visitors 130
CASE SUMMARIES 138
SUMMARY 140
DISCUSSION QUESTIONS 140
ENDNOTES 142

Chapter 5

EXERCISE OF RELIGIOUS BELIEFS 143

RESTRICTIONS ON THE EXERCISE OF RELIGION 143
SECURITY OF THE INSTITUTION 146
    Maintaining Discipline 147
ECONOMICS 147
OFFICIAL DISCRETION 147
DIET 148
GROOMING 149
CASE SUMMARIES 157
SUMMARY 158

DISCUSSION QUESTIONS 159
ENDNOTES 160

Chapter 6

MAIL 161

INTRODUCTION 161
    Prison Security 161
    Orderly Administration 162
    Rehabilitation 162
REGULATION OF MAIL 162
OBSCENE MATERIAL 165
NUDE PHOTOGRAPHS 166
CASE SUMMARIES 180
SUMMARY 181
DISCUSSION QUESTIONS 182
ENDNOTES 183

Chapter 7

SEARCH AND SEIZURE 185

SEARCHES OF PRISONERS 185
RANDOM PAT-DOWN SEARCHES 187
CROSS-GENDER SEARCHES 187
STRIP SEARCHES 188
URINE AND BLOOD TESTS 189
SEARCH OF VISITORS 190
CASE SUMMARIES 196
SUMMARY 197
DISCUSSION QUESTIONS 198
ENDNOTES 199

Chapter 8

THE EIGHTH AMENDMENT: CRUEL AND UNUSUAL PUNISHMENT 201

INTRODUCTION 201
DISPROPORTIONATE PUNISHMENT 202
MANDATORY SENTENCES AS CRUEL AND
　UNUSUAL PUNISHMENT 203
DEATH PENALTY AS CRUEL AND
　UNUSUAL PUNISHMENT 203
　　Medicate to Execute 206
　　Minimum Age for Capital Punishment 207
　　Delay in Imposition of Death Penalty 208
PUNISHMENT IMPOSED BECAUSE OF
　A PERSON'S STATUS 209
MEDICAL TREATMENT 209
CASE SUMMARIES 220
SUMMARY 221
DISCUSSION QUESTIONS 222
ENDNOTES 223

Chapter 9

THE FOURTH AMENDMENT: USE OF FORCE 225

INTRODUCTION 225
WHEN IS FORCE JUSTIFIED? 225
USE OF RESTRAINTS 226
FAILURE TO PROTECT PRISONERS 227
CRUEL AND UNUSUAL PUNISHMENT 227

USE OF FORCE TO QUELL A RIOT	228
MINOR AND NON-PHYSICAL INJURIES	229
CORPORAL PUNISHMENT	230
SUICIDE	231
CASE SUMMARIES	238
SUMMARY	238
DISCUSSION QUESTIONS	239
ENDNOTES	240

Chapter 10

CIVIL ACTIONS ... 241

INTRODUCTION	241
HABEAS CORPUS	241
CRIMINAL LIABILITY	243
TORT	244
CIVIL LIABILITY (SECTION 1983)	246
Requirement of State Action	248
Scope of Liability	248
Custom	251
Failure to Train	251
CASE SUMMARIES	263
SUMMARY	264
DISCUSSION QUESTIONS	265
ENDNOTES	266

Chapter 11

CIVIL LIABILITY DEFENSES ... 267

IMMUNITY	267
Doctrine of Sovereign Immunity	267

Doctrine of Absolute Immunity 268
Doctrine of Qualified Immunity 268
DOUBLE JEOPARDY 270
STATUTE OF LIMITATIONS 271
SELF-DEFENSE 272
DEFENSE OF OTHERS 274
CASE SUMMARIES 286
SUMMARY 287
DISCUSSION QUESTIONS 287
ENDNOTES 288

INDEX 289

TABLE OF CASES

A

Abel v. United States   195
Allen v. Coughlin   181
Apodica v. Oregon   76
Ashelman v. Wawrzaszek   158

B

Baldwin v. New York   75
Bell v. Wolfish   177, 192
Bell-Bey v. Williams   180, 286
Beville v. Ednie   181
Bivens v. Six Unknown Federal Narcotics Agents   250, 279
Block v. Rutherford   128, 177, 187
Boykin v. Alabama   92
Bradley v. Fisher   280
Brady v. United States   105
Briscoe v. LaHue   281
Brown v. Copeland   221
Butz v. Economou   281, 282

C

Canton v. Harris   257
Camarillo v. McCarthy   286
Carpenter v. Wilkinson   157
Champion v. Artuz   130
Cleavinger v. Saxner   274
Cruz v. Beto   149

D

Diaz v. Coughlin   181

E

Edmund v. Florida   215, 217
Estelle v. Gamble   209

F

Fernandez v. Rapone   196
Francis v. Resweber   214, 215
Freedman v. City of Allentown   231
Furman v. Georgia   205, 212, 214

G

Gabel v. Estelle   221
Gardner v. Florida   104
Gassler v. Woods   164
Giano v. Senkowski   167, 181
Graham v. Connor   234
Gregg v. Georgia   210, 215
Grummett v. Rushen   188

H

Hafter v. Melo   263
Harlow v. Fitzgerald   269
Harper v. Wallingford   164
Harris v. Fleming   221
Helling v. McKinney   218
Hogan v. Carter   286
Houchins v. KQED   124
Hudson v. McMillian   227, 229, 234, 236

Table of Cases

Hudson v. Palmer 186, 191, 283
Hyde v. Texas Dept. of Criminal Justice 157-158

I

In re Kemmler 214
Inmates of Occoquan v. Barry 220

J

Jackson v. Bishop 230
Jihaad v. O'Brien 280
Johnson v. Avery 170, 175, 192
Johnson v. Stephan 124
Jones v. Harrison 196
Jones v. Murray 197
Jones v. North Carolina Prisoners' Labor Union 121, 123, 178
Jordan v. Gardner 188

K

Kensu v. Haigh 180
Kentucky Department of Corrections v. Thompson 130
Kerr v. Farrey 157

L

Lasley v. Godinez 197
Lawson v. Singletary 157
Lee v. Washington 192

M

Mack v. O'Leary 157
Malik v. Brown 181
Marbury v. Madison 56
Martinez v. California 282
Martucci v. Johnson 163
Mary v. Ramsden 279
Massiah v. United States 253
McCleskey v. Zant 253
McKenzie v. Day 208
McKnight v. Rees 286
McLaurin v. Morton 263
McLaurin v. Prater 238
Merritt-Bey v. Salts 196
Michenfeder v. Sumner 188
Mitchell v. United States 94
Monell v. New York City Dept. of Social Services 249, 258
Monroe v. Pape 249
Moody v. Proctor 238

N

Neal v. Clark 264
Nixon v. Fitzgerald 282
North Carolina v. Alford 100

O

O'Banion v. Bowman 238
O'Leary v. Iowa State Men's Reformatory 221
O'Lone v. Shabazz 151
Owens v. City of Independence 250

P

Payne v. District of Columbia 130
Pell v. Procunier 123
Penry v. Lynaugh 208
Pepperling v. Crist 167

Peters v. Dept. of Corrections 263
Pierson v. Ray 280, 283
Prins v. Coughlin 157
Procunier v. Martinez 162, 167, 175
Procunier v. Navarette 269

R

Richardson v. McKnight 286
Roberts v. U.S. Jacyees 121
Robinson v. California 209
Romo v. Champion 196

S

Sanderfer v. Nichols 220
Santobello v. New York 103
Saxbe v. Washington 124
Saxner v. Benson 280
Screws v. United States 248
Sheets v. Moore 180
Smith v. Copeland 264
Smith v. Coughlin 129
Smith v. Wade 260
Snipes v. Detella 220
Sosa v. Jefferson County 238
Spear v. Sowders 190
Stanford v. Kentucky 207
State v. Berard 197
Stefanow v. McFadden 158
Stow v. Grimaldi 163

T

Thompson v. City of Los Angeles 251
Thompson v. Oklahoma 207
Thornburgh v. Abbot 163, 164

Trop v. Dulles 214
Turner v. Safley 163, 173

U

U.S. v. State of Michigan 221
United States v. Benchimol 104
United States v. Classic 248
United States v. Edwards 193
United States v. Jackson 106

V

Vance v. Peters 220
Vaughan v. Lacey 220
Von Moltke v. Gillies 94

W

Wainwright v. Sykes 254
Ward v. Johnson 280
Warren v. Humphrey 238
Weems v. United States 214
White v. Keller 129
Whitley v. Albers 227, 228
Wilkerson v. Utah 214
Williams v. New York 104
Wilson v. Seiter 217, 263
Wolff v. McDonnell 175, 186, 192, 284, 285
Wood v. Strickland 268

Y

Young v. Berks County Prison 264

Z

Zunker v. Bertrand 197

Chapter 1

THE CORRECTIONAL PROCESS

The mood and temper of the public with regard to the treatment of crime and criminals is one of the most unfailing tests of the civilization of any country.[1]

Winston Churchill

PUNISHMENT

The natural starting place for the study of the law of corrections or prison law is with an examination of our concepts of punishment. To understand where we are today, we must examine the past. During this process, according to the leading researchers on sentencing, we should ask the following questions:

> How civilized is our country's system of punishing criminals?

> And from a practical perspective, how effective are our efforts to punish and control crime?[2]

Our system of punishment today is vastly different from those of Colonial America. Whipping and pubic humiliation were probably the most popular forms of punishment then, and confinement and threat of confinement (probation) are the most popular forms of punishment now. Under our present system, which relies heavily on confinement, our per-capita imprisonment rate in the United States is exceeded only by the former Soviet Union.

Beginning of Legal Punishments

In primitive societies, the remedy for wrongs done to one's person or property was personal retaliation against the wrongdoer. Unlike modern society, personal retaliation was encouraged. *Blood feuds* developed from the concept of personal retaliation and occurred when the victim's family or tribe took revenge on the offender's family or tribe. Blood feuds often escalated and resulted in continuing vendettas between families or tribes. In many cases, individuals were expected to avenge the death of a kinsman for religious reasons. The duty of *retaliation* was imposed by universal practice upon the victim or, in case of death, the nearest male relative.

To lessen costly and damaging vendettas, the custom developed of accepting money or property in place of blood vengeance. At first, the acceptance of payments instead of blood vengeance was not compulsory. The victim's family was still free to choose whatever form of vengeance they wished. Often the relative power of the families or tribes determined whether payments or blood vengeance was used.

The acceptance of money or property as atonement for wrongs became known as *les salica* or *wergeld*. The amount of payment was based on the rank or position of the victim. This practice is still used in some Middle Eastern countries. The tradition of accepting money or property damages was the beginning of the development of a system of criminal law.

To many, crime was also a sin against the church and later the state. Therefore, one problem with the acceptance of payment as complete satisfaction for the wrong was the concept that punishment of an individual wrongdoer should also include some religious aspects. Accordingly, there developed the concept that punishment in the form of wergeld (payment to the victim) should also be supplemented with friedensgeld (payment to the church, or later, to the crown).

Fines and other forms of punishment replaced personal retaliation as tribal leaders began to exert their authority during the negotiations or proceedings concerning the damages caused by the wrongs committed.[3] The wrongdoers were not required to attend the proceedings. If, however, they failed to follow the recommendations of the tribal leaders, they were banished or exiled, and thus considered to be "outlaws."

Many present day researchers consider the development of this custom as the beginning of criminal law as we know it today. Subsequent legal codes and punishments for different crimes have either stressed or refined the vengeance principle. The concept that a society expresses its vengeance within a system of rules was present in the ethics of primitive societies.

Early Codes

The two earliest codes involving criminal punishments were the Sumerian and Hammurabic codes. The punishment phases of these codes contained the concept of personal vengeance. The listed punishments in the codes were harsh and, in many cases, the victim or nearest relative was allowed to inflict punishment personally. Permitted punishments included mutilation, whipping, or forced labor. At first, the punishments were applied almost exclusively to slaves and bond servants and indicated the assumption of a base or servile mentality on the part of those being punished. Later they were extended to all offenders.

The use of *penal servitude* also developed. Penal servitude involved the use of hard labor as punishment and was generally reserved for the lower classes of citizens. Penal servitude included the loss of citizenship and liberty, i.e., civil death. With the civil death, the offender's property was confiscated in the name of the state and his wife was declared a widow. Later, the use of penal servitude by the Romans was encouraged by the need for workers to perform hard labor.

The fact that early punishments were considered synonymous with slavery is indicated by the practice of shaving the heads of those punished as a *mark of slavery*. Other marks of slavery used on punished wrongdoers included branding on the forehead or use of a heavy metal collar that could not be easily removed.

The Greek Code of Draco used the same penalties for both citizens and slaves and incorporated many of the concepts used in primitive societies, e.g., vengeance, outlawry, and blood feuds. The Greeks apparently were the first society to allow any citizen to prosecute an offender on behalf of the victim. This practice appears to indicate that public interest and protection of society had accepted the concept that crimes affected not only the victim, but society in general.

Middle Ages

During the Middle Ages, rapid changes were made in the social structure of societies. In addition, the growing influence of the church on everyday life helped create a divided system of justice. In committing a crime, the offender also committed a sin. Accordingly, he or she had two debts to pay—one to the victim and one to the Church. *Trials by ordeal* were used by the church as substitutes for trials. In a trial by ordeal, the accused was subjected to dangerous or painful tests in the belief that God would protect the innocent. The brutality of the trial by ordeal ensured that most would die and thus be considered guilty. The practice of trial by ordeal was not abolished until about the year 1215.

It was also during the Middle Ages that the Church expanded the concept of crime to include newly prohibited areas. This concept is still present in our modern day codes. Sexual offenses were among the new areas now covered by law. Sex offenses, which include either public or "unnatural" acts, were dealt with by horrible punishments. Heresy and witchcraft were also included in the newly prohibited areas of conduct. The Church inflicted cruel punishments and justified the punishments as necessary to save the "unfortunate sinners." For example, the zealous movement to stamp out heresy resulted in the Inquisition. The Inquisition was a tribunal established by the Church with very broad powers to use for the suppression of heresy. The Inquisition searched out offenders rather than waiting for charges to be brought forward.

Whipping was the usual method of punishing persons for minor offenses. Whipping was inflicted on women while kneeling and on men while lying on the ground. Generally the victims were stripped to the waist and the blows inflicted on their backs.[4]

PHILOSOPHY OF PUNISHMENT

Purposes of Criminal Sanctions

In discussing the purposes of criminal sanctions, various ideologies are presented. *Ideology* refers to the belief system adopted by a group and consists of assumptions and values. The assumptions are beliefs about the way the world is constituted and organized. *Values*, however, are beliefs about what is moral and desirable.[5] There are numerous methods to classify ideologies. Three popular classifications based on political theories that influence our corrections system are conservative, liberal, and radical.

The *conservative ideology* tends to accept the concept that human beings are rational, possess free will, and voluntarily commit criminal misconduct. Accordingly, criminals should be held accountable for the actions. Punishment should be imposed to inflict suffering on the criminal because the suffering is deserved and because it will deter future crime. The punishment imposed should fit the crime. Because of its view on the causes of human behavior, this ideology generally does not accept the concept of rehabilitation as an attractive objective of punishment.

The *liberal ideology* tends to view human behavior as greatly influenced by social circumstances: one's upbringing, material affluence, education, peer relationships. Accordingly, human behavior is more than a simple product of free choice. All of the social influences are important factors in shaping our conduct. Liberals viewing criminal behavior as a product of both social circumstances and individual actions are more likely to support rehabilitation as the proper purposes of criminal punishment. Most liberals tend to be receptive to a wider range of aims for criminal punishment, including deterrence.

The *radical ideology* rejects both the conservative and liberal ideologies. To radicals, crime is a reflection of the status of our present social system, and crime is only a natural consequence of our social system. According to the radicals, fundamental changes in the socioeconomic basis of society are required in order to control crime.

The ultimate purpose of criminal sanctions is generally considered to be the maintenance of our social order. Herbert Packer contends that the two major goals of criminal sanctions are to inflict suffering upon the wrongdoers and the prevention of crime.[6] Robert Dawson suggests that the major purpose of the criminal justice system is the identification in a legally acceptable manner of those persons who should be subjected to control and treatment in the correctional process.[7] According to Dawson, if corrections does not properly perform its task, the entire criminal justice system suffers. An inefficient or unfair correctional process can nullify the courts, prosecutors, and police alike. Conversely, the manner in which the other agencies involved perform their tasks has an important impact upon the success of the process. A person who has been unfairly dealt with prior to conviction is a poor subject for rehabilitation.

The four popular goals of criminal sanctions are retribution, deterrence, incapacitation, and rehabilitation. From the 1940s to the 1980s, rehabilitation was considered by most as the primary goal of our system. Since the 1980s, retribution has received popular support. Each of these four commonly accepted goals are discussed in this chapter.

Retribution

Retribution generally means "getting even." Retribution is based on the ideology that the criminal is an enemy of society and deserves severe punishment for willfully breaking its rules. Retribution is often misunderstood as revenge. However, there are important differences between the two. Both retribution and revenge are primarily concerned with punishing the offender and neither is overly concerned with the impact of the punishment on the offender's future behavior or the behavior of others. Unlike revenge, however, retribution attempts to match the severity of the punishment to the seriousness of the crime. Revenge acts on passion, whereas retribution follows specific rules regarding the types and amounts of punishment that may be inflicted. The Biblical response of an "eye for an eye" is a retributive response to punishment. While the "eye for an eye" concept is often cited as an excuse to use harsh punishment, it is less harsh than revenge-based punishment, which does not rule out "two eyes for an eye" punishment. Sir James Stephen, an English judge, expressed the retributive view by stating that "the punishment of criminals was simply a desirable expression of the hatred and fear aroused in the community by criminal acts."[8] This line of reasoning conveys the message that punishment is justifiable because it provides an orderly outlet for emotions that if denied may express themselves in socially less acceptable ways. Another justification under the retribution ideology is that only through suffering punishment can the criminal expiate his sin. In one manner, retribution treats all crimes as if they were financial transactions. The criminal got something or did something, therefore the criminal must give equivalent value (suffering).

Retribution is also referred to as "just deserts." The just desserts movement reflects the retribution viewpoint and provides a justifiable rationale for support of the death penalty. This viewpoint has its roots in a societal need for retribution. It can be traced back to the individual need for retaliation and vengeance. The transfer of the vengeance motive from the individual to the state has been justified based on theories involving theological, aesthetic, and expiatory views. According to the theological view, retaliation fulfills the religious need to punish the sinner. Under the aesthetic view, punishment helps reestablish a sense of harmony through requital and thus solves the social discord created by the crime. The expiatory view is that guilt must be washed away (cleansed) through suffering. There is even a utilitarian view that punishment is the means of achieving beneficial and social consequences through the application of a specific form and degree of punishment deemed most appropriate to the particular offender after careful individualized study of the offender.[9]

Deterrence

Deterrence is a punishment viewpoint that focuses on future outcomes rather than past misconduct. It is also based on the theory that creating a fear of future punishments will deter crime. It is based on the belief that punishments have a deterrent effect. There is substantial debate as to the validity of this concept. *Specific deterrence* deters specifically the offender, whereas *general deterrence* works generally on others who might consider similar acts. According to this viewpoint, the fear of future suffering motivates individuals to avoid involvement in criminal misconduct. This concept assumes that the criminal is a rational being who will weigh the consequences of his or her criminal actions before deciding to commit them.

One of the problems with deterrence is determining the appropriate magnitude and nature of punishment to be imposed in order to deter future criminal misconduct. For example, an individual who commits a serious crime and then feels badly about the act may need only slight punishment to achieve deterrent effects, whereas a professional shoplifter may need severe fear-producing punishments to prevent future shoplifting.

Increases in crime rates and high rates of recidivism are often used to cast doubt that the deterrence approach is effective. Recidivism may cause some doubt regarding the efficacy of special deterrence, but it says nothing about the effect of general deterrence. In addition, unless we know what the crime rate or rates of recidivism would be if we did not attempt to deter criminal misconduct, the assertions are unfounded. Are we certain that the rates would not be higher had we not attempted to deter criminals?

Incapacitation

At least while the prisoner is in confinement, he is unlikely to commit crimes on innocent persons outside of prison. To this extent, confinement clearly helps reduce criminal behavior. Under this viewpoint, there is no hope for rehabilitating the individual; therefore, the only solution is to incapacitate the offender. Marvin Wolfgang's famous study of crime in Philadelphia indicated that although chronic offenders constituted only

23 percent of the offenders in the study, they committed over 61 percent of all the violent crimes.[10] Accordingly, the supporters of the incapacitation viewpoint contend that incapacitating the 23 percent would have prevented 61 percent of the future violent crimes. This approach has often been labeled the "nothing else works" approach to corrections. According to this viewpoint, we should make maximum effective use of the scarce prison cells to protect society from the depredations of such dangerous and repetitive offenders. This approach is expressed in California's "Three Strikes and You're Out" statute.

There are two variations in the incapacitation viewpoint. *Collective incapacitation* refers to sanctions imposed on offenders without regard to their personal characteristics, such as whether they are all violent offenders. *Selective incapacitation* refers to incapacitation of certain groups of individuals who have been identified as high risk offenders, such as robbers with a history of drug use. Under selective incapacitation, offenders with certain characteristics or history would receive longer prison terms than others convicted of the same crime. The purpose of incapacitation is to prevent future crimes, and the moral concerns associated with retribution are not as important as the reduction of future victimization.[11] As Herbert Packer states, "Incapacitation is a mode of punishment that uses the fact that a person has committed a crime as a basis for predicting that he will commit future crimes."[12] Packer also states that the logic of the incapacitative position is that until the offender stops being a danger, we will continue to restrain him. Accordingly, he contends that pushed to its logical conclusion, offenses that are regarded as relatively trivial may be punished by imprisonment for life.

Rehabilitation

The rehabilitation approach contends that punishment should be directed toward correcting the offender. This approach is also considered the "treatment" approach. It considers the criminal misconduct as a manifestation of a pathology that can be handled by some form of therapeutic activity. Although this viewpoint may consider the offender as "sick," it is not the same as the medical approach. Under the rehabilitation viewpoint, we need to teach offenders to recognize the undesirability of their criminal behavior and make significant efforts to rid themselves of that behavior. The main difference between the rehabilitation approach and the retribution approach is that under the rehabilitation approach, offenders are assigned to programs designed to prepare them for readjustment or reintegration into the community, whereas the latter approach is more concerned with the punishment aspects of the sentence. Packer sees two major objections to making rehabilitation the primary justification for punishment. First, we do not know how to rehabilitate offenders. Second, we know little about who is likely to commit crimes and less about what makes them apt to do so. As long as we are ignorant in these matters, Packard contends that punishment in the name of rehabilitation is gratuitous cruelty.[13]

Social Purposes of Punishment

C. Ray Jeffery, a noted criminologist, contends that the more glaring defect in most analyses of punishment is that punishment is always in the context of what it means to the individual offender and never in terms of what it means to society. According to Jeffery, the purpose of punishment should be to establish to the public social disapproval of the act. The use of punishment by society is not as important in terms of whether or not it reforms the individual as in terms of what it does for society. He also contends that punishment serves an important social function in that it creates social solidarity and re-enforces social norms.[14]

CHANGES TO THE "JUSTICE" PHILOSOPHY

The Violent Crime Control and Law Enforcement Act of 1994 was one of the most ambitious crime bills in our history.[15] The act allocated more than $22 billion to expand prisons, impose longer sentences, hire more police officers, and, to a very limited extent, fund prevention programs. However, the following year the money allocated to prevention programs was eliminated. This act, and similar acts, have great political appeal but little support among criminal justice professionals. Most professionals feel that such efforts will do little to reduce crime. This approach has been labeled as the "enforcement model."[16] The popular criticisms of the present "enforcement model approach" are that it is racist, it costs too much, and it fails to prevent young people from entering and continuing lives of crime. The popularity of prison as a response to crime has resulted in changes in the public and professional perceptions of the role of corrections.

The various approaches to correctional philosophy fall into one of three categories: punishment, treatment, or prevention. They often overlap as punishment and treatment can be argued as an approach to prevent crime. The 1960s was a period in which treatment was the dominant approach. This changed in the late 1970s. Since that time, society, in general, has preferred the punishment approach. As will be discussed in later chapters, the punishment approach has resulted in overcrowded institutions, and budgets are stripped of so-called frills needed for treatment and prevention programs. It appears that in the 1990s the punishment approach may have reached its height, and the future may see the pendulum swing back toward the treatment or prevention emphasis.

Until recent years, the determination of whether a convicted defendant went to prison and for how long was left largely to the courts. Judicial decisions were made with few statutory guidelines except for the stated statutory maximum sentence that may be imposed on the conviction of an offense. In recent decades, however, many restrictions have been placed on the discretion of judges regarding the types of sentences, and whether to suspend sentences or grant probation. Concerns regarding disparate sentences and abuses, or perceived abuses, in sentencing have resulted in six common strategies used by legislatures to maintain control over the sentencing process and reduce the discretion of the judiciary and correctional administrators. The common theme of the six strategies is to "reduce judicial and correctional imperialism." The six strategies are as follows:

> **Determinate sentencing.** Establishment of set sentences whereby parole boards are restricted from releasing prisoners before their sentences (minus good time) have expired.

- ➤ **Mandatory prison terms.** Statutes that require the courts to impose mandatory prison terms for convictions of certain offenses or for certain defendants.
- ➤ **Sentencing guidelines.** Guidelines designed to structure sentences based on the severity of the offense and the criminal history of the defendant.
- ➤ **Parole guidelines.** Guidelines designed to require parole decisions to be based on measurable offender criteria.
- ➤ **Good-time guidelines.** Guidelines that allow for reducing prison terms based on an inmate's behavior in prison.
- ➤ **Emergency overcrowding provisions.** Regulations that allow early release of prisoners based on systematic provisions to relieve overcrowding.

Sentencing Guidelines

In most states, a judge must follow required guidelines and statutory restrictions to determine the appropriate sentence. To assist judges, most states require that a *presentence report* (PSI) be prepared and submitted to the court. The PSI contains a variety of information, such as statements describing the seriousness of the crime, the defendant's past criminal history, any history of substance abuse, and any aggravating or mitigating circumstances.

Sentencing guidelines are being used by the federal government and many states to guide the judges in making their determinations of appropriate sentences. The guidelines were developed in an attempt to limit disparity and discretion, and to establish more detailed criteria for sentencing. A sentencing commission monitors the use of the guidelines. Written explanations are required when a judge departs from the guideline ranges. For example, Minnesota provides that while sentencing guidelines are advisory to the judge, departures from the guideline sentences established should be made only when substantial and compelling circumstances exist. In Pennsylvania, failure of the court to explain sentences deviating from the guidelines is grounds for vacating the sentence and resentencing the defendant. In addition, if the appellate court considers that the guidelines were inaccurately or inappropriately applied, the appellate court may vacate the sentence and order a resentencing.

The U.S. Sentencing Reform Act of 1984 advocated the "least restrictive alternative" in sentencing federal prisoners. The U.S. Sentencing Commission has established guidelines that authorize prison terms for all felony convictions. Research indicates that since the adoption of the federal sentencing guidelines, the use of probation and other non-incarcerative sentences has declined.[17]

The Federal Sentencing Guidelines were enacted in 1984 and have governed federal sentencing decisions since 1989. The guidelines that were promulgated by the Sentencing Commission created 43 offense levels, with each level reflecting increased severity of crime. In addition, offenders were divided into six categories based on their criminal history. The net result is a grid containing 258 cells, each of which has a sentencing range expressed in terms of months. The intent was to have the grids serve as an advisory to judical decision making on sentencing. While the stated objective of the federal sentencing reform was to encourage alternative sanctions to prison, the guidelines are constructed in such a manner that they discourage judges from imposing alternative sanctions.

The sentencing court must select a sentence from within the guideline range. If, however, a particular case presents atypical features, the act allows the court to depart from the guidelines and sentence outside the prescribed range. In that case, the court must specify reasons for departure.[18]

In 1984, before the use of the guidelines, approximately 52 percent of felony federal offenders were sentenced to prison. In 1991, the percentage had increased to 71 percent. Since adoption of the guidelines, there has been widespread criticism of the guidelines among federal district court judges. The judges have called them unduly harsh and mechanical. Other judges consider that, in addition to being harsh, the guidelines are very inflexible. Most agree that the guidelines rely too heavily on imprisonment as a sanction.

Presumptive Sentences

One alternative used to limit the discretion of sentencing judges is the use of presumptive sentences. Under this system, the state legislature sets minimum, average, and maximum prison terms. The judges select the term appropriate for the defendant based on the characteristics of the offender and aggravating circumstances. California has used this system since 1979. For example, in California, if a defendant is convicted of burglary, the punishment range is set forth in section 461 of the Penal Code. That section provides: "Burglary in the first degree: by imprisonment in the state prison for two, four, or six years."

The first decision that the judge would need to make is the "out or in" decision: whether the defendant should be placed on probation (out) or sentenced (in) to prison. If the judge decides that imprisonment is the correct sentence, the judge would award four years, the average sentence, unless there were mitigating or aggravating circumstances. Under aggravating circumstances, the sentence would be six years, and under mitigating circumstances, the sentence would be two years. Examples of mitigating circumstances would be that the defendant is a first-time offender or the crime was committed under strong peer pressure. Examples of aggravating circumstances include a prior criminal record or great harm to the victim.

JUDICIAL PROCESS FOR MISDEMEANANTS

Misdemeanants are individuals convicted of minor crimes (misdemeanors). Their sentences are to jails for periods normally not to exceed one year, fines, community service, and/or attendance at some type of behavior modification course. In studying corrections, we rarely consider the roles of our minor courts and their handling of misdemeanants. However, more citizens become involved at this level than at the felony level. It is estimated that on any given day approximately 500,000 individuals are confined in local jails. The lower courts of America are truly involved in an "assembly-line" type of justice.

JUDICIAL PROCESS FOR FELONS

In most states, sentences to prison or correctional institutions are decided by judges. Several states, such as Texas, allow the defendants to opt for jury sentencing. The incarceration of an individual in a state prison is a dramatic, but all too often used, sanction. The Model Penal Code addresses the problems involved in selecting the appropriate sentence. The code provides that imprisonment should be used as the last resort.[19] The code provides that imprisonment should be used only when one of these conditions exists:

1. There is undue risk that during the period of probation the defendant will commit another crime.
2. The defendant is in need of correctional treatment that can be provided most effectively by commitment to an institution.
3. A lesser sentence will depreciate the seriousness of the defendant's crime.

ALTERNATIVE SENTENCING AND DIVERSION

Alternative sentencing involves the use of nontraditional programs in lieu of fines and custody. One of the most popular alternative sentencing procedures is the use of deferred adjudication. *Deferred adjudication* is a form of probation that is used without a finding of guilt. In deferred adjudication, the defendant pleads guilty and agrees to defer further proceeding. The defendant is then placed on probation or directed to attend counseling or behavior modification courses. After the defendant has successfully completed the requirements, the guilty or *nolo contendere* plea is withdrawn and the case is dismissed. When the charges are dismissed, the defendant does not have a criminal conviction for this misconduct. If the defendant fails to comply with the requirements, the court sentences the defendant based on his or her original plea.

Pretrial diversion is a form of probation that is granted prior to trial. Under this process, the defendant agrees to waive time and to complete a program or process. Pretrial diversion is used primarily for offenders who need treatment or supervision and for whom criminal sanctions would be excessive. Like deferred adjudication, there is no finding of guilt and, thus, no conviction if the program is successfully completed. If the program is not successfully completed, the defendant is then brought to trial on the charges. One of the popular criticisms of pretrial diversion is based on research that indicates that many people are diverted who would not have been prosecuted because of the lack of evidence against them. If this is correct, such action increases the number of persons involved in the criminal justice system.

PRISON DISCIPLINE

Inmates confined in institutions are required to obey a lengthy list of rules. When an institution employee observes an inmate commit an infraction, the employee is generally required to submit a disciplinary report. The inmate receives notice of the report with written notification of the charge and a hearing date. At the hearing, the hearing officer receives the evidence presented by the institutional division and any that is presented by the inmate. The formal rules of evidence do not apply at these hearings. The hearing officer decides whether the inmate committed the infraction. Possible punishments include loss of time credited for good conduct or participation credit, solitary confinement, extra work, loss of certain privileges (recreation, commissary, television, access to personal property, or contact visits) for stated periods of time. Generally, the inmate may appeal the hearing officer's finding and/or punishment to the unit warden.

Disciplinary Hearing Procedures

ABA Standard 23-3.2 Relating to the Legal Status of Prisoners provides:

(a) At a hearing where a minor sanction is imposed, the prisoner should be entitled to:

(1) written notice of the charge, in a language the prisoner understands, within seventy-two hours of the time he or she is suspected of having committed an offense; within another twenty-four hours the prisoner should be given copies of any further written information the hearing officer may consider;

(2) a hearing within three working days of the time the written notice of the charge was received.

(3) be present and speak on his or her own behalf;

(4) a written decision based upon a preponderance of the evidence, with specified reasons for the decision. The decision should be rendered promptly and in all cases within five days after conclusion of the hearing; and

(5) appeal, within five days, to the chief executive officer of the institution, and the right to a written decision by that officer within thirty days, based upon a written summary of the hearing, any documentary evidence considered at the hearing, and the prisoner's written reason for appealing. The chief executive officer should either affirm or reverse the determination of misconduct and decrease or approve the punishment imposed. Execution of punishment should be suspended during the appeal unless individual safety or individual security will be adversely affected thereby.

(b) At a hearing where a major sanction is imposed, in addition to the requirements of paragraph (a), the prisoner should be entitled to have in attendance any person within the local institution community who has relevant information, and to examine or cross-examine such witnesses except when the hearing officer(s):

(1) exclude testimony as unduly cumulative; or

(2) receive testimony outside the presence of the prisoner pursuant to a finding that the physical safety of a person

would be endangered by the presence of a particular witness or disclosure of his or her identity.

(c) Disciplinary hearings should be conducted by one or more impartial persons.

(d) Unless the prisoner is found guilty, no record relating to the charge should be retained in the prisoner's file or used against the prisoner in any way.

The Supreme Court has approved a distinction between disciplinary proceedings that may result in the imposition of major punishments, such as loss of good time and solitary confinement and minor punishments that affect only privileges.[20] Regarding the requirement that the person or persons conducting the hearing be impartial, the courts have held that no hearing officer should have been involved in the circumstances or investigation of the alleged violation.

When the misconduct involves the violation of a prison rule and criminal misconduct, there is no formal bar to disciplinary action as well as referral of the matter to criminal courts. The drafters of the standards contend that it is preferable administrative policy to refrain from pursuing both actions concurrently. Many states, such as Texas, pursue both avenues as a matter of routine. In one recent Texas case, a prisoner lost three years good time credit at a disciplinary hearing for assaulting a correctional officer and was then prosecuted in the local district court for assault on a peace officer.

Grievances

Most state prisons and local jails have grievance procedures for inmates who feel that they have been mistreated or have not received proper credit. Generally, the inmate must file a written claim on an approved form. In most states, if the grievance is denied and the inmate has exhausted his or her administrative remedies, the inmate may file a petition with a district or superior court.

The American Bar Association (ABA) Standards provide:

(a) Correctional authorities should authorize and encourage correctional employees to resolve prisoner grievances on an informal basis whenever possible.

(b) Every correctional institution should adopt a formal procedure to resolve specific prisoner grievances, including any complaint arising out of institutional policies, rules, practices, and procedures or the action of any correctional employee or official. Grievance procedures should not be used as a substitute appellate procedure for individual decisions reached by adjudicative bodies, for example, parole, classification, and disciplinary boards, although a complaint involving the procedures or general policies employed by any correctional adjudicative body should be subject to grievance procedures.

(c) Correctional authorities should make forms available so that a grievant may initiate review by describing briefly the nature of the grievance, the persons involved, and the remedy sought.

(d) The institution's grievance procedure should be designed to ensure the cooperation and confidence of prisoners and correctional officials and should include:

   (1) provisions for written responses to all grievances, including the reasons for the decision;

   (2) provision for response within a prescribed, reasonable time limit. A request that is not responded to or resolved within thirty working days should be deemed to have been denied;

   (3) special provision for responding to emergencies;

   (4) provision for advisory review of grievances;

   (5) provision for participation by staff and prisoners in the design of the grievance procedure;

   (6) provision for access by all prisoners, with guarantees against reprisal;

(7) applicability over a broad range of issues; and

(8) means for resolving questions of jurisdiction.

Courts have held that the right to petition for redress of grievances is a First Amendment right.[21] It appears that common sense would also indicate that as many disputes as possible between prisoners and administrators should be worked out informally. In addition, an effective grievance procedure should reduce the number of cases filed in court involving inmate complaints. As a general rule, before filing a court action regarding the conditions of confinement, the prisoner must exhaust his or her administrative remedies. A formal grievance process is considered as an administrative remedy that should be exhausted prior to the inmate filing judicial papers. By filing a grievance, the inmate provides the institution with an opportunity to correct any wrongs without resorting to court action.

Rules of Conduct

The American Bar Association's (ABA) Joint Task Force on the Legal Status of Prisoners contains this standard regarding rules of conduct:

(a) Correctional authorities should promulgate clear written rules for prisoner conduct. These rules and implementing criteria should include:

   (1) a specific definition of offenses, a statement that the least severe punishment appropriate to each offense should be imposed, and a schedule indicating the minimum and maximum possible punishment for each offense, proportionate to the offense, and

   (2) specific criteria and procedures for prison discipline and classification decisions, including decisions involving security status and work and housing assignments.

(b) A personal copy of the rules should be provided to each prisoner upon entry to the institution. For the benefit of illiterate and foreign-language prisoners, a detailed oral explanation of the rules should be given. In addition, a written translation should be provided in any language spoken by a significant number of prisoners.[22]

The authors of the above standards feel that many prison rule books contain ambiguities and that correctional officers often believe that publications of this sort provide sufficient guides for ascertaining violations. According to the authors, prison regulations should not be vague and over broad. The courts have held that due process requires a schedule of penalties for violation of penal rules and that the punishment must bear some proportionality to punishable misconduct, measured in some objective fashion. Disproportionate penalties will be struck down by the courts, both within and without prison walls.[23] However, when challenging a prison rule for disproportionate penalty, the prisoner must "demonstrate disparities in punishment that are not reasonably related to legitimate state interests."[24]

RELEASE FROM CONFINEMENT

In most states, there are three ways in which an inmate may be released from confinement: parole, mandatory supervision, and discharge.

Parole is the discretionary release of an inmate from prison when he or she completes a prescribed portion of his or her sentence and the parole board agrees that the release will not increase the likelihood of harm to the public. Parole is discussed in the next section.

Mandatory supervision is the release of an inmate from prison when he or she completes a prescribed portion of his or her sentence and is then under the close supervision of a parole officer. For example, an inmate could receive a sentence of confinement for two years with two years mandatory supervision when released. Mandatory supervision differs from parole in that the defendant is informed when sentenced as to the release date, whereas a parole date must be approved by a parole board. Not all states use the concept of mandatory supervision. Once released, the inmate is on mandatory supervision for as long as the inmate follows the conditions of his or her supervision. Should the parolee violate the conditions of supervision, the parolee may be returned to confinement.

Discharge is the outright release of the inmate after serving the entire sentence, minus any participation or good time credit given. An inmate who serves his or her time, often referred to as serving "flat time," is not subject to any form of supervision.

INTENSIVE SUPERVISION

Intensive supervision probation (ISP) is commonly considered as "a response to pressures created by a demand for incarceration that exceeds prison capacity."[25] ISP was developed to meet the need for another type of intermediate sanction—something stronger than traditional probation, but not as harsh as incarceration. ISP programs vary from traditional probation by the requirement of more intense level of supervision. This intense level of supervision is achieved by the use of such measures as:

- Smaller caseloads
- More frequent face-to-face contacts
- Home confinement
- Electronic monitoring
- Regular visits to client's home and workplace
- Drug and alcohol screening
- Clear revocation guidelines

SEX OFFENDER REGISTRATION LAWS

Most states have some form of sex offender registration law that requires a convicted sex offender to register when he or she moves into the community. Sex offender registration laws are often called Megan's laws because most were enacted as the result of the death of a juvenile named Megan by a known sex offender.

In 1994, Jesse K. Timmendequas confessed to the strangling and raping of Megan Kanka. Megan was seven years old, and she had just finished the first grade. Timmendequas lived across the street. He is described as a slight man with the dirty blond hair and a nervous preoccupation with himself. He had pleaded guilty twice before to sexually assaulting small children.

In 1981, a judge had labeled him a "compulsive, repetitive sexual offender." After he had served more than seven years for a 1981 crime, he was released. He and two other convicted child molesters had quietly moved into a neighborhood in which people tend to mind their children well. Before the killing, he appeared to the neighbors as pleasant. He had helped an elderly man move furniture. His classmates in high school considered him "one of those quiet kids." A therapist stated, "He was a pouter, and then he'd go hide. He spent a lot of time in bed."

The cases against him stemming from the assaults in 1979 and 1981 were handled routinely in the legal system. He benefitted from plea bargains in both cases. One prosecutor justified the plea bargain on the fact that since child victims make poor witnesses he was reluctant to take the case to trial.

His first known case occurred in 1979. He was 18 years old and his victim was 5 years old. He told police that he just wanted to look at her vagina. But the little girl stated that he smelled her and touched her. For that offense he pleaded guilty to attempted aggravated sexual assault. The judge in that case concluded that "While he certainly has mental or psychiatric problems, these seem to be of the type that can be dealt with best in an outpatient setting." He was given a suspended sentence on the condition that he go for counseling. Later cited for violating the terms of his suspended sentence, he served nine months in the Middlesex County Adult Correctional Center.

His second known case occurred in 1981, only months after he was released from the correctional center. The victim, who was seven years old at the time, was found unconscious in the woods near her neighborhood home. Examination revealed that sexual contact had occurred. There were blue marks on her neck where she had been choked and her stomach had black and blue marks on it. He was charged with five felonies and attempted murder. As the results of his plea bargain, all charges except the attempt were dropped. The judge imposed the maximum ten-year sentence and stated that he "constituted a danger to the public at large and to young children in particular."

At that time, a ten-year sentence in New Jersey really meant six years and eight months with credit for good behavior. He was sent to Avenel, New Jersey's Center for sexual offenders. Avenel's therapeutic approach to sexual offenders has been criticized for years by many officials who claim that they coddle offenders. Supporters contend that the therapy represents the only chance that some child molesters and rapists, who are destined to return to the streets, can get to gain enough insight to control themselves. Both sides admit that sex-offender treatment programs are particularly frustrated by the many offenders who do not open up for treatment. Individuals who were at Avenel at the time say that Timmendequas never seemed engaged in therapy.

Megan's death has since become a part of the national psyche. Many states have passed laws named for her requiring that communities be notified when sex offenders move in. On May 17, 1996, President Clinton signed a federal "Megan's Law." The *Random House Webster's College Dictionary* added "Megan's Law" as a new term in the language. Megan's mother speaks often around the country, lobbying for the law and warning parents to take care of their children.

Public records in New Jersey and interviews with people who knew him and with psychologists, detectives, lawyers, a judge and other professionals who dealt with him picture him as the type of sex offender who defies efforts at rehabilitation.[26] His 1981 victim, in describing the turmoil she felt 15 years later when she heard he was accused of killing Megan, said that she "wanted to kill him herself" and "that they didn't stop him the first time."

Under Megan's Law, when an individual is released from prison, the warden has a duty to notify him or her of this requirement. If the individual moves or intends to reside in a new location for a period of time (normally about seven days) he or she must register with the local law enforcement agency. In most states, the individual must submit a photograph and fingerprints at the time that he or she registers. Except for certain identifying data on the registration form, the information is available to the public.

One of the issues involved in Megan's Law is whether it may be applied to persons already convicted before the state act was passed. A sex offender who had completed his sentence before the enactment of the statute argued that it was a violation of his constitutional rights to require him to comply with the statute. The U.S. Court of Appeals for the Third Circuit held that the purpose of the statutes was not to punish the plaintiff, but to safeguard the public. Accordingly, the registration requirement can be explained only in terms of helping law enforcement agencies keep tabs on certain offenders, and the impact of the registration was not significant enough to brand it punishment.[27]

The New Jersey statute is typical of the notification statutes. Under it, all persons who complete sentences for certain crimes involving sexual assault must register with local law enforcement agencies. The registrant must provide certain identifying information to the local agency in the municipality in which he or she lives. He or she must confirm the address every 90 days and notify the agency if he or she moves. In addition, when the offender moves, he or she must notify the law enforcement agency in his or her new municipality. The prosecutor in the county in which the offender lives must determine whether the registrant poses a low, moderate, or high risk of reoffense. Under Tier I (low risk) notification is the only requirement. Under Tier II (moderate risk), the prosecutor must ensure that schools, licensed day care centers, summer camps, scout organizations, etc. are notified. Notification is not shared with the public under Tier II. Under Tier III (high risk) the law enforcement agencies are required to notify members of the public who are likely to encounter the registrant. Notification of individuals and organizations under Tiers II and III include the registrant's name, a recent photograph, his physical description, offense, address, place of employment or schooling, and a description and license number of his or her automobile.

PRISONERS' RIGHTS

Prior to the 1960s, the courts stayed out of the area of prisoners' rights. In the late 1960s, the U.S. Supreme Court began to involve itself in this area and has since decided more than 30 cases on the subject. The courts' involvement in prisoners' rights can be divided into three periods: the hands-off period (prior to 1964), the rights period (1964-1978), and the deference period (since 1979).[28]

During the *hands-off period*, the courts rarely accepted a case involving the conditions of confinement or prisoners' rights based on the concept that prison administrators were the ones best qualified to determine the appropriate conditions of confinement. Although the courts apparently recognized that prisoners have constitutional rights, the courts felt that it was not their role to intervene to protect those rights. One theory as to the reluctance of the courts to intervene during this period was that the courts perceived that intervention would usurp the proper functions of the legislative and executive branches of the government. A second reason given is that the courts felt that they lacked the expertise necessary to protect prisoners' rights and therefore ran a risk of interfering with the proper functioning of the prisons. The third popular reason given was that most prisoners were confined in state institutions and they attempted to protect their rights in federal courts. The federal courts were hesitant to interfere in state governmental operations.

During the *rights period*, the courts became actively involved in prison administration. The movement started when the lower federal courts demonstrated a willingness to identify prisoners' rights and moved to protect those rights. In addition, the legal profession developed a cadre of public interest lawyers who were more willing than in the past to fight the system.

The *deference period* is marked by the policy of the courts to defer to prison administrators' judgments unless constitutional violations are apparent. The present climate can be described as one in which prisoners will lose on most rights issues, while the courts stress the need to give deference to the expertise of correctional officials. The federal Prison Litigation Reform Act of 1996 is designed to limit federal court intervention into prison administration.[29] This legislation is discussed later in this chapter.

Areas of Involvement

Prisoners' rights can be divided into four broad areas:

- Right of access to the courts
- Individual rights
- Due process issues
- Cruel and unusual punishment[30]

The general consensus is that the courts tend to favor inmates when the issue involves the right of access to the courts, and to favor prison officials when the other three areas are involved.

Due Process Rights

Except for those cases brought by pretrial detainees regarding the conditions of their confinement, most due process rights issues concern procedural protections that must be afforded an inmate. For example, the inmate does not contend that the prison officials can not take the action that they have taken, only that before taking the action, the officials failed to provide him or her with the procedural protections to which the prisoner was entitled. In this area, it appears that the Court generally holds that if a liberty interest is involved, such as the loss of good time, prior to taking the action the inmate has a right to written notice, an opportunity to be heard, a written statement of the reasons for the decisions, and the right to be represented by a representative (not necessarily an attorney).

Torts

In most situations, prisoners challenging actions of prison officials do so by tort actions. A *tort* is a civil wrong or injury, other than a breach of contract, resulting from a violation of a duty. Most tort cases involving prisoners are filed under the Civil Rights Act, Section 1983.

> ## Civil Rights Act
>
> ### Title 42, Section 1983, U.S. Code
>
> Any person who, under color of any statute, ordinance, regulation, custom, or usage, or any state, or territory, subjects or causes to be subjected, any citizen of the United States or other person within the jurisdiction thereof to the deprivation of any rights, privileges, or immunities secured by the Constitution and laws, shall be liable to the party injured in an action at law, suit in equity, or other proper proceedings for redress.

Less than two percent of the section 1983 cases filed by inmates are successful in obtaining any redress. Despite this low rate of success, the number of cases filed each year continues to increase. It was estimated that more than 50,000 suits were filed nationwide by prisoners in 1999.

Conditions of Confinement

Prisoners who are detained in pretrial confinement facilities may challenge the conditions of their confinement under the Fifth or Fourteenth Amendments' due process clause. Prisoners who have been convicted may challenge their conditions under the Eighth Amendment's prohibition against cruel and unusual punishments.

Habeas Corpus

Traditionally, prisoners have filed *writs of habeas corpus* to attack the state court convictions. This writ, traditionally known as the "Great Writ," is a constitutionally protected writ designed to require the government to justify why the individual is being held in confinement. Under the process, the prisoner can file a writ in federal court alleging that he is being illegally held in confinement because his conviction was in violation of a state or federal constitutional right. If the writ involves only state issues, then the state courts make the final decision. If the writ is based on a federal issue, e.g., his conviction was based on the violation of a federal constitutional right, then the final decisionmakers are the federal courts. After the prisoner files the writ, the receiving court determines whether a writ should be issued. If the court issues a writ, then the warden (actually a representative from the attorney general's office) must come forward and justify the confinement. The justification usually consists of filing proof of the conviction, at which point the burden shifts to the defendant to establish the illegality of the conviction. Less than one percent of the writs filed are successful. The problem is that a vast number of writs flood the court system.

The writ is also the way that the death penalty from state criminal trials is traditionally attacked in federal court. In the past, convictions have been voided years after the defendants were found guilty. The process has also been used to delay the imposition of the death penalty. To eliminate this, the U.S. Congress passed the Antiterrorism and Effective Death Penalty Act in 1976. This act establishes limitation periods for the bringing of *habeas* actions and requires that federal courts generally defer to state courts' determinations. Under the act, a *habeas* petitioner will normally have one year in which to seek relief. If the claim has been adjudicated in state court, relief will not be available unless the state court's adjudication resulted in a decision that is either contrary to, or involved an unreasonable application of, clearly established federal law as determined by the U.S. Supreme Court, or was based on an unreasonable determination of the facts in light of the evidence presented in the state court proceedings. The presumption of correctness accorded state courts' factual findings was also strengthened. Second or successive *habeas* actions presenting new claims must be dismissed unless the claim is shown to rely on a new, previously unavailable rule of constitutional law, or the factual predicate for the claim could not have been discovered previously through due diligence and the new facts would be sufficient to establish by clear and convincing evidence that, except for the error, no reasonable factfinder would have convicted.[31]

Prison Litigation Reform Act

In an attempt to reduce federal involvement in the operation of state correctional systems, the U.S. Congress passed the Prison Litigation Reform Act in 1996. This act was an amendment to the 1994 Crime Bill.[32] Under this act, federal courts are instructed to extend no further than necessary prospective relief in prison overcrowding orders. The act sets two minimum conditions for the entry of prisoner release orders. [One popular method used by federal courts was to order the correction of a problem or in the alternative to release the prisoners held under the conditions complained of in the case.] First, a prior order of less intrusive relief must have failed; and second, the prison official must have had a reasonable opportunity to comply with the previous order. In addition, a single judge may not issue a prisoner release order based on overcrowding. Any order issued must be approved by an appellate court or a three judge federal court. Before issuing an order for relief, the court must find by clear and convincing evidence that overcrowding is the primary cause of the violation of a federal right and that no relief other than an order releasing prisoners will remedy the violation. Prior to filing for a release order, the prisoner must first exhaust state remedies. In addition, prisoners may not bring federal civil rights actions for mental or emotional injury suffered while in custody without a prior showing of physical injury. The award of attorney fees to successful prisoner litigators was also limited to only that which was directly and reasonably incurred in enforcing the relief.

BACK TO THE BASICS

Starting in the mid-1990s, legislatures have decided that they were tired of "coddling" prison inmates and have attempted to make prison conditions harsher for the inmates. A Mississippi state senator stated, "We want a prisoner to look like a prisoner and to smell like one." In 1996, Mississippi banned individual television sets from inmate cells, banned air conditioning, prohibited weight-lifting equipment, and required inmates to dress in striped uniforms with CONVICT stamped on the back. Ohio, Wisconsin, and North Carolina have enacted similar legislation. California is now charging inmates $3 to initiate court actions and has banned R-rated movies. South Carolina has banned conjugal visits for minimum security inmates, ending a 50-year tradition. New Jersey is considering legislation that would require inmates to work 10-hour days with no educational programs, no gyms, and no television sets. The U.S. Congress has eliminated educational grants for federal prisoners. Chain gangs are once again being used in some Southern states.[33] Although the above perks may be considered as rights by some, it appears that the courts will defer to the prison administrators regarding the new trend in making prison a harsher place. As one judge stated, it appears that none of these types of measures will deter crime, but they do not infringe on any prisoner's constitutional rights.

CASE ON POINT

Assume that you are the district court judge and responsible for determining the sentence in a case involving a popular 64-year-old Jewish rabbi who plead guilty to two counts involving knowing and willful participation in a scheme to defraud the United States. The scheme involved federal Medicaid funds being paid to nursing homes. This case was widely reported in the New York newspapers.

What factors would you consider in determining the correct sentence?

Would you send the rabbi to prison?

The following sentencing memorandum was issued by the trial court judge to justify his sentence.

United States v. Bergman
416 F.Supp. 496 (S.D.N.Y., 1976)

SENTENCING MEMORANDUM
FRANKEL, District Judge.
    Defendant is being sentenced upon his plea of guilty to two counts of an 11-count indictment. The sentencing proceeding is unusual in some respects. It has been the subject of more extensive submissions, written and oral, than this court has ever received upon such an occasion. The court has studied some hundreds of pages of memoranda and exhibits, plus scores of volunteered letters. A broad array of issues has been addressed. Imaginative suggestions of law and penology have been tendered. A preliminary conversation with counsel, on the record, preceded the usual sentencing hearing. Having heard counsel again and the defendant speaking for himself, the court postponed the pronouncement of sentence for further reconsideration of thoughts generated during the days of studying the briefs and oral pleas. It seems fitting now to report in writing the reasons upon which the court concludes that defendant must be sentenced to a term of four months in prison.[34]

I. DEFENDANT AND HIS CRIMES

    Defendant appeared, until the last couple of years, to be a man of unimpeachably high character, attainments, and distinction. A doctor of divinity and an ordained rabbi, he has been acclaimed by people around the world for his works of public philanthropy, private charity, and leadership in educational enterprises. Scores of letters have come to the court from across this and other countries reporting debts of personal gratitude to him for numerous acts of extraordinary generosity. (The court has also received a kind of petition, with fifty-odd signatures, in which the signers, based upon learning acquired as newspaper readers, denounce the defendant and urge a severe sentence. Unlike the pleas for mercy, which appear to reflect unquestioned facts inviting compassion, this document should and will be disregarded.) In addition to his good works, defendant has managed to amass considerable wealth in the ownership and operation of nursing homes, in real estate ventures, and in a course of substantial investments.

Beginning about two years ago, investigations of nursing homes in this area, including questions of fraudulent claims for Medicaid funds, drew to a focus upon this defendant among several others. The results that concern us were the present indictment and two state indictments. After extensive pretrial proceedings, defendant embarked upon elaborate plea negotiations with both state and federal prosecutors. A state guilty plea and the instant plea were entered in March of this year. (Another state indictment is expected to be dismissed after defendant is sentenced on those to which he has pled guilty.) As part of the detailed plea arrangements, it is expected that the prison sentence imposed by this court will comprise the total covering the state as well as the federal convictions.[35]

For purposes of the sentence now imposed, the precise details of the charges, and of defendant's carefully phrased admissions of guilt, are not matters of prime importance. Suffice it to say that the plea on Count One (carrying a maximum of five years in prison and a $10,000 fine) confesses defendant's knowing and wilful participation in a scheme to defraud the United States in various ways, including the presentation of wrongfully padded claims for payments under the Medicaid program to defendant's nursing homes. Count Three, for which the guilty plea carries a theoretical maximum of three more years in Prison and another $5,000 fine, is a somewhat more "technical" charge. Here, defendant admits to having participated in the filing of a Partnership return which was false and fraudulent in failing to list people who had bought Partnership interests from him in one of his nursing homes, had paid for such interests, and had made certain capital withdrawals.

The conspiracy to defraud, as defendant has admitted it, is by no means the worst of its kind; it is by no means as flagrant or extensive as has been portrayed in the press; it is evidently less grave than other nursing home wrongs for which others have been convicted or publicized. At the same time, the sentence, as defendant has acknowledged, is imposed for two federal felonies including, as the more important, a knowing and purposeful conspiracy to mislead and defraud the Federal Government

II. The Guiding Principles of Sentencing

Proceeding through the short list of the supposed justifications for criminal sanctions, defense counsel urges that no licit purpose could be served by defendant's incarceration. Some of these arguments are plainly sound; others are not.

The court agrees that this defendant should not be sent to prison for "rehabilitation." Apart from the patent inappositeness of the concept to this individual, this court shares the growing understanding that no one should ever be sent to prison for *rehabilitation*. That is to say, nobody who would not otherwise be locked up should suffer that fate on the incongruous premise that it will be good for him or her. Imprisonment is punishment. Facing the simple reality should help us to be civilized. It is less agreeable to confine someone when we deem it an affliction rather than a benefaction. If someone must be imprisoned—for other, valid reasons—we should seek to make rehabilitative resources available to him or her. But the goal of rehabilitation cannot fairly serve in itself as grounds for the sentence to confinement.[36]

Equally clearly, this defendant should not be confined to incapacitate him. He is not dangerous. It is most improbable that he will commit similar, or any, offenses in the future. There is no need for "specific deterrence."

Contrary to counsel's submissions, however, two sentencing considerations demand a prison sentence in this case:

First, the aim of *general deterrence,* the effort to discourage similar wrongdoing by others through a reminder that the law's warnings are real and that the grim consequence of imprisonment is likely to follow from crimes of deception for gain like those defendant has admitted.

Second, the related, but not identical, concern that any lesser penalty would, in the words of the Model Penal Code, 7.01(1)(c), "depreciate the seriousness of the defendant's crime."

Resisting the first of these propositions, defense counsel invoked Immanuel Kant's axiom that "one man ought never to be dealt with merely as a means subservient to the purposes of another."[37] In a more novel, but equally futile effort, counsel urge that a sentence for general deterrence "would violate the Eighth Amendment proscription against cruel and unusual punishment." Treating the latter point first, because it is a short subject, it may be observed simply that if general deterrence as a sentencing purpose were now to be outlawed, as against a near unanimity of views among state and federal jurists, the bolt would have to come from a place higher than this.[38]

As for Dr. Kant, it may well be that defense counsel mistake his meaning in the present context.[39] Whether or not that is so, and without pretending to be an authority on that score, we take the widely accepted stance that a criminal punished in the interest of general deterrence is not being employed "*merely* as a means...." Reading Kant to mean that every man must be deemed *more* than the instrument of others, and must "always be treated as an end in himself,"[40] the humane principle is not offended here. Each of us is served by the enforcement of the law—not least a person like the defendant in this case, whose wealth and privileges, so long enjoyed, are so much founded upon law. More broadly, we are driven regularly in our ultimate interests as members of the community to use ourselves and each other, in war and in peace, for social ends. One who has transgressed against the criminal laws is certainly among the more fitting candidates for a role of this nature. This is no arbitrary selection. Warned in advance of the prospect, the transgressor has chosen, in the law's premises, "between keeping the law required for society's protection or paying the penalty."[41]

But the whole business, defendant argues further, is guesswork; we are by no means certain that deterrence "works." The position is somewhat overstated; there is, in fact, some reasonably "scientific" evidence for the efficacy of criminal sanctions as deterrents, at least as against some kinds of crimes.[42] Moreover, the time is not yet here when all we can "know" must be quantifiable and digestible by computers. The shared wisdom of generations teaches meaningfully, if somewhat amorphously, that the utilitarians have a point; we do, indeed, lapse often into rationality and act to seek pleasure and avoid pain.[43] It would be better, to be sure, if we had more certainty and precision. Lacking these comforts, we continue to include among our working hypotheses a belief (with some concrete evidence in its support) that crimes like those in this case—deliberate, purposeful, continuing, non-impulsive, and committed for profit—are among those most likely to be generally deferrable by sanctions most shunned by those exposed to temptation.[44]

    The idea of avoiding depreciation of the seriousness of the offense implicates two or three thoughts, not always perfectly clear or universally agreed upon, beyond the idea of deterrence. It should be proclaimed by the court's judgment that the offenses are grave, not minor or purely technical. Some attention must be paid to the demand for equal justice; it will not do to leave the penalty of imprisonment a dead letter as against "privileged" violators while it is employed regularly, and with vigor, against others. There probably is in these conceptions an element of retributiveness, as counsel urge. And retribution, so denominated, is in some disfavor as a reason for punishment. It remains a factor, however, as Holmes perceived,[45] and as is known to any one who talks to judges, lawyers, defendants, or people generally. It may become more palatable, and probably more humanely understood, under the rubric of "deserts" or "just deserts."[46] However the concept is formulated, we have not yet reached a state, supposing we ever should, in which the infliction of punishments for crime may be divorced generally from ideas of blame worthiness, recompense, and proportionality.

III. An Alternative, "Behavioral Sanction"

Resisting prison above all else, defense counsel included in their thorough memorandum on sentencing two proposals for what they call a "constructive," and therefore a "preferable" form of "behavioral sanction." One is a plan for Dr. Bergman to create and run a program of Jewish vocational and religious high school training. The other is for him to take charge of a "Committee on Holocaust Studies," again concerned with education at the secondary school level.

A third suggestion was made orally at yesterday's sentencing hearing. It was proposed that Dr. Bergman might be ordered to work as a volunteer in some established agency as a visitor and aide to the sick and the otherwise incapacitated. The proposal was that he could read, provide various forms of physical assistance, and otherwise give comfort to afflicted people.

No one can doubt either the worthiness of these proposals or Dr. Bergman's ability to make successes of them. But both of the carefully formulated "sanctions" in the memorandum involve work of an honorific nature, not unlike that done in other projects to which the defendant has devoted himself in the past. It is difficult to conceive of them as "punishments" at all. The more recent proposal is somewhat more suitable in character, but it is still an insufficient penalty. The seriousness of the crimes to which Dr. Bergman has pled guilty demands something more than "requiring" him to lend his talents and efforts to further philanthropic enterprises. It remains open to him, of course, to pursue the interesting suggestions later on as a matter of unforced personal choice.

IV. "Measuring" the Sentence

In cases like this one, the decision of greatest moment is whether to imprison or not. As reflected in the eloquent submissions for defendant, the prospect of the closing prison doors is the most appalling concern; the feeling is that the length of the sojourn is a lesser question once that threshold is passed. Nevertheless, the setting of a term remains to be accomplished. And in some respects it is a subject even more perplexing, unregulated, and unprincipled.

Days and months and years are countable with a sound of exactitude. But there can be no exactitude in the deliberations from which a number emerges. Without pretending to a nonexistent precision, the court notes at least the major factors.

The criminal behavior, as has been noted, is blatant in character and unmitigated by any suggestion of necessitous circumstance or other pressures difficult to resist. However metaphysicians may conjure with issues about free will, it is a fundamental premise of our efforts to do criminal justice that competent people, possessed of their faculties, make choices and are accountable for them. In this sometimes harsh light, the case of the present defendant is among the clearest and least relieved. Viewed against the maxima Congress ordained, and against the run of sentences in other federal criminal cases, it calls for more than a token sentence.[47]

On the other side are factors that take longer to enumerate. Defendant's illustrious public life and works are in his favor, though diminished, of course, by what this case discloses. This is a first, probably a last, conviction. Defendant is 64 years old and in imperfect health, though by no means so ill, from what the court is told, that he could be expected to suffer inordinately more than many others of advanced years who go to prison.

Defendant invokes an understandable, but somewhat unworkable, notion of "disparity." He says others involved in recent nursing home fraud cases have received relatively light sentences for behavior more culpable than his. He lays special emphasis upon one defendant whose frauds appear indeed to have involved larger amounts and who was sentenced to a maximum of six months' incarceration, to be confined for that time only on week nights, not on week days or weekends. This court has examined the minutes of that sentencing proceeding and finds the case distinguishable in material respects. But even if there were a threat of such disparity as defendant warns against, it could not be a major weight on the scales.

Our sentencing system, deeply flawed, is characterized by disparity. We are to seek to "individualize" sentences, but no clear or clearly agreed standards govern the individualization. The lack of meaningful criteria does indeed leave sentencing judges far too much at large. But the result, with its nagging burdens on conscience, cannot be meaningfully alleviated by allowing any handful of sentences in a short series to fetter later judgments. The point is easy, of course, where Sentence No. 1 or Sentences 1–5 are notably harsh. It cannot be that a later judge, disposed to more leniency, should feel in any degree "bound." The converse is not identical, but it is not totally different. The net of this is that this court has considered and has given some weight to the trend of the other cited sentences (though strict logic might call for none), but without treating them as forceful "precedents" in any familiar sense.

How, then, is the particular sentence adjudged in this case? As has been mentioned, the case calls for a sentence that is more than nominal. Given the other circumstances, however—including that this is a first offense, by a man no longer young and not perfectly well, where danger of recidivism is not a concern—it verges on cruelty to think of confinement for a term of years. We sit, to be sure, in a nation where prison sentences of extravagant length are more common than they are almost anywhere else. By that light, the term imposed today is not notably long. For this sentencing court, however, for a nonviolent first offense involving no direct assaults or invasions of others' security (as in bank robbery, narcotics, etc.), it is a stern sentence. For people like Dr. Bergman, who might be disposed to engage in similar wrongdoing, it should be sufficiently frightening to serve the major end of general deterrence. For all but the profoundly vengeful, it should not depreciate the seriousness of his offenses.

V. Punishment in or for the Media

Much of defendant's sentencing memorandum is devoted to the extensive barrage of hostile publicity to which he has been subjected during the years before and since his indictment. He argues, and it appears to be undisputed, that the media (and people desiring to be featured in the media) have vilified him for many kinds of evildoing of which he has in fact been innocent. Two main points are made on this score with respect to the problem of sentencing.

First, as has been mentioned, counsel express the concern that the court may be pressured toward severity by the force of the seeming public outcry. That the court should not allow itself to be affected in this way is clear beyond discussion.[48] Nevertheless, it is not merely permissible, but entirely wholesome and responsible, for counsel to bring the expressed concern out in the open. Whatever our ideals and mixed images about judges, it would be naive to doubt that judges have sometimes been swept by a sense of popular demand toward draconian sentencing decisions. It cannot hurt for the sentencing judge to be reminded of this and cautioned about it. There can be no guarantees. The sentencer must confront and regulate himself. But it bears reaffirmance that the court must seek to discount utterly the fact of notoriety in passing its judgment upon the defendant. Defense counsel cite reported opinions of this court reflecting what happens in a large number of unreported cases, by the present sentencer and many others, in which "unknown" defendants have received prison sentences, longer or shorter than today's, for white-collar or comparably nonviolent crimes. The overall run of cases, with all their individual variations, will reflect, it is hoped, earnest efforts to hew to the principle of equal treatment, with or without publicity.

Defendant's second point about his public humiliation is the frequently heard contention that he should not be incarcerated because he "has been punished enough." The thought is not without some initial appeal. If punishment were wholly or mainly retributive, it might be a weighty factor. In the end, however, it must be a matter of little or no force. Defendant's notoriety should not in the last analysis serve to lighten, any more than it may be permitted to aggravate, his sentence. The fact that he has been pilloried by journalists is essentially a consequence of the prestige and privileges he enjoyed before he was exposed as a wrongdoer. The long fall from grace was possible only because of the height he had reached. The suffering from loss of public esteem reflects a body of opinion that the esteem had been, in at least some wrongly bestowed and enjoyed. It is not possible to justify the notion that this mode of nonjudicial punishment should be an occasion for leniency not given to a defendant who never basked in such an admiring light at all. The quest for both the appearance and the substance of equal justice prompts the court to discount the thought that the public humiliation serves the function of imprisonment.

Writing, as judges rarely do, about a particular sentence concentrates the mind with possibly special force upon the experience of the sentencer as well as the person sentenced. Consigning someone to prison, this defendant or any other, "is a sad necessity." There are impulses of avoidance from time to time—toward a personally gratifying leniency or toward an opposite extreme. But there is, obviously, no place for private impulse in the judgment of the court. The course of justice must be sought with such objective rationality as we can muster, tempered with mercy, but obedient to the law, which, we do well to remember, is all that empowers a judge to make other people suffer.

CASE SUMMARIES

The interest in confidentiality of measures taken to capture escaped inmates was sufficient to justify denying prisoner access to prison internal memoranda in disciplinary hearing concerning his escape. *Ryan v. Pico*, 642 N.Y.S.2d 436 (A.D. 1996).

The failure to call previously requested witness at prisoner's disciplinary hearing did not violate his due process rights when prisoner failed to repeat request when given opportunity to do so and failed to object to hearing being closed after his own testimony; prisoner waived his right to call witness by his silence. *Bedoya v. Coughlin*, 91 F.3d 349 (2nd Cir. 1996).

A New York prison regulation setting aside some prisoner wages until prisoners are released did not violate any constitutional rights; federal court also upholds regulations imposing a $5 surcharge on such wages after prisoners are found guilty, following a disciplinary hearing, of infractions of prison rules. *Rudolph v. Cuomo*, 916 F. Supp. 1308 (S.D.N.Y. 1996).

A prisoner was properly found guilty of disciplinary charges of assault even though later acquitted of criminal charges arising from same incident; requiring him to defend himself against disciplinary charges first did not violate his Fifth Amendment right against self-incrimination in the criminal trial. *Bellum v. Vose*, 848 F. Supp. 1065 (D. Mass. 1994).

The prisoner was not entitled to counsel substitute at disciplinary hearing when the issues presented were not complex and he was able to understand the issues and clearly present his defense. *Giles v. State*, 511 N.W.2d 622 (Iowa 1994).

U.S. Supreme Court rules that prisoner placed in disciplinary segregation following charges of misconduct was not entitled to due process procedural protections; state regulation simply requiring that disciplinary guilt be supported by substantial evidence did not result in a state-created constitutionally protected "liberty" interest; focus in determining whether state creates a liberty interest to shift from search for mandatory language in state laws or regulations to the nature of the deprivation imposed. *Sandin v. Conner,* 115 S. Ct. 2293 (1995).

An inmate was properly confined in isolation until he consents to blood test to determine venereal disease. *Smallwood-El v. Coughlin*, 589 F. Supp. 692 (S.D. N.Y. 1984)

A federal appeals court rules that Prison Litigation Reform Act of 1996 applies retroactively to plaintiff prisoner's pending appeal as a pauper of dismissal of federal civil rights lawsuit as frivolous. *Marks v. Solcum*, 98 F.3d 494 (9th Cir. 1996).

A federal appeals court rules that requirements of Prison Litigation Reform Act that prisoners pay filing fees applied both to $5 filing fee and $100 "docketing" fee required for appeal; obligation on prisoner to be imposed prior to determination as to whether or not appeal was frivolous. *Leonard v. Lacy*, 88 F.3d 181 (2nd Cir. 1996).

A prisoner was not required to comply with fee provisions of Prison Litigation Reform Act when his appeal was fully submitted for consideration to the appeals court prior to the Act's effective date. *Ramsey v. Coughlin*, 94 F.3d 71 (2nd Cir. 1996).

The compensation of special master appointed to oversee implementation of court orders concerning inadequate medical care of inmates was not subject to limitations in Prison Litigation Reform Act when master was appointed before effective date of the law. *Coleman v. Wilson,* 933 F. Supp. 954 (E.D. Cal. 1996).

SUMMARY

- In primitive societies, the remedy for wrongs done to one's person or property was personal retaliation against the wrongdoer. From the concept of personal retaliation, developed blood feuds. To lessen the costly and damaging vendettas, the custom of accepting money or property in place of blood vengeance developed. At first, the acceptance of payments instead of blood vengeance was not compulsory. The victim's family was still free to choose whatever form of vengeance they wished.

- Fines and other forms of punishment replaced personal retaliation as tribal leaders began to exert their authority during the negotiations or proceedings concerning the damages caused or the wrongs committed.

- During the Middle Ages, rapid changes were made in the social structure of societies. In addition, the growing influence of the church on everyday life helped create a divided system of justice. The offender, in committing a crime, also committed a sin. Accordingly, he or she had two debts to pay.

- There are numerous methods to classify ideologies. Three popular classifications based on political theories that influence our corrections system are conservative, liberal, and radical.

- The four popular goals of criminal sanctions are retribution, deterrence, incapacitation, and rehabilitation.

From the 1940s to the 1980s, rehabilitation was considered by most as the primary goal of our system. Since the 1980s, retribution as received popular support. The various approaches to correctional philosophy fall into one of three categories: punishment, treatment, or prevention. Often, they overlap as punishment and treatment can be argued as an approach to prevent crime.

- The common theme of the six strategies is to "reduce judicial and correctional imperialism." The six strategies are determinate sentencing, mandatory prison terms, sentencing guidelines, parole guidelines, good-time guidelines and emergency overcrowding provisions.

- The Violent Crime Control and Law Enforcement Act of 1994 and similar acts use the enforcement model approach to reducing crime.

- Formal rules of evidence do not apply in prison discipline cases. Due process requirements impose the requirement that prison discipline cases provide the inmate with the right to written notice, a hearing and, in many cases, the right to appeal.

- Most correctional institutions have formal grievance procedures for inmates who feel that they have been mistreated or not received proper credit for good time.

- The three ways that an inmate may be released from prison are parole, mandatory supervison and discharge. Certain inmates may be required to register as sex offenders on their release from prison.

- Prisoners' rights can be divided into three periods: the hands-off period, the rights period, and the deference period. The rights can be divided into four broad areas; right to access to the courts, individual rights, due process rights, and cruel and unusual punishment issues.

DISCUSSION QUESTIONS

1. Explain the development of the concepts of punishment as we know it today.
2. What should be the goals of punishment?
3. What rights should prisoners have?
4. What was the purpose of the Prison Litigation Reform Act?

ENDNOTES

1. As reported by Marvin E. Frankel, *Criminal Sentences: Law Without Order*, (1973) p.9.
2. Lynn S. Branharm and Sheldon Krantz, *Cases and Materials on the Law of Sentencing, Corrections, and Prisoners' Rights*, 5th ed. (St. Paul: West, 1997) p. 2.
3. Albert Kocourek and John Wigmore, *Evolution of Law*, Vol. II, (Boston: Little, Brown and Company, 1915) p.15.
4. John Swain, *The Pleasures of the Torture Chamber,* (New York: Dorset Press, 1931) p. 27.
5. Alexis M. Durham III, *Crisis and Reform: Current Issues in American Punishment,* (Boston: Little, Brown and Company, 1994) pp. 16–18.
6. Herbert L. Packer, *The Limits of Criminal Sanction* (Stanford, Ca.: Stanford University Press, 1968) p. 33.
7. Robert O. Dawson, *Sentencing: The Decision as to Type, Length, and Conditions of Sentence,* (Boston:Little, Brown and Company, 1969).
8. Herbert L. Packer, *The Limits of Criminal Sanction,* (Stanford: Univ. of Stanford Press, 1968) p. 37.
9. Elmer H. Johnson, *Crime, Correction, and Society,* (Homewood, Ill.: Dorsey Press, 1974) p. 173.
10. Marianne W. Zawitz, ed., *Report to the Nation on Crime and Justice* (Washington, D.C.:, Bureau of Justice Statistics, U.S. Government Printing Office, 1983) p. 35.
11. Durham, 1994:26.
12. Packer, 1963:49.
13. Packer, 1963:55-57.
14. C. Ray Jeffery, "The Historical Development of Criminology," in *Pioneers in Criminology*, 2d ed. Hermann Mannheim, ed. (Montclair, NJ: Patterson Smith, 1973) p. 487.
15. Joan Petersilia, "A Crime Control Rationale For Reinvesting in Community Corrections," *The Prison Journal*, Vol. 75, No. 4, December 1995, pp. 479-496.
16. Petersilia, 1995:479.
17. Elaine Wolf and Marsha Weissman, "Revising Federal Sentencing Policy: Some Consequences of Expanding Eligibility for Alternative Sanctions," *Crime and Delinquency*, Vol. 42, No. 2, April 1996, p. 192-197.

18. United States Sentencing Commission, *Guidelines Manual,* (Nov. 1995).
19. American Law Institute, *Model Penal Code Proposed Official Draft*, (Philadelphia, 1962).
20. *Hughes v. Rowe*, 449 U.S. 5 (1980).
21. *Nickens v. White*, 622 F.2d 967 (8th Cir. 1973).
22. ABA Standards for Criminal Justice, Legal Status of Prisoners, Standard 23-3.1.
23. *Weems v. United States*, 217 U.S. 349 (1910).
24. *Rhodes v. Robinson*, 612 F.2d 766 (3d Cir. 1972).
25. Bureau of Justice Assistance, *Intensive Supervision Probation and Parole: Program Brief*, (Washington, D.C.: U.S. Department of Justice, 1988) p. 7.
26. *New York Times*, May 26, 1996, page B6.
27. *Artway v. Attorney General of New Jersey*, CA3, decided April 12, 1996.
28. Jack E. Call, "The Supreme Court and Prisoners' Rights," *Federal Probation*, Vol. 59, No. 1, March 1995, pp. 36-46.
29. 28 U.S. Code 3626, as amended.
30. Call, 1995: 41.
31. 18 U.S.Code 3663A.
32. 28 U.S. Code 3626.
33. *Time*, September 4, 1995, p. 31 and *Newsweek*, October 17, 1994, p.87.
34. The court considered, and finally rejected, imposing a fine in addition to the prison term. Defendant seems destined to pay hundreds of thousands of dollars in restitution. The amount is being worked out in connection with a state criminal indictment. Apart from defendant's further liabilities for federal taxes, any additional money exaction is appropriately left for the state court.
35. This is not absolutely certain. Defendant has been told, however, that the imposition of any additional prison sentence by the state court will be an occasion for reconsidering today's judgment.
36. This important point, correcting misconceptions still widely prevalent, is developed more fully by Dean Norval Morris in *The Future of Imprisonment* (1974).
37. Quoting from I. Kant, *Philosophy of Law,* 1986 (Hastie Trans. 1887).

38. To a large extent, the defendant's Eighth Amendment argument is that imprisoning him because he has been "newsworthy" would be cruelly wrong.
39. See H.L.A. Hart, *Punishment and Responsibility,* (1968) pp. 243-44.
40. Andenaes, "The Morality of Deterrence," 37 U. Chi. L.Rev. 649 (1970). See also O. Holmes, *Common Law*, (1881) pp. 43-44, 46-47.
41. H.L.A. Hart, supra note 6, at 23.
42. See, e.g., F. Zimring and G. Hawkins, *Deterence* 168-71, (1973) p. 282.
43. See Andenaes, supra note 7, at 663-64.
44. For some supporting evidence that "white-collar" offenses are somewhat specially deterrable, see Chambliss, "Types of Deviance and the Effectiveness of Legal Sanctions," 1967 Wis. L. Rev. 703, 708-10.
45. See O. Holmes, *Common Law* 41-42, 45 (1881).
46. See A. von Hirsch, *Doing Justice* (1976) pp. 45-55 ; see also N. Morris, *The Future of Imprisonment* (1974) pp. 73-77.
47. Despite Biblical teachings concerning what is expected from those to whom much is given, the court has not, as his counsel feared might happen, held Dr. Bergman to a higher standard of responsibility because of his position in the community. But he has not been judged under a lower standard either.
48. Cf. Andenaes, supra note 7, at 656.

CHAPTER 2

THE COURT SYSTEM

> *Justice, though due to the accused, is due to the accuser also. The concept of fairness must not be strained till it is narrowed to a filament. We are to keep the balance true.*
>
> Justice Cardozo
> *Snyder v. Massachusetts,* 291 U.S. 97 (1934)

COURT STRUCTURE

Introduction

In order to understand the role of federal and state law in sentencing, prisoners' rights, and corrections, it is essential to have a firm grasp of the principles of how the American criminal justice system functions. There is no more confusing, frustrating, and complex environment in the legal system than the criminal court system.

The court system in the United States is based upon the principle of federalism. The first Congress established a federal court system and the individual states were permitted to continue their own judicial structure. There was general agreement among our nation's founding fathers that individual states needed to retain significant autonomy from federal control. Under this concept of federalism, the United States developed as a loose confederation of semi-independent states with the federal court system acting in a very limited manner. In the early history of our nation, most cases were tried in state courts, and it was only later that the federal government and the federal judiciary began to exercise jurisdiction over crimes and civil matters. *Jurisdiction,* in this context, simply means the ability of the court to enforce laws and punish individuals who violate those laws.

As a result of this historical evolution, a dual system, consisting of state and federal courts, exists today. Therefore, federal and state courts may have concurrent jurisdiction over specific crimes. For example, a person who robs a bank may be tried and convicted in state court for robbery and then tried and convicted in federal court for the federal offense of robbery of a federally chartered savings institution.

Another characteristic of the American court system is that it performs its duties with little or no supervision. A supreme court justice does not exercise supervision over lower court judges in the same way that a government supervisor or manager exercises control over his or her employees. The U.S. Supreme Court and the various state supreme courts exercise supervision only in the sense that they hear appellate cases from lower courts and establish certain procedures for these courts.

A third feature of our court system is one of specialization that occurs primarily at the state and local level. In many states, courts of limited jurisdiction hear misdemeanor cases. Other state courts of general jurisdiction try felonies. Still other courts may be designated to hear only matters involving juveniles. This process also occurs in certain civil courts that hear only family law matters, probate matters, or civil cases involving damages. At the federal level, there are courts such as bankruptcy that hear only cases dealing with specific matters.

The fourth characteristic of the American court system is its geographic organization. State and federal courts are organized into geographic areas. In many jurisdictions, these are called judicial districts and contain various levels of courts. For example, on the federal level, the 9th Circuit Court of Appeals has district (trial) courts that hear matters within certain specific boundaries and an appellate court that hears all appeals from cases within that area. Several studies have been conducted regarding the difference in sentences for the same type of crime in geographic distinct courts. For example the average sentence for motor vehicle theft in Iowa was 47 months, while the average sentence for the same offense in New York was fourteen months.[1] This shouldn't be taken as a criticism; rather, it may reflect different social values and attitudes within specific geographic areas.

The State System

Historically, each of the 13 states had its own unique court structure. This independence continued after the American Revolution and resulted in widespread differences among the various states, some of which still exist today. Because each state adopted its own system of courts, the consequence was a poorly planned and confusing judicial structure. As a result, there have been several reform movements whose purpose has been to streamline and modernize this system. Many state courts can be divided into three levels: trial courts, appellate courts, and state supreme courts.

Trial Courts

Trial courts are where criminal cases start and finish. The trial court conducts the entire series of acts that culminate in either the defendant's release or sentencing. State trial courts can be further divided into courts of limited or special jurisdiction and courts of general jurisdiction.

The nature and type of case determines which court will have jurisdiction. Courts that only hear and decide certain limited legal issues are courts of limited jurisdiction. Typically, these courts hear certain types of minor civil or criminal cases. There are approximately 13,000 local courts in the United States. They are county, magistrate, justice, or municipal courts. Judges in these courts may be either appointed or elected. In many jurisdictions, these are part-time positions and the incumbent may have another job or position in addition to serving as a judge. However, simply because they handle minor civil and criminal matters does not mean that these courts do not perform important duties. Many times the only contact the average citizen will have with the judicial system occurs at this level. Courts of limited jurisdiction hear and decide issues, such as traffic tickets, or set bail for criminal defendants.

In addition, courts of limited jurisdiction may hear certain types of specialized matters, such as probate of wills and estates, divorces, child custody matters and juvenile hearings. These types of courts may be local courts or, depending on the state, courts of general jurisdiction that are designated by statute to hear and decide specific types of cases. For example, in California, a superior court is considered a court of general jurisdiction; however, certain superior courts are designated to hear only juvenile matters, thereby becoming a court of limited jurisdiction when sitting as a juvenile court.

Courts of general jurisdiction are granted authority to hear and decide all issues that are brought before them. These are the courts that normally hear all major civil or criminal cases. These courts are known by a variety of names, such as superior courts, circuit courts, district courts, or courts of common pleas. Because they are courts of general jurisdiction, they have authority to decide issues that occur anywhere within the state. Some larger jurisdictions, such as Los Angeles or New York, may have hundreds of courts of general jurisdiction within the city limits. Typically, these courts hear civil cases involving the same types of issues that courts of limited jurisdiction hear, although the amount of damages will be higher and may reach millions. These courts also hear the most serious forms of criminal matters, including death penalty cases.

Courts of general jurisdiction traditionally have the power to order individuals to do, or refrain from doing, certain acts. These courts may issue injunctions which prohibit performing certain acts or require individuals to do certain functions or duties. This authority is derived from the equity power that resides in courts of general jurisdiction. *Equity* is the concept that justice is administrated according to fairness as contrasted with the strict rules of law. In early English Common Law such separate courts of equity were known as Courts of Chancery. These early courts were not concerned with technical legal issues; rather, they focused on rendering decisions or orders that were fair or equitable. In modern times, the power of these courts has been merged with courts of general jurisdiction, allowing them to rule on matters that require fairness as well as the strict application of the law. The power to issue Temporary Restraining Orders in spousal abuse cases comes from this authority.

Appellate jurisdiction is reserved for courts that hear appeals from both limited and general jurisdiction courts. These courts do not hold trials or hear evidence. They decide matters of law and issue formal written decisions or "opinions." There are two classes of appellate courts: intermediate and final.

Courts of Appeals

The intermediate appellate courts are known as courts of appeals. Approximately half the states have designated intermediate appellate courts. These courts may be divided into judicial districts that hear all appeals within their district. They will hear and decide all issues of law that are raised on appeal in both civil and criminal cases. Because these courts deal strictly with legal or equitable issues, there is no jury to decide factual disputes. These courts accept the facts as determined by the trial courts. Intermediate appellate courts have the authority to reverse the decision of the lower courts and to send the matter back with instructions to retry the case in accordance with their opinion. They also may uphold the decision of the lower court. In either situation, the party who loses the appeal at this level may file an appeal with the next higher appellate court.

Supreme Courts

Final appellate courts are the highest state appellate courts. They may be known as supreme courts or courts of last resort. There may be five, seven, or nine justices sitting on this court, depending on the state. This court has jurisdiction to hear and decide issues dealing with all matters decided by lower courts, including ruling on state constitutional or statutory issues. This decision is binding on all other courts within the state. Once this court had decided an issue, the only appeal left is to file in the federal court system.

The Federal System

State courts had their origin in historical accident and custom, but federal courts were created by the U.S. Constitution. Section 1 of Article III established the federal court system with the words providing for "one supreme Court, and . . . such inferior Courts as the Congress may from time to time ordain and establish." From this beginning, Congress has engaged in a series of acts that has resulted in today's federal court system. The Judiciary Act of 1789 created the U.S. Supreme Court and established district and circuit courts of appeals.

Federal District Courts

Federal district courts are the lowest level of the federal court system. These courts have original jurisdiction over all cases involving a violation of federal statutes. These district courts handle thousands of criminal cases per year and questions have been raised as to the quality of justice that can be delivered by overworked judges.

Federal Circuit Courts

Federal circuit courts of appeals are the intermediate appellate level courts within the federal system. These courts are called circuit courts because the federal system is divided into 11 circuits. A twelfth circuit court of appeals serves the Washington D.C. area. These courts hear all criminal appeals from the district courts. These appeals are usually heard by panels of three appellate court judges, rather than by all the judges of each circuit.

U.S. Supreme Court

The United States Supreme Court is the highest court in the land. It has the capacity for judicial review of all lower court decisions, as well as state and federal statutes. By exercising this power, the Supreme Court determines what laws and lower court decisions conform to the mandates set forth in the U.S. Constitution. The concept of judicial review was first referred to by Alexander Hamilton in the Federalist Papers where he referred to the Supreme Court as ensuring that the will of the people will be supreme over the will of the legislature.[2] This concept was firmly and finally established in our system when the Supreme Court asserted its power of judicial review in the case of *Marbury v. Madison*.[3]

The Supreme Court has original jurisdiction in the following cases: cases between the United States and a state; cases between states; cases involving foreign ambassadors, ministers, and consuls; and cases between a state and a citizen of another state or country. The court hears appeals from lower courts, including the various state supreme courts. If four justices of the U.S. Supreme Court vote to hear a case, the court will issue a *writ of certiorari*. This is an order to a lower court to send the records of the case to the Supreme Court for review. The court meets on the first Monday of October and usually remains in session until June. The court may review any case it deems worthy of review but it actually hears very few of the cases filed with it. Of approximately 5000 appeals each year, the court hears approximately 200.

THE PARTIES

The Victim

The victim of any crime is often the forgotten party in the criminal justice system. For many years, victims were perceived as simply another witness to the crime. The prevailing attitude was that the real victim was the "People of the State" in which the crime was committed. Families of murder victims could not obtain information regarding the case, and were often ignored by overworked and understaffed criminal justice personnel. Within the last twenty years this attitude has begun to change as we become more aware of the needs and desires of crime victims.

Professionals dealing with crime victims must understand that they may be suffering emotional and/or physical trauma as a result of the offense.[4] Care must be taken to ensure that victims understand their rights and how the process works. It is also important to realize that there are individuals other than the original victim who have an interest in the process. These parties include the victim's family and friends and, in some situations, the victim's employer. All the appropriate parties should be notified of every significant event within the criminal justice process. Victim-service providers must also respect and protect the victim's right to privacy if that is the victim's desire.

Victims of crime will normally have a number of questions and concerns regarding the court system and their involvement in it. One of the most frustrating aspects of this process is the fact that victims often perceive that the defendant has more rights and faster access to the courts than they do.

The Defendant

The defendant is guaranteed certain rights within our form of government. Many aspects of the criminal procedure process are controlled by the U.S. Constitution, specifically the Bill of Rights (the original ten amendments to the Constitution). These federal constitutional protections concerning individual rights are, for the most part, binding on state courts.[5]

These rights attach to the defendant early in the criminal procedure process, and violation of these rights may result in the case being dismissed. For example, if the defendant confesses to the crime of murder, and that confession is obtained in violation of his or her constitutional rights, it may be suppressed.[6] If the confession is the only link connecting the defendant to the crime, the case may have to be dismissed. When this type of incident occurs, it is very difficult for the victim to understand why the defendant goes free when there has been a confession. If this happens, professionals working with victims must attempt to offer other alternatives such as availability of filing civil lawsuits against the defendant.

Law Enforcement

The law enforcement officer's role in the court system is critical. Here, it is important to remember that law enforcement officers' duties do not end with the apprehension of the suspect. They must continue to work the case until it is sent to the jury by the judge. It is common in larger prosecutors' offices to have the lead detective sit with the prosecutor during the trial. That detective may know the case as well as the prosecutor and many times will provide critical advice.

The Prosecutor

> *The prosecutor has absolute and unrestricted discretion to choose who is prosecuted and who is not.*
>
> *Anonymous*

One of the most important roles in the system is that of the prosecutor. This individual is charged with the responsibility of filing criminal cases. Until the case is filed, it does not become a part of the court system.

We often think that the prosecutor's role is to convict the defendant. This is erroneous. The prosecutor has the duty to ensure justice, not merely to convict. Accordingly, if the prosecutor has a reasonable basis for believing that the defendant is not guilty, the prosecutor should not attempt to obtain a conviction. In such a case, if the prosecutor is the decision maker (e.g., district attorney), then the prosecutor should request that the case be dismissed. If the prosecutor is not the decision maker (e.g., an assistant district attorney), the prosecutor should present the facts to the district attorney and request either that he or she be relieved from the case or that the case be dismissed. It would be unethical for an attorney to attempt to convict an innocent person.

The prosecutor in federal court is the U.S. Attorney or Assistant U.S. Attorney, usually the latter. In state courts, he or she is known as the district attorney, state's attorney, commonwealth's attorney, or county attorney. The American Bar Association's Canons of Professional Responsibility mandate that the prosecutor's primary duty is not to convict but to seek justice. If the prosecutor believes that the defendant is guilty and there is sufficient evidence to support the charges, then, and only then, is the prosecutor under a duty to enforce the criminal charge against the defendant.

> ## Ethics in the Courtroom
>
> The American Bar Association's Code of Professional Responsibility, Canon 7-103 provides:
>
> 7-103: Performing the Duty of Public Prosecutor or Other Government Counsel
>
> A. A public prosecutor or other government lawyer shall not institute or cause to be instituted criminal charges when he knows or it is obvious that the charges are not supported by probable cause.
>
> B. A public prosecutor or other government lawyer in criminal litigation shall make timely disclosure to counsel for the defendant, or to the defendant if the defendant does not have counsel, of the existence of evidence, known to the prosecutor or other government lawyer, that tends to negate the guilt of the accused, mitigates the degree of the offense, or reduces the punishment.

Prosecutors often forget this and attempt to obtain as many convictions as possible to build a reputation as a "tough" prosecutor on crime. This conflict can lead to prosecutorial misconduct. Because appellate courts generally uphold convictions in those cases in which the misconduct is not serious, some prosecutors who are overzealous or motivated by personal or political gain attempt to prosecute using questionable tactics that are marginally acceptable.

Under our adversarial system, only the prosecutor has the authority to refer charges to the courts. A case does not begin until the prosecutor files the charges or grand jury indictment with the court. In most jurisdictions, if the prosecutor refuses to prosecute, the only remedy is to remove the prosecutor for misconduct or elect a new one. The courts will refuse to order a prosecutor to prosecute a case. Prosecutors do not have sufficient assets to prosecute all cases. Accordingly, they select which cases to prosecute. In deciding which cases to prosecute, prosecutors tend to focus on certain types of crimes. The decisions are often made based on the personal behavioral norms of the elected district attorney. The prosecutor cannot, however, forget that he or she may soon be up for reelection and may have to answer to the voters for his or her actions.

The reference to prosecutor in the above paragraphs has generally been to the elected or appointed prosecutor. In most jurisdictions, this individual, as the head of the prosecutor's office, makes policy decisions and rarely tries a case in trial court. Most cases are tried, however, by the assistant district attorneys or assistant state's attorneys. There are approximately 2,300 chief prosecutors in the United States. They employ some 20,000 assistants. Approximately 97 percent of the chief prosecutors are elected to office. The others are usually appointed by the governor.

The general duties of an assistant district attorney or assistant state's attorney include:

- Helping investigate possible violations of the law
- Cooperating with police in investigating crimes
- Interviewing witnesses
- Subpoenaing witnesses to appear in court
- Plea bargaining in accordance with policy directions from the elected prosecutor
- Trying the cases in court
- Recommending sentences to the court
- Representing the government in appeals

Assistants must make many decisions regarding the processing and prosecution of cases. Often there is neither time nor the opportunity to check with the elected prosecutor. The elected prosecutor is, however, held responsible for decisions made by his or her assistants. In most prosecutors' offices, the elected prosecutor provides detailed guidelines or standards for the assistant prosecutors to follow in making decisions. For example, in most offices there are specific guidelines regarding plea bargaining.

The high number of part-time prosecutors in small jurisdictions is another problem. Many states, such as California, have taken steps to consolidate the prosecutors' offices in order to eliminate the need for part-time prosecutors. The part-time prosecutor generally practices law to supplement his or her income. Conflicts may arise if the prosecutor is also a part-time civil attorney. In addition, most part-time prosecutors receive little or no formal training to handle the complex duties of prosecutor.

Justice George Sutherland described the role of the U.S. Attorney as follows:

> The United States Attorney is the representative not of an ordinary party to a controversy, but of a sovereignty whose obligation to govern impartially is as compelling as its obligation to govern at all; and whose interest, therefore, in a criminal prosecution is not that it shall win a case, but that Justice shall be done. As such, he is in a peculiar and very definite sense the servant of the law, the twofold aim of which is that the guilty shall not escape or innocence suffer. He may prosecute with earnestness and vigor—indeed, he should do so. But while he may strike foul ones, it is as much his duty to refrain from improper methods calculated to produce wrongful conviction as it is to use ever legitimate means to bring about a just one.[7]

There is a U.S. attorney for each federal district court. They are appointed by the president and serve at the pleasure of the president. It is customary for every new president to request the resignation of all U.S. attorneys at the start of a new administration.

The U.S. attorneys, therefore, tend to have the same political outlook as the president and probably supported the president during the election process. Accordingly, to some extent the U.S. attorney is a political person.

As the chief federal prosecutor for the district court, the U.S. attorney determines which federal crimes will be prosecuted. However, the new federal court sentencing guidelines limit the plea bargaining that the U.S. attorney may do.

The Defense Attorney

> *Defending people accused of a crime is the most distasteful function performed by lawyers.*
>
> *F. Lee Bailey*

At a trial in Leningrad in 1974, the first thing that the accused's attorney did was to apologize to the court for defending "an enemy of the people." This would never happen in our courts. Under our system of justice, the accused has the right to a counsel whose duty is to serve the interests of the accused. Although the defense counsel is an officer of the court, he or she is also the representative of the defendant in our adversarial process. The Sixth Amendment provides that in all criminal cases the accused shall have the right to the assistance of counsel. As a member of the courthouse work group, the defense counsel should represent the interests of the accused.

Right to Assistance of Counsel

... in all criminal prosecutions, the accused shall enjoy the right ... to have the assistance of counsel for his defense.

Sixth Amendment, U.S. Constitution

The Sixth Amendment of the U.S. Constitution guarantees that the accused shall have the right to the assistance of counsel in all criminal cases. This means that no matter how petty the offense, the accused has the right to assistance of counsel. This issue has never been seriously questioned. The controversial issue is, when the accused cannot afford an attorney, when is the government required to provide the accused with counsel?"

As a general rule, the accused is entitled to the appointment of a counsel any time that the accused is subject to punishment which may include jail or prison time and the accused cannot afford to retain an attorney.[8] [Note: If the accused can afford counsel, he or she has the right to counsel in all criminal proceedings.] Typically, the indigent accused has the right to counsel at every significant phase of the trial.

Another problem in our system is that of providing counsel in those cases where the accused cannot afford an attorney. States and the federal government use several different methods. The three methods generally used are public defender, assigned counsel, and contract counsel.

The first public defender's office was established in Los Angeles County, California, in 1914. Thirty states and the federal government use a public defender system to provide legal services to indigent defendants. The *public defender* is an attorney who is employed by the state or federal government to serve as counsel for indigent defendants. In those jurisdictions using a public defender, a public defender will generally be available in court to be appointed as counsel for the accused when the trial judge conducts arraignments.

In some jurisdictions, the public defenders receive less pay than the prosecutors and their positions are considered less prestigious than those of the prosecutors. Most states have corrected this situation and have attempted to make public defenders' positions as prestigious as that of the assistant prosecutors.

Most public defenders' offices are struggling under a massive caseload, and often the attorneys do not have sufficient time to spend on particular cases. The quality of services provided by public defenders are often criticized. It appears that public defenders' offices, like other state agencies, vary in the quality of services provided. In each office one is likely to encounter individuals who fail to adequately perform their assigned duties as counsel. But, one can also find many well-qualified and highly competent attorneys. In both the public defender and the assigned counsel systems, attorneys may be found who do not wish to anger judges through the use of extensive motions, arguments, or demands for jury trials. It appears that the quality of service provided by public defenders is very similar to that provided by individual attorneys who have been selected and hired by the defendant. In both situations, one can find good attorneys and bad ones.

Most jurisdictions that do not have a public defender system normally use the assigned counsel method to represent indigent defendants. Judges use several methods to decide which attorney should be appointed. The most common is the use of a list of all attorneys practicing in the local court. From this list, the judge appoints the next available attorney to defend the accused. Assigned counsel generally receives a small fee from the state for the representation of the defendant.

The assigned counsel system is the oldest and, until recently, the most widely-used method for providing representation to indigent defendants in criminal cases. The problems with this system include:

- In many jurisdictions, only new and inexperienced counsel are assigned.
- In some jurisdictions, "has beens" are assigned to supplement their retirement income.
- In those jurisdictions that use all members of the local bar, frequently counsel will be assigned who do not normally practice criminal law.
- For those counsel assigned, the pay is substantially lower than the counsel would make on a non-assigned case and most of their out-of-pocket expenses are not reimbursed; accordingly, this discourages attorneys from accepting appointments.
- Additional funds are seldom available to hire investigators to assist in these cases.
- The few attorneys who are financially dependent upon the assignments will be hesitant to vigorously defend the cases for fear of angering the judge.

Despite these problems, there are some definite advantages in using the assigned counsel system. They include:

> Counsel may bring a different perspective to the case because counsel is not a part of the courthouse work group.

> The accused generally feels more comfortable when represented by a private attorney rather than a public defender.

Presently, six states exclusively use the *contract system*, and several other states use the contract system to supplement the public defender system. It is the newest system, but appears to be growing as more states attempt to obtain more for their limited resources. Under the contract system, the jurisdiction publishes a *request for proposals* (RFP). An RFP invites private law firms to bid for the services. The law firms submit proposals on establishing a defender system and the costs involved. The government then selects the firm with the best bid. That firm is responsible for providing indigent defendants with representation in court.

The most popular grounds for appeal in criminal courts is that of ineffective assistance of counsel. The appellate courts generally require not only that the defendant establish that his or her counsel made errors at trial, but also that the errors prejudiced the defendant. The courts are hesitant to engage in second guessing trial counsel. In addition, a defendant who is represented by a retained attorney (one hired by defendant) has a more difficult time in establishing ineffective assistance of counsel. The rationale for the latter rule is that the accused should not be rewarded for selecting a bad attorney.

No one person has a more demanding and more misunderstood role than that of the defense counsel. Too often we associate the defense counsel with the person he or she represents. The defense attorney's role is to be the spokesperson and representative for the accused. If the attorney can legally prevent the state from proving the accused's guilt, the attorney must do so.

The defense attorney is an officer of the court and, as such, he or she cannot present false evidence, allow perjury to be committed, or break the law in defending the accused. However, the defense attorney is required to use any legal method to prevent the accused's conviction or, in the case of conviction, to obtain the lightest sentence possible for the accused. It is not the attorney's duty to determine what sentence is best for the accused, it is his or her duty to obtain the lightest sentence unless requested otherwise by the defendant. An undecided issue in this regard is the defense counsel's duty to fight the death penalty or to attempt to ensure that the death penalty is imposed when the accused is being tried for a capital offense and requests the death penalty.

> You are representing an accused. Prior to trial, the accused tells you he is going to commit perjury at trial. What do you do?

As noted earlier, the defense counsel cannot violate the law in defending the accused. If, for example, the accused tells the counsel that he is going to testify falsely at the trial, the counsel should encourage the accused not to. If the accused insists on testifying and indicates that he will commit perjury, the defense counsel should request that the judge relieve the counsel from the duties to represent the accused before the accused testifies. The problem is that the counsel cannot tell the judge why he or she wants to be relieved, due to the rules of confidentiality. All the counsel can tell the judge is that there is a conflict between the accused and counsel. This problem could last indefinitely, because if the accused tells the newly appointed counsel that he intends to commit perjury, the new counsel should also be excused. What normally happens, however, is that once a counsel has been excused, the accused realizes the problem and doesn't tell all to the new counsel.

> A young girl is missing, and the girl's parents offer a reward for information regarding her whereabouts. You are defending an accused man on an unrelated murder charge. He informs you that he killed the young girl and buried her body in the local cemetery. If the police find the body, evidence on the body will lead the police to your client. What do you do?[9]

Information that an attorney receives from his or her client is privileged and cannot be divulged without the client's consent. Accordingly, if an accused tells his attorney that he committed a murder, the attorney cannot divulge this information without the client's consent. This privileged communication is based on the theory that the accused needs to be able to communicate with his or her attorney without fear of the communications being used against him or her. In this situation, the New York Bar Association ruled that the communication was privileged and the attorney should not have revealed the information regarding the girl's death.

In one Virginia case, the accused told his counsel that the money from a bank robbery was in a locker in a bus station. The counsel advised the accused to hide the money elsewhere. The attorney was convicted of being an accessory after the fact. While the communications as to the location of the money was privileged, the attorney went beyond that when he advised the accused to hide the money in a different location. This conversation was overheard by a nosey telephone operator, who reported it to the police. [Note: The privileged communication extends to the attorney and the attorney's secretary and paralegal, but not to a third person such as a telephone operator who overhears the conversation.]

The courts have recognized that there is an important relationship between the accused and his or her counsel. Accordingly, an accused has the right to refuse a counsel and, in turn, counsel has a right to refuse to represent any accused. An occasional problem in this area arises when the accused is assigned a counsel at government expense and the accused does not like his or her attorney. As a general rule when dealing with "appointed" counsel, the judge will allow the defendant to "fire" one attorney, but will require reasons before allowing the defendant to fire the second attorney. Normally a defendant can fire his or her "retained" counsel at any time. The judge, however, may decide not to delay a scheduled trial or other court appearance to allow the defendant time to obtain new retained counsel. [Note: *Appointed counsel* is one provided by the government to indigent defendants. *Retained counsel* is an attorney who has been hired and paid by the defendant.]

The Judge

 The judges are the weakest link in our system of justice, and they are also the most protected.

Alan M. Dershowitz

> ### Functions of the Trial Judge
>
> The American Bar Association Standards for Criminal Justice makes this statement regarding the responsibility of the trial judge:
>
> The trial judge has the responsibility for safeguarding both the rights of the accused and the interests of the public in the administration of criminal justice. The adversarial nature of the proceedings does not relieve the trial judge of the obligations of raising on his own initiative, at all appropriate times and in an appropriate manner, matters which may significantly promote a just determination of the trial. The only purpose of a criminal trial is to determine whether the prosecution has established the guilt of the accused as required by law, and the trial judge should not allow the proceedings to be used for any other purpose.[10]

The *trial judge* is an officer of the court. It would be more accurate to describe him or her as the "master of the court." The trial judge's duties are varied and far more extensive than would appear on the surface. During the trial, judges rule on appropriateness of the conduct of all others involved in the court process, including spectators. Judges determine what evidence is admissible and, during jury trials, which instructions of law the juries will receive. Any motions, questions of law, objections, and, in most states, the sentence to impose are questions decided only by the judges. The senior judge in any one court or the presiding judge is responsible for the docketing (scheduling) of cases, motions, etc. Judges also have extensive control over probation officers, the court clerks and indirectly, to some extent, the police.

The duties and responsibilities of an *appellate judge* are very different from those of a trial judge. The responsibilities of an appellate judge include:

- Examining the record of trial, trial brief, notice of appeal, and other matter submitted with the appeal to determine whether the appeal is properly presented and the appropriate issues are properly before the court
- Presiding over oral arguments
- Negotiating a decision among the justices considering the appeal
- Writing an opinion that explains the logic and reasons for the decision

The appellate justice's work is largely confined to reviewing cases tried by trial judges. Instead of the noisy, crowded trial court with numerous distractions, the appellate justice deals mainly with paperwork, (e.g., briefs, records of trial, and research regarding prior court decisions).

There are approximately 26,000 judges in the United States. The vast majority of them are lower court judges. Most states now require that a judge have a law degree and be licensed to practice law in the jurisdiction. Many states, such as California, Florida, and New Jersey, require the judges to be admitted to practice in that jurisdiction and at least "learned in the law." However, there are still a number of lower court judges who do not have formal legal training.

Judge Selection

Although judges have the most important role in the judicial process, the current methods used to select judges do not guarantee that the best-suited and best-trained persons are appointed as judges. Judges are selected by one of three methods: popular election, appointment, or merit plan. Thirty-two states elect their judges. Some elections are partisan (candidates run as members of a political party) and some are nonpartisan (candidates run without a party designation). Some states and the federal system appoint their judges. Other states use a form of merit system or the Missouri Plan.

The Missouri Plan was created in the 1940s to overcome the widespread use of political patronage in the appointment of judges. Judges are selected based on their records of achievement in the legal field. After serving an initial term of office, the judge's name is then placed on the ballot for confirmation. When the judge's confirmation is presented to the voters, it is normally by a yes or no vote.

California elects its judges. However, in most situations in California, when a vacancy occurs the governor appoints a new judge. At the next election, the judge stands for election. In 1992, 88 percent of the trial court judges in California were placed on the bench initially by gubernatorial appointments to fill vacancies. In states using nonpartisan elections, only 43 percent of the judges were initially elected; the majority were initially appointed by the governor.[11]

In most states, such as California, it is rare that a sitting judge is defeated by an opponent. An exception to this is Texas, where the judges are elected in partisan elections and the judicial races are very political in nature. A problem with the partisan election of judges is illustrated in a Texas case. In the 1970s, an individual was elected to the state supreme court who was being investigated for criminal homicide in another state and had little prior legal experience. This individual's last name was very similar to that of a popular politician in the state, and it is assumed that many voters thought they were voting for the politician. [Note: This individual resigned from the state supreme court as part of a criminal plea bargain.]

A few states, such as New York, use a variety of methods for selecting judges. Appellate court judges are appointed by the governor from a group of candidates selected by a judicial nominating commission and approved by the state senate. Partisan elections are used to select major court trial judges. Municipal judges in New York City are appointed by the mayor of New York City.

Terms

As noted earlier, federal judges in constitutional courts hold office "during good behavior" for life. In most states, the judges serve terms of four to seven years. The most common method of removing judges is the failure to reelect a judge when his or her term expires. In those states, such as California, where judges are subject to being removed by a "fail-to-retain" vote, they can be removed by a negative vote. The opportunity to remove by not reelecting the judge occurs only when the judge's term is expiring.

In some states, the judges are subject to being recalled. The general recall procedure is to file a recall petition with a sufficient percentage of voter signatures with the state election commission and place the recall question on the next general election ballot. A majority vote at the recall election will remove the judge. This process is time consuming and expensive.

Federal judges and some state judges may be removed by impeachment. The U.S. Constitution provides, in part, that any civil officer of the United States (including judges) may be removed by impeachment for crimes of "treason, bribery, or other high crimes and misdemeanors."[12] In federal cases, the House of Representatives must vote on the articles of impeachment, which is an accusation of criminal wrongdoing. The actual trial occurs before the Senate. Two-thirds vote of the Senate is required before the judge is removed from office. As with recall procedures, impeachment is time consuming and expensive.

The most workable method of judicial removal is by use of the Judicial Conduct Commission. In 1960, California was the first state to establish a judicial conduct commission. Now all states have some form of judicial removal commission. The judicial commission normally consists of judges, nonlawyer citizens, and attorneys. For example, Florida's 13-member commission is comprised of six judges (two from circuit courts, two from county courts, and two from the district courts of appeal); two attorneys appointed by the state bar; and five non-lawyer citizens appointed by the governor. The members serve staggered six-year terms. The Florida commission is empowered to deal with charges of misconduct, persistent failure to perform judicial duties, and any physical or mental disability that interferes with the performance of duties.

Generally, federal court judges hold their offices for life "during good behavior." The judges are nominated by the president and confirmed by the Senate. In most cases, the president nominates judges of the same political party as the president. In fact, of the 107 Supreme Court justices, only 12 were not of the same party as the president. This power to nominate federal judges is an important political power, because the judges appointed by a president generally remain in office years after the president's term has expired. Accordingly, a president's influence will be felt for many years after the president has been replaced.

For many years, the president appointed his friends or political supporters to the courts. However, President Reagan changed this practice. He started the trend that has been followed by both Bush and Clinton—to appoint judges that seemed most ideologically suited to the president's agenda. In addition, Reagan started the trend of appointing younger judges who would most likely serve longer terms of office.

The practice of selecting judges based on their ideology has had the effect of making the appointments more controversial and more difficult to achieve Senate confirmation. Previously, most presidential appointments were quickly approved by the Senate. Now, the confirmation hearings are more adversarial in nature and the candidates face an in-depth examination of their past career activities and personal conduct.

Federal Magistrates

For many years U.S. commissioners served the same functions that justices of the peace served for state courts. Commissioners had the authority to issue search and arrest warrants, arraign defendants, hold preliminary hearings, and try cases involving petty offenses. In 1967, the President's Commission on Law Enforcement and Administration of Justice noted that 30 percent of the commissioners were not lawyers and all but 7 of the 700 commissioners had other jobs. The president's commission recommended that the system be either eliminated or reformed. As the result of the recommendations, Congress established the federal magistrate system and provided for phasing out the commissioners over a three-year period.

Federal magistrates are appointed to assist district courts. There are presently 452 federal magistrates. Magistrates are lawyers appointed by district court judges for eight-year terms. Part-time magistrates are appointed for four-year terms. The Federal Magistrates Act of 1968 empowers them to issue search warrants, hear preliminary stages of felony cases, set bail, and try misdemeanor cases.[13] In 1976, the magistrates were given the authority to review civil rights and *habeas corpus* petitions and make recommendations regarding them to the district court judges.

It is estimated that magistrates perform about 475,000 separate tasks a year for the federal districts. Misdemeanor and petty offense trials account for 20 percent of the magistrate's time. Approximately 30 percent of their time is involved with preliminary proceedings in criminal cases, 40 percent involves the disposition of motions and pretrial conferences, and the remaining 10 percent in miscellaneous duties.[14]

The Jury

Even though most cases are handled with a guilty plea and only a few cases are tried by a jury, the jury is the focal point of the criminal justice system. The Sixth Amendment also guarantees the accused the right to trial by jury. The major issues regarding the right to a jury trial are

- Whether all offenders, including those being tried on minor offenses, have a right to jury trial
- The size of the jury
- Whether the jury verdict must be unanimous

In felony cases, there has never been a question regarding the right to a jury trial. Prior to 1970, the general rule for state criminal trials was that the accused had a right to a jury trial in serious crimes but not in minor offenses. In *Baldwin v. New York*, the court moved away from the serious/minor classification and established the rule that if the accused is facing a possible sentence of six months or more in jail, the accused has a right to a jury trial.[15] If the accused is facing a possible sentence of less than six months, then the accused has no right to a jury trial unless provided by state statute. Many states, such as California, provide the right to a jury trial any time the accused faces a possible jail sentence.

The U.S. Supreme Court discussed this issue again in *Blanton v. North Las Vegas*. The issue in this case was whether the accused had a right to a jury trial in cases involving driving under the influence (DUI). The court stated that if the state considered the offense a petty offense, the accused has no right to a jury trial. However, if the state treats the crime as a serious crime, then the accused has a right to a speedy trial. [Note: Nevada had a statute that classified DUI as a petty offense unless aggravating circumstances were present.[16]]

A related issue is whether the accused has a right to a trial by a jury consisting of at least 12 jurors. Historically, trial juries have consisted of 12 jurors. As the result of *Williams v. Florida*, the U.S. Supreme Court has approved trial by a six-person jury. The court stated:

> We conclude, in short, as we began: the fact that a jury at common law was composed of precisely 12 is an historical accident, unnecessary to effect the purposes of the jury system and wholly without significance....[17]

After the *Williams* case, many states adopted the six-person jury for misdemeanor cases. In some states, such as Florida, a six-person jury may be used in felony cases. The U.S. Supreme Court has set six as the minimum size for a jury.

A related issue is the requirement for unanimous verdicts in jury cases. The Supreme Court has ruled that in trials with six-person juries, the verdict must be unanimous. The Court has approved statutes that allow less than unanimous verdicts in cases with 12 person juries. In *Apodica v. Oregon*, the court approved a state statute that allowed conviction based on the vote of 10 jury members in a 12 person jury.[18] The Supreme Court has never approved a less than unanimous verdict in cases with fewer than 12 jurors.

PRETRIAL

Decision to Prosecute

The decision to prosecute is a function of the prosecutor and is generally not reviewable. In many states and the federal government, before the prosecutor may file felony charges with a court, he or she must obtain a grand jury indictment. In other states, the prosecutor files "an information" with the lower court.

Generally, after an arrest or on the completion of an investigation, the case is referred to the prosecutor's office. In some jurisdictions, however, the case is not referred until after the accused has made an initial appearance in court. When the case is received in the prosecutor's office, it is reviewed to determine if the case merits prosecution. Because of a lack of resources, prosecutors cannot try all cases referred to their offices.

Additional reasons that prosecution may be declined in a case include:

- Insufficient evidence
- Witness problems
- Interests of justice
- Defendant pleas in another case
- Pretrial diversion
- Referral to another jurisdiction for prosecution
- Due process problems (e.g., questionable search)
- Referral to treatment programs (e.g., alcohol rehabilitation programs)

The prosecutor may also reduce the charge to a misdemeanor. Of the above reasons for declining prosecution, insufficient evidence is the most common reason for rejection. For example, approximately one-half of all drug cases that prosecution declined to try are based on insufficient evidence. The second most common reason involves witness problems, in that the witnesses are unavailable or unwilling to be involved.[19]

Bail

Traditionally, the bail system required the defendant to guarantee his or her appearance at trial by posting a money bond. This money would be forfeited should the defendant fail to appear in court for trial. The Eighth Amendment of the U.S. Constitution states that excessive bail shall not be required. While the amendment does not grant the right to bail in all cases, all states and the federal government give the defendant the right to bail except in limited situations.

The traditional bail system discriminates against the poor who cannot afford bail. Accordingly, alternatives to the bail system include release on recognizance, conditional release, third-party custody, and citation release.

Pretrial Releases

Traditional Bail Bond. In this situation, the defendant, or someone on the defendant's behalf, posts the full amount of the bail.

Privately Secured Bail. A professional bondsperson signs a promissory note to the court for the bail amount and charges the defendant a fee for the service (usually 10 percent of the face amount of the bond). If the defendant fails to appear in court as required, the bondsperson may be required to pay the court the full amount of the bond. Frequently, a bondsperson will require the accused or the accused's family to post collateral in addition to the fee. If the accused fails to appear, the accused owes the bondsperson the amount of money that the bondsperson has to pay the court. This amount is in addition to the 10 percent fee already paid by the accused for bail services.

Deposit Bond. The courts in many states allow the defendant to post a deposit, usually 10 percent of the full bail with the court. This is also frequently referred to as the "10 percent Bail" program. If the defendant fails to appear, he or she owes the full amount of the bond to the court. If the defendant appears, most of the deposit is returned. Generally the courts keep one percent of the bond amount for administrative costs.

Unsecured Bail. In this situation, the defendant pays no money to the court, but is liable for the full amount of the bail if the accused fails to appear.

Release on Recognizance (ROR). In this situation, the court releases the defendant on the defendant's *promise* to appear in court as required.

Conditional Release. The court releases the defendant subject to the defendant agreeing to follow certain specified conditions. For example, the judge may release a defendant providing he or she will not leave the city, or bother the witnesses.

Third Party Custody. The defendant is released to the custody of a third person who promises to ensure the accused's presence in court. No monetary transactions are involved in this type of release. This type of release is very common with juvenile defendants released into the custody of their guardians.

Citation Release. The defendant is released pending the first court appearance by signing a citation issued by a law enforcement person. Normally the citation release is used only in traffic cases and cases involving minor offenses.

The U.S. Supreme Court made it clear in 1950 that the purpose of bail was "to assure the defendant's attendance in court when his presence is required."[20] Accordingly, we assume that any bail higher than that necessary to ensure the accused's presence at trial is excessive and, thus, unconstitutional.

The U.S. Bail Reform Act of 1984 added the duty to consider the safety of the community when making the pretrial release decision. The act provided that bail could be refused in those cases in which the accused is charged with a violent offense, has a serious criminal record and is considered a danger to the community, or is a flight risk.

Other key features of the act were its establishment of a "no-bail" presumption for certain types of cases. Many scholars thought that the "no-bail" presumption denied the accused due process because it authorized punishment before trial. The U.S. Supreme Court, in upholding the constitutionality of the Bail Reform Act, stated: "The legislative history clearly shows that Congress formulated the Bail Reform Act to prevent danger to the community—a legitimate regulatory goal—not to punish dangerous individuals."[21]

When the U.S. Supreme Court held this act constitutional, most states enacted similar statutes. Accordingly, in determining whether to release a defendant from custody prior to the trial, the judge must now consider both the

- Likelihood that the accused will be present for trial, and
- The safety of the community

Pretrial Hearings

Felony cases are processed either by indictment or appearance at a preliminary hearing. In those states that require indictments by a grand jury, the case is normally presented to the grand jury by the prosecutor. If the grand jury returns an indictment, the indictment is then filed with the superior or district court.

In states, such as California, that do not require an indictment by grand jury, an *information* is presented to a lower court. The information is a charging document similar to the complaint in a misdemeanor case. The information is presented to the municipal or justice court in which a preliminary hearing is held. Approximately half the states use preliminary hearings rather than grand juries. The purpose of the preliminary hearing is to determine whether there is probable cause to have the defendant answer to the charge in a felony court. At the preliminary hearing, the judge can dismiss the charges, reduce the charge to a misdemeanor and try the case, or order the defendant to be bound over for trial in felony court.

After the indictment is filed or the accused is bound over by the municipal or justice court on an information, the accused is arraigned before the trial court. In some states, the arraignment may be before the lower court. At the *arraignment*, the accused is informed of the charge(s) against him or her and advised of the right to counsel, and a plea is entered. In addition, the judge must decide whether the accused should be released on bail or some other form of release while awaiting trial.

At the preliminary hearing, the prosecution presents its evidence, including witnesses, to the judge. The defense counsel may also present evidence favorable to the accused. At this hearing, the judge determines whether probable cause indicates that the accused has committed a felony.

The accused may plea guilty, not guilty, or *nolo contendere* when asked to plead. A plea of *nolo contendere* means that the accused does not contest the charges. It is treated as if the accused entered a plea of guilty. If the accused enters a guilty plea, he or she admits all of the elements of the offense charged. If the accused enters a plea of not guilty, the case is set for trial. Normally, both a trial date and a date for pretrial motions are set by the judge after the judge accepts the not guilty plea. At the pretrial motion date, the counsel are afforded an opportunity to present motions. Typical motions include motion to suppress certain items of evidence, motion for speedy trial, and motion for dismissal of charges.

Pleas

Plea of Not Guilty. A plea of not guilty denies placing the burden of proving guilt beyond a reasonable doubt on the prosecution. If the defendant stands mute and refuses to enter any plea, a plea of not guilty will be entered on the defendant's behalf by the judge. [Note: An accused has a constitutional right to be assumed innocent until proven guilty beyond a reasonable doubt.]

Guilty Plea. A guilty plea is not only an admission of guilt but is also a waiver of the right to jury, the right to remain silent, the right to confront witnesses, and the right to require the prosecution to establish guilt beyond a reasonable doubt by admissible evidence. Although an accused has a right to plead guilty, the trial judge is not required to accept this plea. If the judge feels that the accused's plea is not providently entered, the judge can enter a plea of not guilty for the accused. In addition, in capital cases the accused cannot enter a plea of guilty if the state is requesting the death penalty. The rationale for this rule is to allow the accused to plead guilty in a death penalty case would be the same as allowing the accused to commit suicide.

Nolo Contendere. This is a plea of "no contest." It is essentially a guilty plea. By entering a *nolo* plea, the accused waives the above rights, the same as if he or she had plead guilty. The *nolo contendere* plea is often used in those cases where the accused is also liable in civil court. By pleading *nolo contendere*, the accused does not admit commission of the act in question. The accused does not have a *right* to plead *nolo contendere*. This form of plea is acceptable in only about one half of the states and the federal government.

Not Guilty by Reasons of Insanity. In most states, the accused may plead not guilty by reasons of insanity. In states that do not allow the accused to plead insanity, the accused must plead not guilty and raise the issue of insanity as an affirmative (acceptable) defense. The normal plea in insanity cases is "not guilty and not guilty by reasons of insanity." This plea requires that the government prove that the defendant committed the offense, then the issue of the accused's sanity is determined. In all states and the federal government, insanity is an affirmative defense, so the burden of producing evidence as to the sanity or insanity of the accused is first upon the defense. If no evidence is entered at trial regarding the sanity of the accused, it is assumed that the accused is sane.

Statute of Limitations or Double Jeopardy. In most states, before the accused enters a plea as to his or her guilt, the defense of statute of limitations or double jeopardy must be pled. In most cases, if these defenses are not pled before the guilty or not guilty plea, these defenses are relinquished.

TRIAL

Jury Selection

The Sixth Amendment guarantees a defendant the right to an impartial jury. In addition, the due process clause of the Fifth and Fourteenth Amendments prohibits juries that exclude members of the defendant's racial, gender, ethnic, religious, or similar groups. To ensure an impartial jury, states and the federal government require that the jury panel (potential members of the jury) be selected from a fair cross-section of the community wherein the court convenes. Most jurisdictions randomly select the jury panel from the local census, tax rolls, city directories, telephone books, drivers' license lists, etc.

After the jury panel is selected, the members are directed to appear at a certain time and place. It is from the jury panel that the actual jury is selected. The principal method used by the counsel to ensure that the jury is impartial is the *voir dire* of the jury. *Voir dire* is the questioning of the prospective jury members about matters that could influence their ability to serve on a jury. In some jurisdictions, counsel submit their questions to the judge, who then asks the questions of the individual jury members. In other jurisdictions, both counsel have the opportunity to question the prospective jurors. Counsel can then challenge the prospective jury members. If the counsel's challenge is sustained (approved) by the judge, the prospective jury member is excused.

There are two types of challenges: challenges for cause and peremptory challenges. A *challenge for cause* is based on something that indicates that the person would not be an impartial juror or would not follow the judge's instructions. Both sides have unlimited challenges for cause, but the judge may overrule (disapprove) the challenge. An example of a challenge for cause is if a juror indicates that he was the victim of a robbery and, therefore, would be prejudiced against the defendant who is charged with robbery.

In capital cases, one may often hear the term "death qualified jury." This refers to the fact that all the members selected for the jury have indicated that in the appropriate circumstances they would vote for the death penalty. The prosecutor asking for the death penalty has the right to challenge for cause any prospective juror who indicates that under no circumstances would the juror vote for the death penalty.

After the *voir dire* is completed and the jury members have been selected, they are empaneled (sworn in). The judge then gives preliminary instructions to the jury. The jurors are instructed that they are not to talk to others about the case, to read the newspapers, or decide on the case until all the evidence has been submitted and the jury has received their instructions from the judge.

Opening Statements

After preliminary matters have been disposed of, the jury is seated in the jury box. The prosecutor has the opportunity to make an *opening statement*. This statement is not evidence, but may be used to inform the jury of the direction that the prosecutor is attempting to go. The defense counsel may make his or her opening statement immediately after the prosecution finishes, or the defense may wait until the defense presents its case.

Case in Chief

The prosecutor, having the burden of proof, begins the trial. Witnesses are called and evidence is presented. After the prosecution rests its case, the defense presents its case. The prosecution may then present evidence in rebuttal to counter the defense.

Closing Arguments

After both sides have finished, the prosecution presents its closing argument. The defense then presents its closing argument. Finally, the prosecution may present an argument in rebuttal to the defense's closing argument. The reason that the prosecutor goes first and is afforded the last word is based on the concept that the side with the burden of proof has the right to open and close the case. In the arguments presented by counsel, it is unethical for counsel to indicate a personal belief on whether or not the accused is guilty. The prosecutor may argue that the government has proven the guilt of the defendant beyond a reasonable doubt, but it is unethical for the prosecutor to state that he or she believes that the defendant is guilty.

After arguments have been completed, the judge gives instructions to the jury. This is also called *charging the jury*. The instructions are used to explain the law of the case to the jurors. The subjects covered in the instructions include burden of proof, the elements of the offense, and voting procedures to be used by the jury.

The Verdict

Generally in jury trials, the jury makes a finding of guilty or not guilty. After a guilty finding, the judge sets the sentencing. If the jury is unable to reach a verdict, the jury is considered a *hung jury*, and the jury is excused. The prosecution either retries the case or the charges are dismissed.

Although there are no provisions for it in the statutes, juries have nullification power. *Nullification* occurs when a jury brings in a verdict of not guilty despite the fact that the evidence established the guilt of the accused. When jury nullification occurs, the accused cannot be retried for that offense. The power of nullification is a common-law right. It is based on the concept that the jury is not required to explain any findings of not guilty.

Before the death penalty may be imposed by a judge, the jury must not only find that the accused is guilty but also that the special circumstances that allow the imposition of the death penalty exist. Death penalty cases are generally bifurcated (two-part) trials. The first part deals with the question of guilt and the second deals with the question of whether special circumstances are present which would allow the death sentence.

CASE SUMMARIES

An inmate was not entitled to free copy of his 800-page psychiatric treatment record. *Kearney v. Department of Mental Health*, 425 N.W. 2d 161 (Mich. App. 1988).

A Texas state law did not allow inmate to sue correctional officials for alleged negligent failure to enforce rules against excessive noise; suit was properly dismissed as frivolous. *Johnson v. Kinney*, 893 S.W.2d 271 (Tex. App. 1995).

State officials may be sued for damages in their individual capacities in federal civil rights cases, even if they were acting "in their official capacities" during the complained-of conduct, U.S. Supreme Court rules. *Hafter v. Melo*, 60 U.S.L.W. 4001 (U.S., Nov. 5, 1991).

Prison officials cannot be held liable, in federal civil rights suits, for inadequate prison conditions absent a showing of "deliberate indifference" as a mental state; U.S. Supreme Court adopts tougher standard for inmate suits. *Wilson v. Seiter*, 111 S. Ct. 2321 (1991).

Civil rights suit dismissed when plaintiff-inmates did not clearly state that they were suing state corrections officials in their individual capacities; Eleventh Amendment immunity applied to their official capacities. *Wells v. Brown*, 891 F. 2d 591 (6th Cir. 1989).

SUMMARY

- The court system in the United States is based upon the principle of federalism. As a result of a historical evolution, a dual system of state and federal courts exists today. Therefore, federal and state courts may have concurrent jurisdiction over specific crimes.

- Another characteristic of the American court system is that it performs its duties with little or no supervision.

- Many state courts can be divided into three levels: trial courts, appellate courts, and state supreme courts.

- The victim of any crime is often the forgotten party in the criminal justice system. For many years, victims were perceived as simply another witness to the crime.

- One of the most important roles in the system is that of the prosecutor. This individual is charged with the responsibility of filing criminal cases. Until the case is filed, it does not become a part of the court system.

- We often think that the prosecutor's role is to convict the defendant. This is erroneous. The prosecutor has the duty to ensure justice, not merely to convict.

- Under our system of justice, the accused has the right to a counsel whose duty is to serve the interests of the accused. Although the defense counsel is an officer of the court, he or she is also the representative of the defendant in our adversarial process.

- The trial judge is an officer of the court. It would be more accurate to describe him or her as the "master of the court."

- Even though most cases are handled with a guilty plea and only a few cases are tried by a jury, the jury is the focal point of the criminal justice system.

- The decision to prosecute is a function of the prosecutor and is generally not reviewable. In many states and the federal government, before the prosecutor may file felony charges with a court, he or she must obtain a grand jury indictment. In other states, the prosecutor files an *information* with the lower court.

- Bail serves several purposes, including protecting society and ensuring the appearance of the defendant at court hearings.
- The criminal trial follows a series of steps that leads to a guilty or not guilty verdict.

DISCUSSION QUESTIONS

1. Explain the differences between the state and federal court system.
2. Name the key players in the court system and compare their roles.
3. Compare and contrast the roles of the defense counsel and the prosecutor.
4. Why doesn't the prosecutor always have a duty to convict?
5. Explain the role and function of the jury.
6. Why does the prosecution have the burden of proof in criminal cases?
7. Explain the process of selecting jurors.
8. Would you qualify for a "death qualified jury"?

ENDNOTES

1. Pursley, *Introduction to Criminal Justice*, 6th Ed.(MacMillan Publishing Company, New York) 1994.
2. *The Supreme Court of the United States* (U.S. Government Printing Office, Washington D.C.) no date.
3. 1 Cranch 137 (1803)
4. M. Randell and L. Haskell, "Sexual Violence in Women's Lives," *Violence Against Women* 6, (1995).
5. The Fifth Amendment's right to grand jury indictment and the Eighth Amendment's right regarding excessive bail have not been applied to the states. See *Hurtado v. California*, 110 U.S. 516 (1884).
6. If the confession was obtained by coercion, it may not be admitted even for impeachment purposes. See *Mincey v. Arizona,* 437 U.S. 385 (1978)
7. *Berger v. United States*, 295 U.S. 78 (1935).
8. *Argersinger v. Hamlin*, 407 U.S. 25 (1972).
9. This was an actual case that occurred in the 1970s in Buffalo, New York.
10. American Bar Association, *Standards for Criminal Justice*, approved draft, (1972).
11. N.Gary Holten and Lawson L. Lamar, *The Criminal Courts*, (New York: McGraw-Hill, 1991), p. 96.
12. U.S. Constitution, Article II.
13. 28 U.S.C. 636 (b).
14. Administrative Office of the United States Courts, *The United States Courts*, (Washington D.C.: Government Printing Office, 1989).
15. 399 U.S. 66 (1970).
16. 489 U.S. 538 (1989).
17. 399 U.S. 78, 90 (1970).
18. 406 U.S. 404 (1972).
19. Bureau of Justice Statistics Study, "Felony Arrests," (1987).
20. 342 U.S.1 (1951).
21. *U.S. v. Salerno*, 55 USLW 4663 (1987).

CHAPTER 3

SENTENCING AND PLEA BARGAINING

PLEAS

More than 90 percent of the convictions in criminal courts are the results of guilty pleas. Accordingly, guilty pleas play a central role in our criminal justice system. Without the high rate of pleas, our presently overloaded judicial system would probably collapse. All individuals charged with a crime may plead guilty or not guilty. In some jurisdictions, they may also enter a plea of *nolo contendere* which literately means no contest. A plea of not guilty by reason of insanity is also allowed in many jurisdictions.

PLEA BARGAINS

Plea bargaining is nothing more than an agreement between the prosecuting attorney and the defense to reduce the charge to a lesser crime, to drop certain charges, or to receive a lessened sentence in return for a guilty or nolo contendere plea. Plea bargaining usually takes place after the initial appearance or the arraignment of the defendant. In most states, the negotiating can continue until the time that a verdict is rendered. In most jurisdictions, the judge is prohibited from being involved in the plea bargaining. The judge generally must be advised of the agreement and in most states must approve it. Plea bargaining has been criticized because it allows a criminal to take advantage of the justice system by not being convicted or sentenced for the crime actually committed.

The National Advisory Commission on Criminal Justice Standards and Goals, Report on Courts suggested the following limitations on prosecutor's conduct during plea bargaining:

STANDARD 3.6

PROHIBITED PROSECUTORIAL INDUCEMENTS TO ENTER A PLEA OF GUILTY

No prosecutor should, in connection with plea negotiations, engage in, perform, or condone any of the following:

- Charging or threatening to charge the defendant with offenses for which the admissible evidence available to the prosecutor is insufficient to support a guilty verdict.

- Charging or threatening to charge the defendant with a crime not ordinarily charged in the jurisdiction for the conduct allegedly engaged in by him.

- Threatening the defendant that if he pleads not guilty, his sentence may be more severe than that which ordinarily is imposed in the jurisdiction in similar cases on defendants who plead not guilty.

- Failing to grant full disclosure before the disposition negotiations of all exculpatory evidence material to guilt or punishment.

Negotiated Pleas

Negotiated pleas are those pleas that are entered by the defendant based on a commitment from the prosecutor. A *blind plea* is a plea that is entered by the defendant without any inducement by the prosecutor or judge. In the latter situation, the defendant simply acknowledges his or her guilt. In the negotiated plea, the defendant has been promised some benefit in return for his or her plea. The benefit may be for a sentence not to exceed an agreed maximum or to plead guilty to a lessor offense in return to dismissing the more serious charge. In some cases, the negotiated plea is based on an agreement to drop unrelated charges, not to seek the death penalty or the habitual sentencing process, or for the prosecutor to recommend a certain sentence. A negotiated plea may also be based on the agreement of the prosecutor not to enter into evidence previous convictions or facts that a dangerous weapon was used, either of which would enhance the sentence.

Negotiated pleas or plea bargaining have been criticized for many reasons including:

- ➢ A favorable plea may induce an innocent person to plead guilty out of fear of the consequences of a trial.
- ➢ The government is making *deals* with criminals.
- ➢ Plea bargaining may allow the unconstitutional actions of law enforcement personnel to be concealed.
- ➢ It results in a compromise in public safety.
- ➢ Behind-the-scenes negotiations invite abuse by the participants.
- ➢ Plea bargaining policies in effect punish individuals who do not plea bargain and invoke their constitutional rights.

Those who support plea-bargaining contend that:

- ➢ Without plea bargaining, the judicial system would simply break down.
- ➢ Plea bargains relieve victims and other witnesses from the burdens of testifying.

> It facilitates law enforcement in those cases in which defendants provide information needed to apprehend or convict other defendants.

> A plea of guilty is the first step toward rehabilitation by the defendant.

Due Process Requirements

Boykin v. Alabama[1] is the leading case on the due process rights of guilty pleas. The petitioner was charged with and plead guilty to five armed robberies that had occurred in Mobile, Alabama. At that time, the crimes were punishable by death. The defendant was sentenced to death for each of the robberies. The Alabama Supreme Court affirmed his sentence and the U.S. Supreme Court granted *certiorari*. The defendant claimed that he was not aware of the consequences of his guilty pleas prior to having them accepted by the trial court. The record of trial did not reflect that the judge asked the defendant any questions when he entered his guilty pleas. In addition, the record fails to reflect that the petitioner [defendant] addressed the court when his pleas were entered.

CASE ON POINT

Justice Douglas, writing for the majority, stated that it was error for the trial judge to accept the petitioner's guilty pleas without an affirmative showing on the record that the pleas were intelligent and voluntary. Douglas pointed out that several constitutional rights are involved when a plea of guilty is involved. First is the privilege against compulsory self-incrimination guaranteed by the Fifth Amendment and applicable to the states by reason of the Fourteenth Amendment. Second is the right to trial by jury. Third is the right to confront one's accusers. And also that the Court cannot presume a wavier of these three important federal rights from a silent record.

Justice Douglas stated that what is at stake for an accused facing death or imprisonment demands the utmost solicitude of which courts are capable in canvassing the matter with the accused to make sure he has a full understanding of what the plea connotes and of its consequences. When a judge discharges that function, he should indicate in the record of trial proceedings adequate for any review that may be later sought and will forestall the spin-off of collateral proceedings that seek to probe murky memories.

Based on the *Boykin* case, there can be no presumption that the defendant was advised of his rights and that the plea was intelligently entered. The record of trial must reflect that the accused was advised of the consequences of his or her guilty plea and that the defendant understood that he or she was waiving certain constitutional rights. Does the same rule apply when the defendant admits to the existence of prior convictions being used to enhance the sentence? This issue was addressed in *Parke v. Raley*.[2] In *Parke*, the defendant was sentenced as a "persistent felony offender" based on two prior felony convictions. He contended on appeal that his guilty plea to the present offense was invalid because there was no indication in the record of trial that he was advised regarding the effects of the two prior convictions. At the time, Kentucky had a statute that created a presumption of the validity of prior convictions based on official records. The burden was on the defendant to produce evidence that the prior convictions were invalid. The court held that the statute created presumption that a prior conviction was valid did not violate due process, and that it was constitutional to apply a presumption of regularity to the prior proceedings.

Generally, for the plea of guilty to withstand challenges on appeal, the accused must be advised of each critical element of the offense to which he or she is pleading guilty.[3] If the defendant is not represented by counsel, the trial court is required to take steps to ensure not only that the guilty plea is otherwise voluntary and intelligent, but that the defendant is validly waiving his or her right to counsel. As stated in *Von Moltke v. Gillies*,[4] the government has the burden of rebutting a "strong presumption" that the defendant did not knowingly, intelligently, and voluntarily waive the right to counsel. Justice Black, in a plurality opinion, stated that to meet this burden, the government must establish that the defendant understood all of the following for the waiver of rights to be valid:

- The nature of the charges
- The statutory offenses included within them
- The range of allowable punishments thereunder
- Possible defenses to the charges
- Circumstances in mitigation thereof

In *Mitchell v. United States,* the Supreme Court held that a defendant who pleads guilty may still invoke the Fifth Amendment's privilege against self-incrimination at the sentencing procedure and no adverse influence may be drawn from the assertion of this right.[5] Amanda Mitchell pled guilty to selling cocaine, but reserved the right to contest the amount of cocaine involved. The quantity was crucial in determining the length of her sentence. At the sentencing hearing, Mitchell did not testify. The sentencing judge expressly said that he was drawing an adverse inference from her assertion of the privilege against self-incrimination at sentencing. The Supreme Court in a 5-to-4 decision held that defendants who plead guilty still retained the right to invoke the Fifth Amendment at sentencing and that no adverse inference can be drawn from their silence.

Statutory and Rule Requirements

In addition to the constitutional due process issues, all states and the federal government have imposed additional requirements that must be met in order for a guilty plea to be valid. The additional requirements are normally imposed by either statutory enactments or court rules. Rule 11 of the Federal Rules of Criminal Procedure, which governs the acceptance of guilty pleas in federal courts, is typical to that in most states.

FEDERAL RULES OF CRIMINAL PROCEDURE,

RULE II. PLEAS

(a) **Alternatives.**
  (1) **In General.** A defendant may plead not guilty, guilty, or *nolo contendere*. If a defendant refuses to plead or if a defendant corporation fails to appear, the court shall enter a plea of not guilty.

  (2) **Conditional Pleas.** With the approval of the court and the consent of the government, a defendant may enter a conditional plea of guilty or *nolo contendere*, reserving in writing the right, on appeal from the judgment, to a review of the adverse determination of any specified pretrial motion. A defendant who prevails on appeal shall be allowed to withdraw the plea.

(b) ***Nolo Contendere.*** A defendant may plead *nolo contendere* only with the consent of the court. Such a plea shall be accepted by the court only after due consideration of the views of the parties and the interest of the public in the effective administration of justice.

(c) **Advice to Defendant.** Before accepting a plea of guilty or *nolo contendere*, the court must address the defendant personally in open court and inform the defendant of, and determine that the defendant understands, the following:
  (1) the nature of the charge to which the plea is offered, the mandatory minimum penalty provided by law, if any, and the maximum

possible penalty provided by law, including the effect of any special parole or supervised release term, the fact that the court is required to consider any applicable sentencing guidelines but may depart from those guidelines under some circumstances, and, when applicable, that the court may also order the defendant to make restitution to any victim of the offense; and

(2) if the defendant is not represented by an attorney, that the defendant has the right to be represented by an attorney at every stage of the proceeding and, if necessary, one will be appointed to represent the defendant; and

(3) that the defendant has the right to plead not guilty or to persist in that plea if it has already been made, the right to be tried by a jury and at that trial the right to the assistance of counsel, the right to confront and cross-examine adverse witnesses, and the right against compelled self-incrimination; and

(4) that if a plea of guilty or *nolo contendere* is accepted by the court there will not be a further trial of any kind, so that by pleading guilty or nolo contendere the defendant waives the right to a trial; and

(5) if the court intends to question the defendant under oath, on the record, and in the presence of counsel about the offense to which the defendant has pleaded, that the defendant's answers may later be used against the defendant in a prosecution for perjury or false statement.

(d) **Insuring That the Plea Is Voluntary**. The court shall not accept a plea of guilty or *nolo contendere* without first, by addressing the defendant personally in open court, determining that the plea is voluntary and not the result of force or threats or of promises apart from a plea agreement. The court shall also inquire as to whether the defendant's willingness to plead guilty or nolo contendere results from prior discussions between the attorney for the government and the defendant or the defendant's attorney.

(e) **Plea Agreement Procedure**.

(1) **In General**. The attorney for the government and the attorney for the defendant or the defendant when acting pro se may engage in discussions with a view toward reaching an agreement that, upon the entering of a plea of guilty or *nolo contendere* to a charged offense or to a lesser or related offense, the attorney for the government will do any of the following:

(A) move for dismissal of other charges; or

(B) make a recommendation, or agree not to oppose the defendant's request, for a particular sentence, with the understanding that such recommendation or request shall not be binding upon the court; or

(C) agree that a specific sentence is the appropriate disposition of the case.

The court shall not participate in any such discussions.

(2) **Notice of Such Agreement**. If a plea agreement has been reached by the parties, the court shall, on the record, require the disclosure of the agreement in open court or, on a showing of good cause, in camera, at the time the plea is offered. If the agreement is of the type specified in subdivision (e)(1)(A) or (C), the court may accept or reject the agreement, or may defer its decision as to the acceptance or rejection until there has been an opportunity to consider the

presentence report. If the agreement is of the type specified in subdivision (e)(1)(B), the court shall advise the defendant that if the court does not accept the recommendation or request, the defendant nevertheless has no right to withdraw the plea.

(3) **Acceptance of a Plea Agreement.** If the court accepts the plea agreement, the court shall inform the defendant that it will embody in the judgment and sentence the disposition provided for in the plea agreement.

4) **Rejection of a Plea Agreement.** If the court rejects the plea agreement, the court shall, on the record, inform the parties of this fact, advise the defendant personally in open court or, on a showing of good cause, in camera, that the court is not bound by the plea agreement, afford the defendant the opportunity to then withdraw the plea, and advise the defendant that if the defendant persists in a guilty plea or plea of *nolo contendere* the disposition of the case may be less favorable to the defendant than that contemplated by the plea agreement.

(5) **Time of Plea Agreement Procedure.** Except for good cause shown, notification to the court of the existence of a plea agreement shall be given at the arraignment or at such other time, prior to trial, as may be fixed by the court.

(6) **Inadmissability of Pleas, Plea Discussions, and Related Statements.** Except as otherwise provided in this paragraph, evidence of the following is not, in any civil or criminal proceeding, admissible against the defendant who made the plea or was a participant in the plea discussions:

    (A)   a plea of guilty which was later withdrawn;

(B) a plea of *nolo contendere*;
(C) any statement made in the course of any proceedings under this rule regarding either of the foregoing pleas; or
(D) any statement made in the course of plea discussions with an attorney for the government which do not result in a plea of guilty or which result in a plea of guilty later withdrawn.

However, such a statement is admissible (i) in any proceeding wherein another statement made in the course of the same plea or plea discussions has been introduced and the statement ought in fairness be considered contemporaneously with it, or (ii) in a criminal proceeding for perjury or false statement if the statement was made by the defendant under oath, on the record, and in the presence of counsel.

(f) Determining Accuracy of Plea. Notwithstanding the acceptance of a plea of guilty, the court should not enter a judgment upon such plea without making such inquiry as shall satisfy it that there is a factual basis for the plea.

(g) Record of Proceedings. A verbatim record of the proceedings at which the defendant enters a plea shall be made and, if there is a plea of guilty or *nolo contendere*, the record shall include, without limitation, the court's advice to the defendant, the inquiry into the voluntariness of the plea including any plea agreement, and the inquiry into the accuracy of a guilty plea.

(h) Harmless Error. Any variance from the procedures required by this rule which does not affect substantial rights shall be disregarded.

> ## CALIFORNIA PENAL CODE
> ## SECTION 1016.5a
>
> ### 1016.5. Advisement concerning status as alien, reconsideration of plea; effect of noncompliance
>
> (a) Prior to acceptance of a plea of guilty or *nolo contendere* to any offense punishable as a crime under state law except offenses designated as infractions under state law, the court shall administer the following advisement on the record to the defendant:
> If you are not a citizen, you are hereby advised that conviction of the offense for which you have been charged may have the consequences of deportation, exclusion from admission to the United States or denial of naturalization pursuant to the laws of the United States.

When sitting in a criminal court listening to the trial judge advise the defendant regarding his or her rights before accepting a guilty plea, one often gets the opinion that the judge is trying to talk the defendant out of pleading guilty. What the judge is trying to do is to prevent appellate issues regarding the validity of the guilty plea. Frequently, prisoners will file writs claiming that they were inadequately advised regarding their rights before they entered their guilty pleas.

Right to Plead Guilty

No discussion of guilty pleas is complete without a review of the *North Carolina v. Alford* case.[6] The *Alford* case answers several important questions:

➢ May a defendant enter a valid plea of guilty without admitting that he or she committed the offense?

➢ Does a defendant have a constitutional right to plead guilty?

➢ Is a trial judge required to accept a plea of guilty that is voluntarily and intelligently entered?

CASE ON POINT

Alford was indicted for first-degree murder, a capital offense in North Carolina. He was represented at trial by a court-appointed attorney. Faced with strong evidence of guilt, Alford's attorney recommended that he plead guilty, but left the ultimate decision to Alford himself. The prosecution agreed to accept a plea of guilty to the reduced charge of second-degree murder. Before the plea was accepted by the trial court, the court heard the sworn testimony of a police officer who summarized the state's case. There were no eyewitnesses to the killing. The testimony indicated that shortly before the killing, Alford took his gun from his house, stated his intention to kill the victim, and returned home with the declaration that he had carried out the killing. Alford testified that he did not commit the murder but that he was pleading guilty because he faced the threat of the death penalty if he did not do so.

Alford acknowledged that his counsel had advised him of his rights and of the difference between first and second degree murder. The judge accepted the plea and sentenced him to 30 years confinement. Alford then pursued his claim in *habeas corpus* proceeding in federal court contending that his plea was invalid because it was the product of fear and coercion.

The Supreme Court held that a trial court could accept the guilty plea of a defendant without the defendant admitting his or her guilt. The test was whether the plea was intelligently and voluntarily entered. The Supreme Court stated that the trial judge did not commit error in accepting the plea even though the defendant maintained his innocence. In footnote 11 of Justice White's opinion, the Court stated:

> Our holding does not mean that a trial judge must accept every constitutionally valid guilty plea merely because a defendant wishes so to plead. A criminal defendant does not have an absolute right under the Constitution to have his guilty plea accepted by the court, although the States may by statute or otherwise confer such a right. Likewise, the States may bar their courts from accepting guilty pleas from any defendants who assert their innocence.. Cf. Fed. Rule Crim. Proc. 11, which gives a trial judge discretion to "refuse to accept a plea of guilty . . ." We need not now delineate the scope of that discretion.

A factual basis is required in some jurisdictions before the accused may enter a plea of guilty. A *factual basis* consists of evidence that the crime was committed and that the defendant could have committed the crime. The factual basis may be established by admissions by the defendant, the recitation of details of the crime by the prosecutor or defense counsel, by testimony of police officers or other witnesses, and by police reports that are stipulated to by both parties. Generally two purposes are served by requiring that a factual basis be established for a guilty plea. First, the existence of a factual basis helps to ensure that the defendant is knowingly pleading guilty to a crime that he or she could have committed. Second, the statement of a factual basis helps ensure that the defendant's plea is in fact voluntary and not the result of impermissible threats, promises, or other pressures.

BREACHES OF PLEA BARGAINS

In *Santobello v. New York,* the defendant plead guilty to a lesser-included offense of the possession of gambling records. As part of the plea bargain, the prosecutor agreed to make no recommendation as to sentence.[7] At the sentencing hearing, another prosecutor had replaced the prosecutor who had negotiated the plea. The second prosecutor, apparently ignorant of his colleague's commitment, recommended a one-year sentence. At that time, the defense counsel requested an adjournment in order to present evidence regarding the issue. The judge stated that:

> I am not at all influenced by what the District Attorney says, so that there is no need to adjourn the sentence, and there is no need to have any testimony. It doesn't make a particle of difference what the District Attorney says he will do, or what he doesn't do.

The judge then imposed the maximum sentence of one year. The Supreme Court reversed the case and stated that:

> It is now conceded that the promise to abstain from a recommendation was made, and at this stage the prosecution is not in a good position to argue that its inadvertent breach of agreement is immaterial. . . . That the breach of agreement was inadvertent does not lessen its impact. . . . We need not reach the question whether the sentencing judge would or would not have been influenced had he known all the details of the negotiations for the plea. He stated that the prosecutor's recommendations did not influence him and we have no reason to doubt that. Nevertheless, we conclude that the interests of justice and appropriate recognition of the duties of the prosecution in relation to promises made in the negotiation of pleas of guilty will be best served by remanding the case to the state courts for further consideration.

In *Santobello*, the prosecutor failed to comply with a portion of the plea agreement and the case was reversed. What if the prosecutor, in return for a plea of guilty, agrees to recommend probation rather than prison, and the judge nonetheless sentenced the defendant to six years in prison? In *United States v. Benchimol,* the parties had agreed that the prosecutor would recommend probation in return for the defendant's plea of guilty.[8] The defendant plead guilty. The prosecution recommended probation and the court sentenced the defendant to six years in prison. The Supreme Court upheld the sentence in this case, based on the concept that the plea bargain was not for probation, but only that the prosecutor would recommend probation and therefore there was no breach of agreement.

RIGHTS DURING SENTENCING

Prior to the verdict, defendants are protected by an array of constitutional rights, including the right to a jury trial in most criminal trials, the right to present witnesses on their behalf, the right to cross-examine government witnesses, and the presumption of innocence. The constitutional protections afforded a defendant during the sentencing process are not as broadly interpreted. For example, in *Williams v. New York,* the Supreme Court held that the trial judge could consider a wide range of information in determining the appropriate sentence even though the information would not have been admissible in the guilt-innocence stage of the criminal proceedings.[9] However, in *Gardner v. Florida*, the Supreme Court held that the defendant has a right to see the entire presentence report in a death penalty case.[10]

Most courts generally assume that defendants have a constitutional right to have their attorneys comment on the evidence and make a statement to the court at sentencing hearings. In most jurisdictions, defendants have the right of *allocution*, i.e., to personally address the court on their behalf before the sentence is announced. It appears that in all jurisdictions, the defendants have a right to be present at the sentencing hearing and to present evidence. Generally, defendants have no right to cross-examine witnesses who do not testify in person, but whose statements are contained in the presentence reports.

In most jurisdictions, the courts have held that the defendant has no constitutional right for a statement of reasons for the sentence imposed. However, if the defendant is retried after a successful appeal, there is the requirement for the court to explain the court's rationale for imposing a more severe sentence in the subsequent trial. This requirement is imposed to ensure that the defendant is not being punished for having exercised his or her right to appeal the first conviction. This requirement does not apply when the second sentence is imposed by a different sentencer.[11]

In addition to the procedural safeguards required by the U.S. Constitution, almost all jurisdictions have provided additional rights to defendants during the sentencing process through state constitutions, statutes, and court rules.

CASES ON POINT

When the defendant pleas guilty in order to avoid the death penalty, is the plea voluntary? The *Brady* case examines this issue.

BRADY v. UNITED STATES
90 S.Ct. 1463 (1970)

MR. JUSTICE WHITE delivered the opinion of the Court.

In 1959, petitioner was charged with kidnaping in violation of 18 U.S.C. § 1201(a). Since the indictment charged that the victim of the kidnaping was not liberated unharmed, petitioner faced a maximum penalty of death if the verdict of the jury should so recommend. Petitioner, represented by competent counsel throughout, first elected to plead not guilty. Apparently because the trial judge was unwilling to try the case without a jury, petitioner made no serious attempt to reduce the possibility of a death penalty by waiving a jury trial. Upon learning that his codefendant, who had confessed to the authorities, would plead guilty and be available to testify against him, petitioner changed his plea to guilty.

His plea was accepted after the trial judge twice questioned him as to the voluntariness of his plea. Petitioner was sentenced to 50 years imprisonment, later reduced to 30.

In 1967, petitioner sought relief under 28 U.S.C. § 2255, claiming that his plea of guilty was not voluntarily given because § 1201(a) operated to coerce his plea, because his counsel exerted impermissible pressure and because his plea was induced by representations with respect to reduction of sentence and clemency.

After a hearing, the District Court for the District of New Mexico denied relief According to the District Court's findings, petitioner's counsel did not put impermissible pressure on petitioner to plead guilty and no representations were made with respect to a reduced sentence or clemency. The court held that § 1201(a) was constitutional and found that petitioner decided to plead guilty when he learned that his co-defendant was going to plead guilty: petitioner pleaded guilty "by reason of other matters and not by reason of the statute" or because of any acts of the trial judge. The court concluded that "the plea was voluntarily and knowingly made."

The Court of Appeals for the Tenth Circuit affirmed, determining that the District Court's findings were supported by substantial evidence and specifically approving the finding that petitioner's plea of guilty was voluntary. 404 F.2d 601(1968). We granted certiorari, 395 U.S. 976 (1969), to consider the claim that the Court of Appeals was in error in not reaching a contrary result on the authority of this Court's decision in *United States v. Jackson*, 390 U.S. 570 (1968). We affirm.

I

In *United States v. Jackson*, supra, the defendants were indicted under § 1201(a). The District Court dismissed the § 1201(a) count of the indictment, holding the statute unconstitutional because it permitted imposition of the death sentence only upon a jury's recommendation and thereby made the risk of death the price of jury trial. This Court held the statute valid, except for the death penalty provision; with respect to the latter, the Court agreed with the trial court "that the death penalty provision . . . imposes an impermissible burden upon the exercise of a constitutional right." The problem was to determine "whether the Constitution permits the establishment of such a death penalty, applicable only to those defendants who assert the right to contest their guilt before a jury." The inevitable effect of the provision was said to be to discourage assertion of the Fifth Amendment right not to plead guilty and to deter exercise of the Sixth Amendment right to demand a jury trial. Because the legitimate goal of limiting the death penalty to cases in which a jury recommends it could be achieved without penalizing those defendants who plead not guilty and elect a jury trial, the death penalty provision "needlessly penalized" the assertion of a constitutional right," 390 U.S., at 583, and was therefore unconstitutional.

Since the "inevitable effect" of the death penalty provision of § 1201(a) was said by the Court to be the needless encouragement of pleas of guilty and waivers of jury trial, *Brady* contends that *Jackson* requires the invalidation of every plea of guilty entered under that section, at least when the fear of death is shown to have been a factor in the plea. Petitioner, however, has read far too much into the *Jackson* opinion.

Plainly, it seems to us, *Jackson* ruled neither that all pleas of guilty encouraged by the fear of a possible death sentence are involuntary pleas nor that such encouraged pleas are invalid whether involuntary or not. *Jackson* prohibits the imposition of the death penalty under § 1201(a), but that decision neither fashioned a new standard for judging the validity of guilty pleas nor mandated a new application of the test theretofore fashioned by courts and since reiterated that guilty pleas are valid if both "voluntary" and "intelligent."

That a guilty plea is a grave and solemn act to be accepted only with care and discernment has long been recognized. Central to the plea and the foundation for entering judgment against the defendant is the defendant's admission in open court that he committed the acts charged in the indictment. He thus stands as a witness against himself and he is shielded by the Fifth Amendment from being compelled to do so—hence the minimum requirement that his plea be the voluntary expression of his own choice. But the idea is more than an admission of past conduct; it is the defendant's consent that judgment of conviction may be entered without a trial—a waiver of his right to trial before a jury or a judge. Waivers of constitutional rights not only must be voluntary but must be knowing, intelligent acts done with sufficient awareness of the relevant circumstances and likely consequences. On neither score was Brady's plea of guilty invalid.

II

The trial judge in 1959 found the plea voluntary before accepting it; the District Court in 1968, after an evidentiary hearing, found that the plea was voluntarily made; the Court of Appeals specifically approved the finding of voluntariness. We see no reason on this record to disturb the judgment of those courts. Petitioner, advised by competent counsel, tendered his plea after his codefendant, who had already given a confession, determined to plead guilty and became available to testify against petitioner. It was this development that the District Court found to have triggered Brady's guilty plea.

The voluntariness of Brady's plea can be determined only by considering all of the relevant circumstances surrounding it. . . . One of these circumstances was the possibility of a heavier sentence following a guilty verdict after a trial. It may be that Brady, faced with a strong case against him and recognizing that his chances for acquittal were slight, preferred to plead guilty and thus limit the penalty to life imprisonment rather than to elect a jury trial which could result in a death penalty. But even if we assume that Brady would not have pled guilty except for the death penalty provision, . . . this assumption merely identifies the penalty provision as a "but for" cause of his plea. That the statute caused the plea in this sense does not necessarily prove that the plea was coerced and invalid as an involuntary act.

The State, to some degree, encourages pleas of guilty at every important step in the criminal process. For some people, their breach of a State's law is alone sufficient reason for surrendering themselves and accepting punishment. For others, apprehension and charge, both threatening acts by the Government, jar them into admitting their guilt. In still other cases, the post-indictment accumulation of evidence may convince the defendant and his counsel that a trial is not worth the agony and expense to the defendant and his family. All these pleas of guilty are valid in spite of the State's responsibility for some of the factors motivating the pleas; the pleas are no more improperly compelled than is the decision by a defendant at the close of the State's evidence at trial that he must take the stand or face certain conviction.

Of course, the agents of the State may not produce a plea "by actual or threatened physical harm or by mental coercion overbearing the will of the defendant." But nothing of the sort is claimed in this case; nor is there evidence that Brady was so gripped by fear of the death penalty or hope of leniency that he did not or could not, with the help of counsel, rationally weigh the advantages of going to trial against the advantages of pleading guilty. Brady's claim is of a different sort: that it violates the Fifth Amendment to influence or encourage a guilty plea by opportunity or promise or leniency that a guilty plea is coerced and invalid if influenced by the fear of a possibly higher penalty for the crime charged if a conviction is obtained after the State has put its proof.

Insofar as the voluntariness of his plea is concerned, there is little to differentiate Brady from (1) the defendant, in a jurisdiction where the judge and jury have the same range of sentencing power, who pleads guilty because his lawyer advises him that the judge will very probably be more lenient than the jury; (2) the defendant, in a jurisdiction where the judge alone has sentencing power, who is advised by counsel that the judge is normally more lenient with defendants who plead guilty than with those who go to trial; (3) the defendant who is permitted by prosecutor and judge to plead guilty to a lesser offense included in the offense charged, and (4) the defendant who pleads guilty to certain counts with the understanding that other charges will be dropped. In each of these situations, as in Brady's case, the defendant might never plead guilty absent the possibility or certainty that the plea will result in a lesser penalty than the sentence that could be imposed after a trial and a verdict of guilty. We decline to hold, however, that a guilty plea is compelled and invalid under the Fifth Amendment whenever motivated by the defendant's desire to accept the certainty or probability of a lesser penalty rather than face a wider range of possibilities extending from acquittal to conviction and a higher penalty authorized by law for the crime charged.

The issue we deal with is inherent in the criminal law and its administration because guilty pleas are not constitutionally forbidden, because the criminal law characteristically extends to judge or jury a range of choice in setting the sentence in individual cases, and because both the State and the defendant often find it advantageous to preclude the possibility of the maximum penalty authorized by law. For a defendant who sees slight possibility of acquittal, the advantages of pleading guilty and limiting the probable penalty are obvious—his exposure is reduced, the correctional processes can begin immediately, and the practical burdens of a trial are eliminated. For the State there are also advantages—the more promptly imposed punishment after an admission of guilt may more effectively attain the objectives of punishment; and with the avoidance of trial, scarce judicial and prosecutorial resources are conserved for those cases in which there is a substantial issue of the defendant's guilt or in which there is substantial doubt that the State can sustain its burden of proof. It is this mutuality of advantage that perhaps explains the fact that at present well over three-fourths of the criminal convictions in this country rest on pleas of guilty, a great many of them no doubt motivated, at least in part, by the hope or assurance of a lesser penalty than might be imposed if there were a guilty verdict after a trial to judge or jury.

Of course, that the prevalence of guilty pleas is explainable does not necessarily validate those pleas or the system which produces them. But we cannot hold that it is unconstitutional for the State to extend a benefit to a defendant who, in turn, extends a substantial benefit to the State and who demonstrates by his plea that he is ready and willing to admit his crime and to enter the correctional system in a frame of mind that affords hope for success in rehabilitation over a shorter period of time than might otherwise be necessary.

A contrary holding would require the States and Federal Government to forbid guilty pleas altogether, to provide a single invariable penalty for each crime defined by the statutes, or to place the sentencing function in a separate authority having no knowledge of the manner in which the conviction in each case was obtained. In any event, it would be necessary to forbid prosecutors and judges to accept guilty pleas to selected counts, to lesser included offenses or to reduced charges. The Fifth Amendment does not reach so far. . . . Affirmed.

[Justice Black noted his concurrence to the judgment and "substantially all" of the Court's opinion. Justice Brennan wrote an opinion concurring in the result, which Justice Douglas and Justice Marshall joined.]

> May a prosecutor threaten to reindict the defendant under the habitual criminal statute in order to induce the defendant to plead guilty to present charges? The following case examines this issue.

BORDENKIRCHER v. HAYES
434 U.S. 357, 98 S.Ct. 663 (1978)

MR. JUSTICE STEWART delivered the opinion of the Court.

The question in this case is whether the Due Process Clause of the Fourteenth Amendment is violated when a state prosecutor carries out a threat made during plea negotiations to reindict the accused on more serious charges if he does not plead guilty to the offense with which he was originally charged.

I

The respondent, Paul Lewis Hayes, was indicted by a Fayette County, Ky., grand jury on a charge of uttering a forged instrument in the amount of $88.30, an offense then punishable by a term of 2 to 10 years in prison. . . .After arraignment, Hayes, his retained counsel, and the Commonwealth's Attorney met in the presence of the Clerk of the Court to discuss a possible plea agreement.

During these conferences the prosecutor offered to recommend a sentence of five years in prison if Hayes would plead guilty to the indictment. He also said that if Hayes did not plead guilty and "save the court the inconvenience and necessity of a trial," he would return to the grand jury to seek an indictment under the Kentucky Habitual Criminal Act. . ., which would subject Hayes to a mandatory sentence of life imprisonment by reason of his two prior felony convictions. Hayes chose not to plead guilty, and the prosecutor did obtain an indictment charging him under the Habitual Criminal Act. It is not disputed that the recidivist charge was fully justified by the evidence, that the prosecutor was in possession of this evidence at the time of the original indictment, and that Hayes' refusal to plead guilty to the original charge was what led to his indictment under the habitual criminal statute.

A jury found Hayes guilty on the principal charge of uttering a forged instrument and, in a separate proceeding, further found that he had twice before been convicted of felonies. As required by the habitual offender statute, he was sentenced to a life term in the penitentiary. The Kentucky Court of Appeals rejected Hayes' constitutional objections to the enhanced sentence, holding in an unpublished opinion that imprisonment for life with the possibility of parole was constitutionally permissible in light of the previous felonies of which Hayes had been convicted, and that the prosecutor's decision to indict him as a habitual offender was a legitimate use of available leverage in the plea-bargaining process.

On Hayes' petition for a federal writ of habeas corpus, the United States District Court for the Eastern District of Kentucky agreed that there had been no constitutional violation in the sentence or the indictment procedure, and denied the writ. The Court of Appeals for the Sixth Circuit reversed the District Court's judgment. . . . We granted certiorari to consider a constitutional question of importance in the administration of criminal justice.

II

It may be helpful to clarify at the outset the nature of the issue in this case. While the prosecutor did not actually obtain the recidivist indictment until after the plea conferences had ended, his intention to do so was clearly expressed at the outset of the plea negotiations. Hayes was thus fully informed of the true terms of the offer when he made his decision to plead not guilty. This is not a situation, therefore, where the prosecutor without notice brought an additional and more serious charge after plea negotiations relating only to the original indictment had ended with the defendant's insistence on pleading not guilty. As a practical matter, in short, this case would be no different if the grand jury had indicted Hayes as a recidivist from the outset, and the prosecutor had offered to drop that charge as part of the plea bargain.

The Court of Appeals nonetheless drew a distinction between "concessions relating to prosecution under an existing indictment," and threats to bring more severe charges not contained in the original indictment—a line it thought necessary in order to establish a prophylactic rule to guard against the evil of prosecutorial vindictiveness. Quite apart from this chronological distinction, however, the Court of Appeals found that the prosecutor had acted vindictively in the present case since he had conceded that the indictment was influenced by his desire to induce a guilty plea. The ultimate conclusion of the Court of Appeals thus seems to have been that a prosecutor acts vindictively and in violation of due process of law whenever his charging decision is influenced by what he hopes to gain in the course of plea bargaining negotiations.

III

...Plea bargains are important components of this country's criminal justice system. Properly administered, they can benefit all concerned." ...The open acknowledgment of this previously clandestine practice has led this Court to recognize the importance of counsel during plea negotiations... the need for a public record indicating that a plea was knowingly and voluntarily made... and the requirement that a prosecutor's plea-bargaining promise must be kept.... The decision of the Court of Appeals in the present case, however, did not deal with considerations such as these, but held that the substance of the plea offer itself violated the limitations imposed by the Due Process Clause of the Fourteenth Amendment.... For the reasons that follow, we have concluded that the Court of Appeals was mistaken in so ruling.

IV

This Court held in *North Carolina v. Pearce*, 395 U.S. 711, 725, that the Due Process Clause of the Fourteenth Amendment "requires that vindictiveness against a defendant for having successfully attacked his first conviction must play no part in the sentence he receives after a new trial." The same principle was later applied to prohibit a prosecutor from reindicting a convicted misdemeanant on a felony charge after the defendant had invoked an appellate remedy, since in this situation there was also a "realistic likelihood of vindictiveness."....In those cases the Court was dealing with the State's unilateral imposition of a penalty upon a defendant who had chosen to exercise a legal right to attack his original conviction-a situation "very different from the give-and-take negotiation common in plea bargaining between the prosecution and defense, which arguably possess relatively equal bargaining power." *Parker v. North Carolina*, 397 U.S. 790, 809 (opinion of Brennan, J.)

To punish a person because he has done what the law plainly allows him to do is a due process violation of the most basic sort, and for an agent of the State to pursue a course of action whose objective is to penalize a person's reliance on his legal rights is "patently unconstitutional." *Chaffin v. Stynchcombe* ...But in the give-and-take of plea bargaining, there is no such element of punishment or retaliation so long as the accused is free to accept or reject the prosecution's offer.

Plea bargaining flows from "the mutuality of advantage" to defendants and prosecutors, each with his own reasons for wanting to avoid trial.... Defendants advised by competent counsel and protected by other procedural safeguards are presumptively capable of intelligent choice in response to prosecutorial persuasion, and unlikely to be driven to false self-condemnation. . . . Indeed, acceptance of the basic legitimacy of plea bargaining necessarily implies rejection of any notion that a guilty plea is involuntary in a constitutional sense simply because it is the end result of the bargaining process. By hypothesis, the plea may have been induced by promises of a recommendation of a lenient sentence or a reduction of charges, and thus by fear of the possibility of a greater penalty upon conviction after a trial.

While confronting a defendant with the risk of more severe punishment clearly may have a discouraging effect on the defendant's assertion of his trial rights, the imposition of these difficult choices [is] an inevitable,"and permissible, attribute of any legitimate system which tolerates and encourages the negotiation of pleas."....It follows that, by tolerating and encouraging the negotiation of pleas, this Court has necessarily accepted as constitutionally legitimate the simple reality that the prosecutor's interest at the bargaining table is to persuade the defendant to forgo his right to plead not guilty.

It is not disputed here that Hayes was properly chargeable under the recidivist statute, since he had in fact been convicted of two previous felonies. In our system, so long as the prosecutor has probable cause to believe that the accused committed an offense defined by statute, the decision whether or not to prosecute, and what charge to file or bring before a grand jury, generally rests entirely in his discretion. Within the limits set by the legislature's constitutionally valid definition of chargeable offenses, the conscious exercise of some selectivity in enforcement is not in itself a federal constitutional violation so long as the selection was not deliberately based upon an unjustifiable standard such as race, religion, or other arbitrary classification." *Ovler v. Boles*, 368 U.S. 448, 456. To hold that the prosecutor's desire to induce a guilty plea is an "unjustifiable standard," which, like race or religion, may play no part in his charging decision, would contradict the very premises that underlie the concept of plea bargaining itself. Moreover, a rigid constitutional rule that would prohibit a prosecutor from acting forthrightly in his dealings with the defense could only invite unhealthy subterfuge that would drive the practice of plea bargaining back into the shadows from which it has so recently emerged....

There is no doubt that the breadth of discretion that our country's legal system vests in prosecuting attorneys carries with it the potential for both individual and institutional abuse. And broad though that discretion may be, there are undoubtedly constitutional limits upon its exercise. We hold only that the course of conduct engaged in by the prosecutor in this case, which no more than openly presented the defendant with the unpleasant alternatives of forgoing trial or facing charges on which he was plainly subject to prosecution, did not violate the Due Process Clause of the Fourteenth Amendment.

Accordingly, the judgment of the Court of Appeals is Reversed.
[Justices Blackmun, Brennan, Powell, and Marshall dissented.]

SUMMARY

- More than 90 percent of the convictions in criminal courts are the result of guilty pleas. Accordingly, guilty pleas play a central role in our criminal justice system. Without the high rate of pleas, our presently overloaded judicial system would probably collapse.
- Negotiated pleas are those pleas that are entered by the defendant based on a commitment from the prosecutor. A blind plea is a plea that is entered by the defendant without any inducement by the prosecutor or judge.
- It is error for the trial judge to accept the petitioner's guilty pleas without an affirmative showing on the record that the pleas were intelligent and voluntary. There is no presumption that the defendant was advised of his

rights and that the plea was intelligently entered. The record of trial must reflect that the accused was advised of the consequences of his or her guilty plea and that the defendant understood that he or she was waiving certain constitutional rights.

- A trial court may accept the guilty plea of a defendant without the defendant admitting his or her guilt. The test is whether the plea was intelligently and voluntarily entered. The Supreme Court has stated that the trial judge did not commit error in accepting the plea even though the defendant maintained his innocence.

- A factual basis is required in some jurisdictions before the accused may enter a plea of guilty. A factual basis consists of evidence that the crime was committed and that the defendant could have committed the crime.

- The constitutional protections afforded a defendant during the sentencing process are not as broadly interpreted as they are during the guilt-innocence phase of the trial.

DISCUSSION QUESTIONS

1. What rights does a defendant have at the sentencing hearing?

2. Should plea bargaining be abolished? Justify your answer.

3. What restrictions should be placed on plea bargaining?

4. What purposes are served by requiring a factual basis for a guilty plea?

5. What must a judge determine before he or she accepts a guilty plea in a felony case?

ENDNOTES

1. 395 U.S. 238 (1969).
2. 506 U.S. 20 (1992).
3. *Henderson v. Morgan*, 426 U.S. 637 (1976).
4. 332 U.S. 708 (1948).
5. 119 S.Ct. 1307 (1999).
6. 400 U.S. 25 (1970).
7. 404 U.S. 257 (1971).
8. 471 U.S. 453 (1985).
9. 337 U.S. 241 (1949).
10. 430 U.S. 349 (1977).
11. *Texas v. McCullough*, 475 U.S. 134 (1986).

CHAPTER 4

FREEDOM OF ASSOCIATION

INTRODUCTION

The fact of confinement and the needs of the penal institution impose limitations on constitutional rights, including those derived from the First Amendment, which are implicit in incarceration...Perhaps the most obvious of the First Amendment rights that are necessarily curtailed are those associational rights that the First Amendment protects outside of prison walls.

Chief Justice Rehnquist in
Jones v. North Carolina Prisoners' Labor Union

The right of freedom of association is not specifically listed in the First Amendment. There is a right to assemble and one can argue that if one has a right to assemble in a group, one must also have a right to associate with those one meets at such an assembly. In *Roberts v. U.S. Jacyees*, the Supreme Court listed two types of protected associations:

➢ The rights of individuals to enter into and maintain intimate family relationships, and

➢ The right of individuals to engage in expressive association or to gather together.[1]

Should prisoners also have the right of freedom of association? If so, to what extent? Does freedom of association include joining unions, contact with the media, visitation, and conjugal visits?

UNION MEMBERSHIP

Labor unions have a long history in the United States. In 1778, the first successful collective action by employees to win a wage increase was won in New York by the New York journeyman printers.[2] From that time to the present, unions have grown, engaged in collective bargaining, and become an accepted part of our society. In some states, correctional officers belong to active statewide unions that represent their interests at the bargaining table.

Starting in the late 1960s, prisoners in North Carolina organized prisoners' unions and associated with the U.S. labor unions. The prisoners organized the Prisoners' Labor Union in many of North Carolina's penal institutions. The union's stated purpose was to seek, through collective bargaining, improved working conditions and to work toward the alteration or elimination of practices and policies of the Department of Corrections with which the union membership did not agree. The union also wanted to serve as a spokesperson for the presentation and resolution of prisoner grievances. At first, the state took no action against the "union." Its membership grew to approximately 2,000 prisoners in forty different institutions. Then, the Department of Corrections issued new regulations prohibiting the solicitation of new members, banning union meetings, and forbidding bulk mailing regarding union matters from outside sources. [Note: the state had and continued to allow some organizations such as the Jaycees, Alcoholics Anonymous, and the Boy Scouts to hold meetings in the institutions and to bulk mail material regarding their organizations.]

The question faced by the courts was, "Should prisoners have a right join together in a union that represents their interests?" Secondary issues involved included:

- Should prisoners have a right to assemble at a union meeting?
- Should prisoners have the right to distribute literature regarding the activities and benefits of union membership?
- Should prisoners have the right to wear union label pins?

The courts have taken different positions regarding union activities by prisoners. One court held that an inmate's status could be changed as a result of his union activities, while other courts allow prisoners to wear union label pins. However, the Supreme Court, in *Jones v. North Carolina Prisoners Labor Union*, stated that prisoners do not have the right to engage in organizing activities while in prison.[3] The Court stated that courts must recognize the wide-ranging deference that should be accorded the decisions of prison administrators.

Regarding the right of prison officials to allow meetings of the Boy Scouts, Jaycees, and Alcoholic Anonymous and their bulk mailing of literature while restricting similar rights by the union, the Court stated that the approach of the Department of Corrections in this area was reasonably related to the objectives of prison administration and therefore was legal. The Court stated that bulk mailing rights were only a question of cost savings and those savings did not fundamentally affect free speech. The Court also held that solicitation is more than a simple expression of ideas and that it was an invitation to engage in illegal collective bargaining. A North Carolina statute existed that made it illegal for any collective bargaining by prisoners regarding conditions of confinement, pay, or work hours. The Court stated that preserving order in the prison was a legitimate primary concern of the prison officials. According to the Court, prison officials should have wide discretion when making decisions regarding the administration of the prison.

NEWS MEDIA CONTACT

In 1974, the Supreme Court decided *Pell v. Procunier*, a case involving the issue of media contact with prisoners.[4] Four California prisoners and three journalists filed suit alleging that their First Amendment rights had been violated by a prison regulation that prohibited face-to-face interviews between the press and prisoners. The prisoners based their claims on the right to free speech under the First Amendment and due process under the Fourteenth Amendment. The Court denied their claims, stating that there were alternate channels of communication available to the prisoners, and the restrictions on their rights had to be balanced against the State's interest in administrating the prison.

The Court denied the journalists' claims, stating that the First Amendment does not guarantee the press a constitutional right of special access to information not available to the general public.

At the same time *Pell* was decided, a companion case, *Saxbe v. Washington* was decided.[5] *Saxbe* also dealt with the constitutionality of a regulation forbidding the media from conducting interviews with prisoners. The Court upheld that regulation, stating that it imposed no more of a burden on the press than the general rule, which was constitutional, that no one can enter the prison and simply designate an inmate he would like to visit.[6]

The next case to deal with the media and prisoners was *Houchins v. KQED*.[7] An operator of a broadcasting company was denied access to the site of an inmate's suicide. A psychiatrist alleged that the prisoner's illness and death resulted from the conditions in that portion of the facility that the media wanted to visit and photograph. It was alleged that several rapes and beatings had occurred at that location. The court denied the media access, reinforcing its holding in *Pell* and *Saxbe* by once again stating that the media has no special right of access different from or greater than that accorded the general public.

More recently, *Johnson v. Stephan* also held that the First Amendment was not violated by denying an inmate permission to conduct a face-to-face interview with personnel of a television news program. The institution argued that its denial was based upon a desire to avoid disruption in the orderly operation of the prison and that the inmate was free to communicate with the news program personnel through use of the mail and telephone conversations.[8]

In deciding the news media cases, the courts have looked at the rights of the prisoners under free speech and the restrictions on the press. As to the restrictions on the prisoners' rights to talk to the press, the Supreme Court has held that this restriction is permitted. The prison officials are restricting only one type of communications and that the prisoners have other means of communication available. They could send and receive mail to the media, as well as to family and friends. They are allowed to have visits with family, members of the clergy, attorneys, and friends. Accordingly, the prisoners are not sealed off from making communications regarding prison conditions. The Court seemed to indicate that a lack of alternative means of communications regarding prison conditions would result in a different holding.

The second aspect of the issue was the limitations on the press. The Court looked at whether this was a violation of the freedom of the press right. The Court noted that the prison authorities were not trying to conceal prison conditions, and that the press were allowed to take tours of the prison. During the tours, the newsmen could stop and speak to any prisoner they encountered. The officials were not trying to deny the press the right to learn about the prison conditions, but were trying to prevent a few prisoners from becoming "big wheels" after they were spotlighted by the press attention. The Court concluded that the regulations were based on the underlying principle of the orderly running of the prison, and were valid.

VISITATION

All jails and prisons have policies regarding visitation. Generally speaking, prisoners are asked to list families and friends he or she would like to visit. These visits are typically of two types: contact and noncontact.

- *Contact visits* allow the inmate and visitors to have physical contact and grant them limited mobility. They may move around in the visiting area, visit at a table, bench, or park area. They may hold hands, hug, or even kiss. As a general rule, it appears that the prison officials may restrict visitation rights as long as those restrictions are reasonably related to legitimate governmental objectives.

- *Noncontact visits* occur when the inmate and visitor cannot physically touch each other. They are usually seated and face each other across a plastic, glass, or wire mesh barrier. They talk via a telephone or through a small opening in the barrier.

Texas Department of Criminal Justice

VISITATION

Visitation serves an important role in preserving the association between offenders and their families and friends. However, offenders are not assigned to specific facilities for the convenience of visitation. Visitation rules are displayed in areas accessible to visitors, and copies of the rules will be provided to the offender upon request. Visits are normally conducted on Saturdays or Sundays between 8:00 a.m. and 5:00 p.m. The names of all visitors, except children under the age of sixteen and the attorney, must be on the approved visitors list, which is limited to ten visitors. All offenders, except those in the reception process, solitary confinement, close custody, lockdown status, or administrative segregation, are allowed one visit every weekend not to exceed two hours and not to exceed two adult visitors. Children under the age of sixteen are not counted as a second visitor, but must be accompanied by an approved adult visitor.

Approved visitors must present photo identification before entering the facility. Identification may include a valid driver's license, a Department of Public Safety I.D. card, an employee I.D. card or badge, a passport, or a student I.D. card. Visitors under the age of sixteen may be required to present identification. Limited physical contact between eligible offenders and their visitors may be allowed if the visitors are immediate family (natural parents, stepparents or grandparents; natural or adopted children, stepchildren or grandchildren; natural siblings or stepsiblings; spouse; or persons related by marriage, if accompanied by an immediate family member). With prior approval from facility administration, non-immediate family members may be allowed contact visits if immediate family members are unable to visit the offender.

Visitors and their vehicles are subject to search prior to entering the facility. Any visitor refusing the search procedure will be required to leave the facility grounds. All visitors will be screened by a metal detector prior to visiting an offender. Intoxicating beverages, drugs, firearms, escape implements, or other items are strictly prohibited by agency rules and policies.

Visitors must abide by a dress code. Shirts and shoes must be worn. Shorts, cut-offs, halter tops, undershirts, and tank tops are prohibited. Shirts and blouses of fishnet, transparent material or open midriff are not allowed. Male visitors must wear long pants, and female visitors must wear dresses, skirts, or long pants. Exceptions for pre-adolescent boys and girls may be made. Dresses or skirts that appear too short will require a decision by the duty officer. Clothing marked by words or pictures considered profane or offensive by current public standards will not be allowed.

Visitors may bring only specific items into the facility. These items include a small wallet or change purse containing no more than $10.00 cash. Visitors with infants or small children may bring no more than three diapers and two baby bottles. Visitors are not permitted to bring items of any kind to offenders. TDCJ facilities are designated as "tobacco free." Visitors shall not be permitted to bring cigarettes, cigarette lighters, matches or any tobacco products into TDCJ facilities. Visitors may purchase soft drinks for offenders to be consumed during the visit.

Visits must be orderly to assure that visitors and offenders are not disturbed. Visitors who cannot control their children will be escorted out of the facility. Visitors are prohibited from loitering, walking the perimeter road, or taking photographs. Radios played at a high volume and shouting at offenders will not be allowed. Visits may be terminated and future visits may be denied for security reasons or because of improper conduct by the visitor or the offender.

Related Links: E-Mail Questions to—
webmaster@tdcj.state.tx.us

Obviously, the main concern during contact visits is the passing of contraband. Searches in connection with visits are discussed in Chapter 6. Because the transfer of contraband is much easier to accomplish during contact visits, one way to eliminate this possibility is to authorize only noncontact visits. Is such a procedure constitutional? In *Block v. Rutherford*, the sheriff for Los Angeles County had a policy that prohibited pretrial detainees from having any contact visits with family and friends.[9] A group of detainees brought suit, alleging that the regulation was punitive in nature and, therefore, a violation of their constitutional rights. The detainees also contended that since they were pretrial detainees, they had not been convicted and thus should not be punished by the denial of contact visits. As will be discussed in the next section, pretrial detainees have different rights from convicted prisoners. However, the U.S. Supreme Court upheld the regulation, stating that there was a valid rational connection between a ban on contact visits and the internal security of a detention faculty. The fact that the court was dealing with pretrial detainees was not a factor because the Court found that there was no reason to conclude that pretrial detainees poised any less security risk than convicted prisoners.

The U.S. Supreme Court has held that prisoners do not have a constitutional right to unrestrained visits; however, the court has not answered the question of whether prisoners have a constitutional right to some form of visitation.[10] Many federal courts have concluded, without stating their reasoning, that inmate visitation is not a constitutionally protected right. In *White v. Keller*, a federal district court simply stated, without any analysis, that prisoners do not have a right to visitation.[11] Other courts have held that visitation is not a constitutional right, but more of a privilege subject to the discretion of the prison authorities.[12]

Some courts have found that prisoners have a constitutionally protected visitation right. These courts rely upon the right to privacy in family relationships. Other authorities have stated that even if there is no federal constitutional right, a state law authorizing visits may create such a right under the state constitution.[13] A New York statute that limited visits to death row prisoners to their family members was upheld in *Smith v. Coughlin* by the U.S. Court of Appeals, Second Circuit.[14]

Does a prisoner have a right to make telephone calls? The courts have upheld the right to limit telephone contact to a certain list of persons and to limit the frequency and length of calls. The question as to whether the prison can prohibit all prisoners from using the telephone has not been answered in recent court cases. The courts have held that prison officials have the right to refuse certain prisoners the right to use the telephone because of custody classifications or for disciplinary reasons.

Pretrial Detainees

Pretrial detainees are those prisoners who have been arrested and incarcerated, but not yet convicted. Pretrial detainees constitute a special category of prisoners. They have the same rights as other citizens except to the extent necessary to ensure their appearance at trial and the security of the institution.[15] The Due Process Clause prohibits punishment of pretrial detainees and protects them from the use of excessive force that amounts to punishment.[16] To determine whether the restriction on a pretrial detainee is valid, courts must determine if the restriction is reasonably related to a legitimate governmental purpose. For example, as long as any restriction on visitation and association of pretrial detainees is not punishment, but rationally related to the goal of maintaining order and security of the institution, the courts will usually uphold the regulation.[17]

Conjugal Visits

Should prisoners have a constitutional right to privacy with their spouse to the degree that they can engage in sexual relations? The U.S. Supreme Court, while upholding the concept of privacy and intimacy among families, has not ruled directly on this issue. One of the earliest cases dealing with this issue, *Payne v. District of Columbia,* held there was no constitutional right for an inmate's wife to engage in conjugal visits with her husband.[18] On the other hand, if an institution desires to establish conjugal visits and does so in a fair and reasonable manner, the courts will uphold such programs. In New York, a federal court upheld the Commissioner of Corrections visitation program that included discretionary conjugal visits by prisoners.[19]

In *Champion v. Artuz,* a federal appeals court upheld the revocation of conjugal visits based upon the spouse's failure to comply with the institutional guidelines.[20] Champion, an inmate in New York state's Green Haven Correctional Facility, was a participant in the Family Reunion program by which prisoners receive conjugal visits from their spouses. Champion's visits were suspended when prison authorities discovered his spouse was an ex-offender and was carrying various items that they perceived as instrumentalities for Champion's escape, including a wig, a camouflage handkerchief, and a man's identification card. The appellate court held that New York's regulations permitting correctional facilities to allow conjugal visits to prisoners did not give Champion a liberty interest in such visits and that they may therefore be suspended or revoked by the institution as a matter of law.

Exclusion of Certain Visitors

The right of the administrators to exclude certain visitors was addressed in *Kentucky Department of Corrections v. Thompson*. The administrators at the Kentucky State Reformatory at LaGrange adopted regulations that restricted visitors who had a record of disruptive conduct or of being under the influence of drugs or alcohol; former residents of the facility; and former employees. Individuals who had violated the visiting regulations in the past were also barred without any kind of hearing. The prisoners brought a class action challenging the enforcement of the regulations. The lower courts held that there was a constitutional right for prisoners to receive visits and that the constitutional right requires prison officials to adopt procedures whereby a prisoner would receive notice of and the reasons why any person was excluded as a visitor. The Supreme Court reversed the lower courts and stated that in order for a prisoner to claim the right to due process protection, there must be a liberty interest protected in either the due process clause of the U.S. Constitution or by state law. First, the Court determined that there was no federal liberty interest in the suspension of visiting privileges and that Kentucky state law did not require a hearing in order to terminate visiting privileges. The Court indicated that had the state adopted "substantive predicates" to guide or limit administrators' discretion, then the state would have created a liberty interest and minimum due process procedures would be required to terminate visiting privileges.

CASES ON POINT

Jones v. N.C. Prisoners' Labor Union
433 U.S. 119 (1977)

MR. JUSTICE REHNQUIST delivered the opinion of the Court.

Pursuant to regulations promulgated by the North Carolina Department of Correction, appellants prohibited prisoners from soliciting other prisoners to join appellee, the North Carolina Prisoners' Labor Union, Inc. (Union), barred all meetings of the Union, and refused to deliver packets of Union publications that had been mailed in bulk to several prisoners for redistribution among other prisoners. The Union instituted this action, based on 42 U.S.C. 1983, to challenge these policies.

It alleged that appellants' efforts to prevent the operation of a prisoners' union violated the First and Fourteenth Amendment rights of it and its members and that the refusal to grant the Union those privileges accorded several other organizations operating within the prison system deprived the Union of equal protection of the laws. A three-judge court was convened. After a hearing, the court found merit in the Union's free speech, association, and equal protection arguments, and enjoined appellants from preventing prisoners from soliciting other prisoners to join the Union and from "refusing receipt of the Union's publications on the ground that they are calculated to encourage membership in the organization or solicit joining." The court also held that the Union "shall be accorded the privilege of holding meetings under such limitations and control as are neutrally applied to all inmate organizations . . . ." We noted probable jurisdiction to consider whether the First and Fourteenth Amendments extend prisoner labor unions such protection. We have decided that they do not, and we accordingly reverse the judgment of the District Court.

. . .The District Court, we believe, got off on the wrong foot in this case by not giving appropriate deference to the decisions of prison administrators and appropriate recognition to the peculiar and restrictive circumstances of penal confinement. While litigation by prison prisoners concerning conditions of confinement, challenged other than under the Eighth Amendment, is of recent vintage, this Court has long recognized that "lawful incarceration brings about the necessary withdrawal or limitation of many privileges and rights, a retraction justified by the considerations underlying our penal system." The fact of confinement and the needs of the penal institution impose limitations on constitutional rights, including those derived from the First Amendment, which are implicit in incarceration.

Perhaps the most obvious of the First Amendment rights that are necessarily curtailed by confinement are those associational rights that the First Amendment protects outside of prison walls. The concept of incarceration itself entails a restriction on the freedom of prisoners to associate with those outside of the penal institution. Equally as obvious, the inmate's "status as a prisoner" and the operational realities of a prison dictate restrictions on the associational rights among prisoners.

Because the realities of running a penal institution are complex and difficult, we have also recognized the wide-ranging deference to be accorded the decisions of prison administrators...

...The invocation of the First Amendment, whether the asserted rights are speech or associational, does not change this analysis. In a prison context, an inmate does not retain those First Amendment rights that are "inconsistent with his status as a prisoner or with the legitimate penological objectives of the corrections system." Prisons, it is obvious, differ in numerous respects from free society. They, to begin with, are populated, involuntarily, by people who have been found to have violated one or more of the criminal laws established by society for its orderly governance.

In seeking a "mutual accommodation between institutional needs and objectives [of prisons] and the provisions of the Constitution that are of general application," this Court has repeatedly recognized the need for major restrictions on a prisoner's rights. These restrictions have applied as well where First Amendment values were implicated.

Case Discussion and Significance. *Jones* is the only U.S. Supreme Court case to discuss organizing activities of unions in prisons. The Supreme Court held that the correctional officials had discretion to prevent a prisoners' union in their institution because its presence would be detrimental to prison order and security. The court denied both claims under the First Amendment and the Equal Protection Clause of the Fourteenth Amendment stating that the inmates' First Amendment rights were not unduly abridged and their Fourteenth Amendment rights were not violated because a union and other service organizations were not the same in purpose or classification.

Pell v. Procunier
417 U.S. 817 (1974)

MR. JUSTICE STEWART delivered the opinion of the Court.

The plaintiffs in the District Court were four California prison prisoners...and three professional journalists. . . .The plaintiffs brought the suit to challenge the constitutionality, under the First and Fourteenth Amendments, of 415.071 of the California Department of Corrections Manual, which provides that "press and other media interviews with specific individual prisoners will not be permitted."

[The press]. . .requested permission from the appropriate corrections officials to interview [certain] prisoners. . . .The requests were all denied. The plaintiffs thereupon sued to enjoin the continued enforcement of this regulation. The inmate plaintiffs contended that the regulation violates their rights of free speech under the First and Fourteenth Amendments. Similarly, the media plaintiffs asserted that the limitation that this regulation places on their news gathering activity unconstitutionally infringes the freedom of the press guaranteed by the First and Fourteenth Amendments.

...Corrections Director Procunier and the other defendants appeal from the judgment of the District Court that 415.071 infringes the inmate plaintiffs' First and Fourteenth Amendment rights. The media plaintiffs appeal the court's rejection of their claims ...

We start with the familiar proposition that "lawful incarceration brings about the necessary withdrawal or limitation of many privileges and rights, a retraction justified by the considerations underlying our penal system." In the First Amendment context a corollary of this principle is that a prison inmate retains those First Amendment rights that are not inconsistent with his status as a prisoner or with the legitimate penological objectives of the corrections system. Thus, challenges to prison restrictions that are asserted to inhibit First Amendment interests must be analyzed in terms of the legitimate policies and goals of the corrections system, to whose custody and care the prisoner has been committed in accordance with due process of law.

An important function of the corrections system is the deterrence of crime. The premise is that by confining criminal offenders in a facility where they are isolated from the rest of society, a condition that most people presumably find undesirable, they and others will be deterred from committing additional criminal offenses. This isolation, of course, also serves a protective function by quarantining criminal offenders for a given period of time while, it is hoped, the rehabilitative processes of the corrections system work to correct the offender's demonstrated criminal proclivity. Thus, since most offenders will eventually return to society, another paramount objective of the corrections system is the rehabilitation of those committed to its custody. Finally, central to all other corrections goals is the institutional consideration of internal security within the corrections facilities themselves. It is in the light of these legitimate penal objectives that a court must assess challenges to prison regulations based on asserted constitutional rights of prisoners.

. . .One alternative available to California prison prisoners is communication by mail. . . .We recently held that "the Department's regulations authorized censorship of prisoner mail far broader than any legitimate interest of penal administration demands," and accordingly affirmed a district court judgment invalidating the regulations. In addition, we held that "the interest of prisoners and their correspondents in uncensored communication by letter, grounded as it is in the First Amendment, is plainly a 'liberty' interest within the meaning of the Fourteenth Amendment even though qualified of necessity by the circumstance of imprisonment." Accordingly, we concluded that any "decision to censor or withhold delivery of a particular letter must be accompanied by minimal procedural safeguards." Thus, it is clear that the medium of written correspondence affords prisoners an open and substantially unimpeded channel for communication with persons outside the prison, including representatives of the news media.

Moreover, the visitation policy of the California Corrections Department does not seal the inmate off from personal contact with those outside the prison. Prisoners are permitted to receive limited visits from members of their families, the clergy, their attorneys, and friends of prior acquaintance. The selection of these categories of visitors is based on the Director's professional judgment that such visits will aid in the rehabilitation of the inmate while not compromising the other legitimate objectives of the corrections system. This is not a case in which the selection is based on the anticipated content of the communication between the inmate and the prospective visitor. If a member of the press fell within any of these categories, there is no suggestion that he would not be permitted to visit with the inmate. More importantly, however, prisoners have an unrestricted opportunity to communicate with the press or any other member of the public through their families, friends, clergy, or attorneys who are permitted to visit them at the prison. Thus, this provides another alternative avenue of communication between prison prisoners and persons outside the prison.

. . .Accordingly, in light of the alternative channels of communication that are open to prison prisoners, we cannot say on the record in this case that this restriction on one manner in which prisoners can communicate with persons outside of prison is unconstitutional. So long as this restriction operates in a neutral fashion, without regard to the content of the expression, it falls within the "appropriate rules and regulations" to which "prisoners necessarily are subject," and does not abridge any First Amendment freedoms retained by prison prisoners.

. . .For the reasons stated, we reverse the District Court's judgment that 415.071 infringes the freedom of speech of the prison prisoners and affirm its judgment that the regulation does not abridge the constitutional right of a free press. Accordingly, the judgment is vacated, and the cases are remanded to the District Court for further proceedings consistent with this opinion.

It is so ordered.

Case Discussion and Significance. *Pell* was the first case decided by the court that discussed First Amendment access rights of prisoners and the media. The Supreme Court denied the prisoners' claim of violation of their First Amendment rights because they had other alternate means by which they could communicate with society including family, friends, the clergy and attorneys.

The court reaffirmed its earlier decision in *Branzburg* that held that the media does not enjoy any greater access in prisons than the general public and therefore denying them individual access to selected prisoners was not a violation of the First Amendment.

CASE SUMMARIES

An inmate was not entitled to judicial order requiring warden to transport him to court clerk's office to sign marriage license, or requiring warden to allow clerk to visit prison to get inmate's signature. *Leach, State Ex Rel. v. Schotten*, 653 N.E.2d 356 (Ohio 1995).

A New York prisoner had no constitutionally protected right to participation in conjugal visits with wife; denial of such visits on basis of wife's status as an ex-offender was not a violation of equal protection of law. *Champion v. Artuz*, 76 F.3d 483 (2nd Cir. 1996).

Prison could require inmates who wished to get married to attend six premarital counseling sessions without violating prisoner rights. *Hanselman v. Fiedler*, 822 F. Supp. 1342 (E.D. Wis. 1993).

Prisoners have a constitutional right to marry, but prison officials may reasonably regulate marriages of inmates to further legitimate penological interests. *Turner v. Safley*, 482 U.S. 78 (1987); *Butler v. Wilson*, 415 U.S. 953 (1974); *Johnson v. Rockefeller*, 365 F. Supp. 377 (S.D.N.Y. 1973).

The denial of inmate's request for furlough to visit his brother on his deathbed or to attend his brother's funeral did not violate his constitutional rights. *Hipes v. Braxton*, 878 F. Supp. 56 (W.D.Va. 1995).

Members of sheriff's department are not liable for kidnapping and rape of woman by violent criminal who was given a weekend pass from county jail. *Lovins v. Lee*, 53 F.3d 1208 (11th Cir. 1995).

A prisoner had no due process liberty interest in participating in furlough program and therefore was not entitled to a hearing prior to suspension from the program. *Bowser v. Vose*, 968 F. 2d 105 (1st Cir. 1992).

An inmate had no constitutional right to attend his father's funeral unescorted by a deputy; requirement that inmate appear there in prison clothing and in leg restraints and handcuffs did not violate federal law or Florida state law. *Farmer v. Crews*, 804 F. Supp. 1516 (M.D. Fla. 1992).

A Missouri prison's stay on face-to-face media video interviews of prisoners did not violate First Amendment; media did not have a constitutional right of access to the prison superior to that of the general public. *Sidebottom v. Schiriro*, 927 F. Supp. 1221 (E.D. Mo. 1996).

Regulations providing for the recording of all inmate phone calls other than those to attorneys did not violate Fourth Amendment or provisions of the Massachusetts state constitution. *Cacicio v. Sec. of Public Safety*, 665 N.E.2d 85 (Mass. 1996).

Telephone rules restricting prisoners to making calls to no more than ten persons on a list did not violate First Amendment rights to communicate with friends and family. *Pope v. Hightower*, 101 F.3d 1382 (11th Cir. 1996).

A hearing impaired inmate was not "similarly situated" to other inmates for purposes of using a standard telephone, federal appeals court rules, so that failure to provide him with a special telephone adapted for his disability was not a violation of equal protection of law. *Hansen v. Rimel*, 104 F.3d 189 (8th Cir. 1997).

A Federal Bureau of Prisons regulations on inmate phone calls on new direct-dial (as opposed to collect call) phone system did not violate First Amendment rights of prisoners or persons called; appeals court upholds, however, injunction against use of commissary profits to fund conversion to new system to extent funds were being used for security measures. *Washington v. Reno*, 35 F.3d 1093 (6th Cir. 1994).

There is no First Amendment right to phone non-attorney, nonrelative males. *Benzel v. Grammer*, 869 F. 2d 1105 (8th Cir. 1989).

SUMMARY

- Freedom of association is based on the right to assemble founded in the First Amendment.
- The U.S. Supreme Court has stated that there are two types of associations.
- Union activities may be regulated by prison officials.
- Media access in prisons may be regulated in two ways: prisoners may be denied the right to be interviewed by the media, and the media has no greater right than the general public when it enters the prison.
- Inmate visitation may be controlled by the institutions.
- There are two types of inmate visits: contact visits and noncontact visits.
- Pretrial detainees have different rights from citizens and sentenced prisoners.
- Conjugal visits may be regulated by prison officials.

DISCUSSION QUESTIONS

1. Define *freedom of association*. Draw a horizontal line on your paper and on the left end list those associations that should be allowed in correctional institutions. On the right end, list those associations that should be regulated or prohibited. Be prepared to justify each of your entries.

2. Should prisoners be allowed to belong to unions if they engage in no union activities while incarcerated? Justify your answer from a warden's perspective and from a union official's point of view.

3. What are the benefits for the institution in a conjugal visitation program? What are the drawbacks of such a program? Does it make any difference if we are dealing with female or male prisoners?

4. Is a prison rule that permits heterosexual, but not homosexual, conjugal visits constitutional? [See *Doe v. Sparks*, 733 F.Supp. 227 (W.D.Pa.1990).]

5. If prison officials permit the formation of a Latin studies group, can they then prohibit the formation of a "white ethic club"? [See *Thomas v. United States Secretary of Defense*, 730 F. Supp. 362 (D. Kan. 1990).]

ENDNOTES

1. 468 U.S. 609 (1984).
2. See *A Brief History of the American Labor Movement*, Bureau of Labor Statistics, U.S. Department of Labor (Washington DC, GPO 1979) p. 99.
3. See *North Carolina Prisoners' Union v. Jones*, 433 U.S. 119 (1977)
4. 417 U.S. 817 (1974).
5. 417 U.S. 843 (1974).
6. *Id.* at 849.
7. 438 U.S. 1 (1978).
8. 6 F.3d 691 (10th Cir. 1993).
9. 468 U.S. 576 (1984).
10. See *Kentucky Department of Corrections v. Thompson*, 490 U.S. 454 (1989) in which the Court stated that a prisoner's interest in visitation is not directly guaranteed by the Due Process Clause.
11. 438 F.Supp. 110 (D. Md. 1977).
12. See *Evans v. Johnson,* 808 F.2d 1427 (11th Cir. 1987).
13. William J. Brennan, Jr., "State Constitutions and the Protection of Individual Rights," 90 *Harv. L. Rev.* 489 (1977).
14. 748 F.2d. 783 (1984).
15. *Bell v. Wolfish*, 441 U.S. 520 (1979).
16. See, for example, *Gobel v. Mariposa County*, 867 F.2d 1201 (9th Cir. 1989) holding that a pretrial detainee's due process rights were violated when he was confined in a police van for four-to-seven hours in 108-degree heat without food or water or adequate ventilation, and compare with *Collazo-Leon v. Bureau of Prisons*, 51 F.3d 315 (1st Cir. 1995) holding no due process violation when detainee accused of attempted escape was denied phone and visitation privileges and received 90-day administrative segregation.
17. *Rhem v. Malcolm*, 396 F.Supp. 1195 (S.D.N.Y. 1975).
18. 253 F.2d 867 (D.C. Cir. 1958).
19. *Cromwell v. Coughlin*, 773 F.Supp. 606 (S.D.N.Y. 1991).
20. ___ F.3d ___ (Docket No. 95-2510)(2nd Cir. 1996).

Chapter 5

EXERCISE OF RELIGIOUS BELIEFS

We do not suggest, of course, that every religious sect or group within a prison—however few in number—must have identical facilities or personnel. A special chapel or place of worship need not be provided for every faith regardless of size; nor must a chaplain, priest, or minister be provided without regard to the extent of the demand. But reasonable opportunities must be afforded to all prisoners to exercise the religious freedom guaranteed by the First and Fourteenth Amendments without fear of penalty.

Cruz v. Beto, 405 U.S. 319, 322 (1972)

RESTRICTIONS ON THE EXERCISE OF RELIGION

As with many other controversies facing correctional officers, the exercise of religion raises serious and often times conflicting issues. The First Amendment to the U.S. Constitution states in part:

> Congress shall make no law respecting an establishment of religion, or prohibiting the exercise thereof. . .

A straightforward reading of this amendment would seem to suggest that neither Congress nor the states can pass any law that deals with the establishment of a religion, nor can they prohibit anyone from exercising his religious beliefs. However, none of these rights are absolute. The courts have traditionally engaged in a balancing of interests to determine how to interpret these seemingly absolute statements in our Constitution.

One of the first issues that must be addressed is whether the act or practice regulated is, in fact, a religion. Obviously, if inmates can obtain special privileges by claiming to worship a new deity, there will be some groups that will try to manipulate the system for their own advantage. Therefore, careful attention must be paid the claims of new or otherwise obscure religion practices.

Defining religion can be difficult, and different courts have set forth different definitions. One court stated that an activity can be determined to be a religion if it possesses the cardinal characteristics associated with traditional recognized religions in that it teaches and preaches a belief in a Supreme Being, a religious discipline, and tenets to guide one's daily existence.[1] In *Theriault v. Sibler*, a federal appeals court attempted to explain how to examine religious issues by stating, "When reconsidering what constitutes a religion, a thorough study of the existing case law should be accompanied by appropriate evidentiary exploration of philosophical, theological, and other related literature and resources on this issue."[2]

The case was remanded to the district court that held that under the appellate court guidelines an inmate-created "religion" was not entitled to First Amendment protection because it was not a true "religion." The court stated that "The professed views of Mr. Theriault that he 'would have established a New World Order' with Harry W. Theriault as the head of the Order... are, in the opinion of the Court, more closely akin to the megalomania of Adolph Hitler. . .than any belief that occupies a place parallel to that filled by the orthodox belief in God."[3] However, other courts have found inmate beliefs and practices to conform to the definition of religion and granted them First Amendment protection.[4]

Prison officials have given a variety of reasons or justifications for denying certain inmates the right to exercise their religion: security of the institution, maintaining discipline, economics, and official discretion.

May a warden constitutionally ban gang-related religious publications?

In *Natural Self-Allah v. Annucci*,[13] the U.S. District Court for Western New York looked at the question of whether the warden of a correctional center could prohibit inmates from subscribing to the *Five Percenter*, a magazine published by the religious group Five Percent Nation of Islam. The plaintiff, an inmate at the Clinton Correctional Facility belonged to the Islamic sect, which believes that black people are gods and excludes white people.

Correctional officials, during a routine inspection of incoming mail, withheld delivery to the inmate of the magazine. In withholding the magazine, the officials cited New York Department of Corrections Inmate Behavior Rule 105.12, which provides that

> Inmates shall not engage or encourage others to engage in unauthorized organizational activities or meetings, display, wear, possess, distribute or use unauthorized organizational insignia or materials. An unauthorized organization is any gang or an organization which has not been approved by the Deputy Commissioner for Program Services.

The inmate filed suit, alleging violation of his First and Fourteenth Amendment rights. At an evidentiary hearing, his witnesses described the Five Percent movement as devoted to self-enlightenment and nonviolence. Defense witnesses testified that the group was involved in criminal activity, used violent methods, and espoused a racist philosophy.

How would you rule on the above question?
The court ruled that the publication, though facially neutral, posed a risk to prison security due to the group's violent and racist tendencies. The court also rejected as unworkable the inmate's proposal that the prison's Facility Media Review Committee review all *Five Percenter* material on an issue-by-issue basis. The court stated that it was not the content of the publication that posed a threat to penological interests, but rather the mere presence of *Five Percenter* material within the facility.

SECURITY OF THE INSTITUTION

A case involving Native Americans illustrates the various positions and alternatives used by prison administrators when faced with the claim of denial of religious freedom as compared to the requirement of maintaining security within the institution.

In *Hamilton v. Schriro*, a Native American inmate desired to use a sweat lodge.[5] The sweat lodge ceremony is an accepted tenet of many Native Americans because it signifies the purification of the participant. Purity is a necessary element of other Native American religious ceremonies. Therefore, there was no question of whether or not this was a valid religious doctrine or activity.

The sweat lodge ceremony takes place inside an enclosed dome-shaped structure covered with hides or blankets. Rocks are heated in separate fires outside the lodge. Several tools are used during the ceremony including an axe to split wood for the fire, a shovel to transfer the heated rocks from the fire to the lodge, and deer antlers. Participants are nude and pour water on the hot rocks to create steam, which causes them to sweat. The ceremony lasts between one and three hours. At the trial, there was testimony that if a Native American could not use a sweat lodge, he could not practice any other aspect of his religion.

The institution provided a number of accommodations to Native Americans including the offering of cross-denominational facilities within the prison. Native Americans were allowed to pray, gather together, meet with outside religious leaders, and to obtain religious material from the institution's library. They were also allowed to carry medicine bags containing ceremonial items. The institution objected to the use of a sweat lodge because permitting inmates to meet in an enclosed area may subject them to assaults that could not be controlled by the institution. Additionally, the institution argued that alternative methods of practicing their religion were available to them in that the institution allowed them to meet and pray and carry their ceremonial medicine bags. The institution also pointed out that erecting a sweat lodge would have an adverse impact on prison staff, other inmates, and prison resources. Finally, the institution argued that the inmate had failed to point out any other alternative to the sweat lodge that could be offered that would meet valid penological interests. The court held, based upon the facts of this case, that the institution's denial of access to a sweat lodge was rationally related to the legitimate penological interest of safety and security of the institution.

Maintaining Discipline

Discipline cases rely for the most part on the same rationale set forth in security cases. Courts have allowed institutions to restrict religious freedom of inmates based upon previous abuse of that privilege.[6] Other courts have used the terms together stating institutions have the ability to control prison security or discipline.

ECONOMICS

The economics of providing for religious activity is a valid consideration. If, for example, providing a special diet or the services of a spiritual leader or advisor is economically prohibitive, the institution may deny such activities based on economics. In *Gittlemacker v. Prasse*, the court upheld the institution's decision to deny a Jewish inmate the regular services of a rabbi.[7] In that case, a Jewish prisoner claimed a violation of his First Amendment right to exercise his religious beliefs because while the institution provided clergymen for Catholics and Protestants, the superintendent refused to do so for those of the Jewish faith. The institution responded that the small number of Jewish inmates, usually two or three, made the use of a full-time rabbi economically unfeasible and unwarranted. On previous occasions, the superintendent had attempted to secure the services of a rabbi on a fee basis. The court held that the institution's rationale was valid and based upon valid economic reasons.

OFFICIAL DISCRETION

When correctional officials exercise their judgment, it is usually based on one or more of the reasons discussed earlier.

The courts have stated that prison regulations may infringe on an inmates' constitutional rights, if it is reasonably related to legitimate correctional interests.[8] The restrictions on the exercise of religion can be upheld if there is a valid articulated reason supported by the exercise of sound discretion. Prison officials must state or explain their reasoning and why their decision is sound from a penological point of view. For example, denying inmates who are segregated from the main population the right to a Catholic service was upheld because the prison officials were able to point out that that was a justified safety issue as well as a concern that non-Catholics in the same unit would have to listen to the service. The court held that such a rule was neither arbitrary or capricious and that there were valid articulated grounds for such a policy.[9]

DIET

Some religions require their members to adhere to certain diets. Outside prison walls, these mandates may not cause a member of that religion any problem. However, once that person is incarcerated it may become more difficult to follow those religious tenets. Institutions have broad discretion to set diets for inmates. Using the justifications discussed above, institutions have successfully resisted lawsuits by inmates that attempt to require special diets based upon religious beliefs.

The Black Muslim religion requires that its members refrain from eating pork. There have been a number of cases in which courts have refused demands by Black Muslim inmates that they be provided with pork-free meals in prisons. One court justified its refusal based upon economic grounds.[10] Another court found that Black Muslims could obtain sufficient nourishment in the regular prison fare and still avoid pork and therefore there was no constitutional issue to be decided.[11]

The same rationale that is used to deny Black Muslims pork-free diets is used by courts in declining to order the preparation and service of Jewish kosher foods. In *Kahane v. Carlson*, a federal appellate court held that the demand for kosher foods was of significant religious importance to orthodox Jews.[12] However, the court refused to require the institution to provide such food; rather, it ordered the prison to provide the inmate with a diet sufficient to exist upon without violating Jew dietary laws. Additionally, the court refused to mandate specific items for the diet, leaving that decision to the institution.

GROOMING

The law on grooming standards and the exercise of religion is one of confusing and contradictory case law. Generally speaking, courts will uphold grooming standards if they are related to a legitimate penal interest and there is no other alternative available. Courts have upheld grooming regulations for purposes of identification photographs.[14] Courts have also thrown out grooming regulations when they are unequally applied, with one religious group allowed to keep its beards and another denied that right. There have been a number of cases decided on the basis of the Religious Freedom Restoration Act of 1993 (RERA). However, as will be discussed later, the U.S. Supreme Court declared that act unconstitutional. Therefore, it seems probable that courts will continue to uphold grooming relations if institutions can articulate legitimate reasons related to penal interest.

CASES ON POINT

Cruz v. Beto 405 U.S. 319 (1972)
PER CURIAM.

The complaint, alleging a cause of action under 42 U.S.C. § 1983, states that Cruz, who is in a Texas prison, is a Buddhist. Although prisoners who are members of other religious sects were allowed to use the prison chapel, Cruz was not. He shared his Buddhist religious material with other prisoners and, according to the allegations, was placed in solitary confinement on a diet of bread and water for two weeks, without access to newspapers, magazines, or other sources of news in retaliation. He also alleged that he was prohibited from corresponding with his religious advisor in the Buddhist sect. Those in the isolation unit spent 22 hours a day in total idleness. Again, according to the allegations, Texas encourages inmates to participate in other religious programs, providing at state expense chaplains of the Catholic, Jewish, and Protestant faiths; providing also at state expense copies of the Jewish and Christian Bibles, and conducting weekly Sunday school classes and religious services. According to the allegations, points of good merit are given prisoners as a reward for attending orthodox religious services, those points enhancing a prisoner's eligibility for desirable job assignments and early parole consideration. Respondent answered, denying the allegations and moving to dismiss. . . .

Federal courts sit not to supervise prisons, but to enforce the constitutional rights of all "persons," including prisoners. We are not unmindful that prison officials must be accorded latitude in the administration of prison affairs, and that prisoners necessarily are subject to appropriate rules and regulations. But persons in prison, like other individuals, have the right to petition the Government for redress of grievances which, of course, includes "access of prisoners to the courts for the purpose of presenting their complaints." Moreover, racial segregation, which is unconstitutional outside prisons, is unconstitutional within prisons, save for "the necessities of prison security and discipline."

If Cruz was a Buddhist, and if he was denied a reasonable opportunity of pursuing his faith comparable to the opportunity afforded fellow prisoners who adhere to conventional religious precepts, then there was palpable discrimination by the State against the Buddhist religion, established

600 B.C., long before the Christian era. The First Amendment, applicable to the States by reason of the Fourteenth Amendment, prohibits government from making a law "prohibiting the free exercise" of religion. If the allegations of this complaint are assumed to be true, as they must be on the motion to dismiss, Texas has violated the First and Fourteenth Amendments.

The motion for leave to proceed *in forma pauperis* is granted. The petition for certiorari is granted, the judgment is vacated, and the cause remanded for a hearing and appropriate findings.

Case Discussion and Significance. *Cruz* was one of the first cases to address religion in prisons. Issued as a "Per Curiam" opinion (a brief summary opinion without a full analysis or discussion), the Supreme Court held that inmates must be given reasonable rights to practice their religion even if it does not fit the mainstream idea of what a religion is. Although an institution does not have to cater to every religion, it must provide access for religious services consistent with other penal interests.

O'Lone v. Shabazz
482 U.S. 342 (1987)

CHIEF JUSTICE REHNQUIST delivered the opinion of the Court.

This case requires us to consider once again the standard of review for prison regulations claimed to inhibit the exercise of constitutional rights. Respondents, members of the Islamic faith, were prisoners in New Jersey's Leesburg State Prison. They challenged policies adopted by prison officials which resulted in their inability to attend Jumu'ah, a weekly Muslim congregational service regularly held in the main prison building and in a separate facility known as "the Farm." Jumu'ah is commanded by the Koran and must be held every Friday after the sun reaches its zenith and before the Asr, or afternoon prayer. See *Koran* 62: 9-10. There is no question that respondents' sincerely held religious beliefs compelled attendance at Jumu'ah. We hold that the prison regulations here challenged did not violate respondents' rights under the Free Exercise Clause of the First Amendment to the United States Constitution.

Inmates at Leesburg are placed in one of three custody classifications. Maximum security and "gang minimum" security inmates are housed in the main prison building, and those with the lowest classification—full minimum—live in the Farm. Both respondents were classified as gang minimum security prisoners when this suit was filed, and respondent Mateen was later classified as full minimum.

Several changes in prison policy prompted this litigation. In April 1983, the New Jersey Department of Corrections issued Standard 853, which provided that inmates could no longer move directly from maximum security to full minimum status, but were instead required to first spend a period of time in the intermediate gang minimum status. This change was designed to redress problems that had arisen when inmates were transferred directly from the restrictive maximum security status to full minimum status, with its markedly higher level of freedom. Because of serious overcrowding in the main building, Standard 853 further mandated that gang minimum inmates ordinarily be assigned jobs outside the main building. *Ibid.* These inmates work in details of 8 to 15 persons, supervised by one guard. Standard 853 also required that full minimum inmates work outside the main institution, whether on or off prison grounds, or in a satellite building such as the Farm.

Corrections officials at Leesburg implemented these policies gradually and, as the District Court noted, with some difficulty. In the initial stages of outside work details for gang minimum prisoners, officials apparently allowed some Muslim inmates to work inside the main building on Fridays so that they could attend Jumu'ah. This alternative was eventually eliminated in March 1984, in light of the directive of Standard 853 that all gang minimum inmates work outside the main building.

Significant problems arose with those inmates assigned to outside work details. Some avoided reporting for their assignments, while others found reasons for returning to the main building during the course of the workday (including their desire to attend religious services). Evidence showed that the return of prisoners during the day resulted in security risks and administrative burdens that prison officials found unacceptable. Because details of inmates were supervised by only one guard, the whole detail was forced to return to the main gate when one prisoner desired to return to the facility. The gate was the site of all incoming foot and vehicle traffic during the day, and prison officials viewed it as a high security risk area. When an inmate returned, vehicle traffic was delayed while the inmate was logged in and searched.

In response to these burdens, Leesburg officials took steps to ensure that those assigned to outside details remained there for the whole day. Thus, arrangements were made to have lunch and required medications brought out to the prisoners, and appointments with doctors and social workers were scheduled for the late afternoon. These changes proved insufficient, however, and prison officials began to study alternatives. After consulting with the director of social services, the director of professional services, and the prison's imam and chaplain, prison officials in March 1984 issued a policy memorandum which prohibited inmates assigned to outside work details from returning to the prison during the day except in the case of emergency.

Several general principles guide our consideration of the issues presented here. First, "convicted prisoners do not forfeit all constitutional protections by reason of their conviction and confinement in prison." Inmates clearly retain protections afforded by the First Amendment, including its directive that no law shall prohibit the free exercise of religion. The limitations on the exercise of constitutional rights arise both from the fact of incarceration and from valid penological objectives—including deterrence of crime, rehabilitation of prisoners, and institutional security.

In considering the appropriate balance of these factors, we have often said that evaluation of penological objectives is committed to the considered judgment of prison administrators, "who are actually charged with and trained in the running of the particular institution under examination." To ensure that courts afford appropriate deference to prison officials, we have determined that prison regulations alleged to infringe constitutional rights are judged under a "reasonableness" test less restrictive than that ordinarily applied to alleged infringements of fundamental constitutional rights. We recently restated the proper standard: "[W]hen a prison regulation impinges on inmates' constitutional rights, the regulation is valid if it is reasonably related to legitimate penological interests." This approach ensures the ability of corrections officials "to anticipate security problems and to adopt innovative solutions to the intractable problems of prison administration," and avoids unnecessary intrusion of the judiciary into problems particularly ill-suited to "resolution by decree."

We think the Court of Appeals decision in this case was wrong when it established a separate burden on prison officials to prove "that no reasonable method exists by which [prisoners'] religious rights can be accommodated without creating bona fide security problems." (Prison officials should be required "to produce convincing evidence that they are unable to satisfy their institutional goals in any way that does not infringe inmates' free exercise rights"). Though the availability of accommodations is relevant to the reasonableness inquiry, we have rejected the notion that "prison officials . . . have to set up and then shoot down every conceivable alternative method of accommodating the claimant's constitutional complaint." By placing the burden on prison officials to disprove the availability of alternatives, the approach articulated by the Court of Appeals fails to reflect the respect and deference that the United States Constitution allows for the judgment of prison administrators.

Turning to consideration of the policies challenged in this case, we think the findings of the District Court establish clearly that prison officials have acted in a reasonable manner. *Turner v. Safley* drew upon our previous decisions to identify several factors relevant to this reasonableness determination. First, a regulation must have a logical connection to legitimate governmental interests invoked to justify it. The policies at issue here clearly meet that standard. The requirement that full minimum and gang minimum prisoners work outside the main facility was justified by concerns of institutional order and security, for the District Court found that it was "at least in part a response to a critical overcrowding in the state's prisons, and ... at least in part designed to ease tension and drain on the facilities during that part of the day when the inmates were outside the confines of the main buildings." 595 F. Supp., at 929. We think it beyond doubt that the standard is related to this legitimate concern.

...The right to congregate for prayer or discussion is "virtually unlimited except during working hours," and the state-provided imam has free access to the prison. Muslim prisoners are given different meals whenever pork is served in the prison cafeteria. Special arrangements are also made during the month-long observance of Ramadan, a period of fasting and prayer. During Ramadan, Muslim prisoners are awakened at 4 a.m. for an early breakfast, and receive dinner at 8:30 each evening. We think this ability on the part of respondents to participate in other religious observances of their faith supports the conclusion that the restrictions at issue here were reasonable.

...We take this opportunity to reaffirm our refusal, even where claims are made under the First Amendment, to "substitute our judgment on . . . difficult and sensitive matters of institutional administration," for the determinations of those charged with the formidable task of running a prison. Here the District Court decided that the regulations alleged to infringe constitutional rights were reasonably related to legitimate penological objectives. We agree with the District Court, and it necessarily follows that the regulations in question do not offend the Free Exercise Clause of the First Amendment to the United States Constitution. The judgment of the Court of Appeals is therefore Reversed.

CASE SUMMARIES

A federal appeals court upholds prison's denial of Moorish prisoner's request to hold banquet in honor of the founder of his religion. *Mack v. O'Leary*, 80 F.3d 1175 (7th Cir. 1996).

Requiring a prisoner to attend "Narcotics Anonymous" substance abuse program or suffer possible classification to higher security risk violated the Establishment Clause of the First Amendment since program was religiously based, with references to God or a "higher power," federal appeals court rules. *Kerr v. Farrey*, 95 F.3d 472 (7th Cir. 1996).

A Florida rule allowing prison officials to delete objectionable portions of religious literature that would pose a threat to prison security, while allowing in the remainder of the text, did not violate the Religious Freedom Restoration Act or the First Amendment. *Lawson v. Singletary*, 85 F.3d 502 (11th Cir. 1996).

A Jewish prisoner could not challenge his transfer to another facility based on his dissatisfaction with the quality of the kosher food diet at the receiving facility. *Prins v. Coughlin*, 76 F.3d 504 (2nd Cir. 1996).

Satanist prisoner could legitimately be denied receipt and possession of the Satanic Bible based on review of the book and determination that it was inflammatory and could create safety and security problems. *Carpenter v. Wilkinson*, 946 F. Supp. 522 (N.D. Ohio 1996).

Jehovah's Witnesses prisoners had to be allowed to meet on the same terms as Muslim prisoners, including meetings of fewer than fifteen people and meetings without an outside religious leader when none was available; federal court notes that each religion must be treated alike when similarly situated; plaintiff prisoner awarded right to not work for ten days and be credited for good time as though he had, as compensation for problems with religious meetings. *Hyde v. Texas Dept. of Criminal Justice*, 948 F. Supp. 625 (S.D. Tex. 1996).

Prison officials did not violate prisoner's right to religious freedom or free speech in withholding *Christian Identity* book that advocated violence against Jews and government; prisoner's religion did not require him to read book, so withholding it did not substantially burden his religious freedom, and decision to withhold it was reasonably related to prison security concerns. *Stefanow v. McFadden*, 103 F.3d 1466 (9th Cir. 1996).

Orthodox Jewish prisoner had a right to a kosher diet; prisoner's right to free exercise of religion outweighed prison's concerns about expense and inconvenience. *Ashelman v. Wawrzaszek*, 111 F.3d 674 (9th Cir. 1997).

SUMMARY

- Religion may be defined as an activity that teaches and preaches a belief in a Supreme Being, a religious discipline, and tenets to guide one's daily existence.
- Prison officials give the following justifications for regulating the exercise of religion:
  - √ Security
  - √ Discipline
  - √ Economics
  - √ Discretion
- Institutions have broad discretion to set diets for inmates.
- Institutions must set forth specific reasons to regulate inmates' grooming if such regulation violates an inmate's religious beliefs.

DISCUSSION QUESTIONS

1. Can you give a more precise definition of "religion"? Is it better to have a narrow precise definition or a broad general definition of religion? What are the advantages and disadvantages of each approach?

2. What is the most compelling justification that an institution can give for regulating an inmate's religious activities? List the justifications in order of importance.

3. When dealing with issues, such as religious beliefs and activities, should the burden of proof be a compelling state interest or a reasonableness test? Justify your answer.

ENDNOTES

1. See *Lipp v. Procunier,* 395 F. Supp. 871 (N.D. Cal. 1975).
2. 547 F.2d 1279 (5th Cir. 1977).
3. 453 F. Supp. 254 (W.D. Tex. 1978).
4. See *Loney v. Scurr,* 474 F. Supp. 1186 (S.D. Iowa 1979).
5. No. 94-3845, ___ F.3d ___ (8th Cir. 1996).
6. See *Cooper v. Pate,* 382 F.2d 518 (7th Cir. 1967).
7. 428 F.2d 1 (3rd Cir. 1970).
8. See *O'Lone v. Shabazz* for a more in depth discussion of this approach to regulating religion.
9. See *McDonald v. Hall,* 576 F.2d 120 (1st Cir. 1978)
10. See *Northern v. Nelson,* 315 F. Supp. 687 (N.D. Calif. 1970).
11. See *Childs v. Pegelow,* 321 F.2d 487 (4th Cir. 1963).
12. 527 F.2d 492 (2d Cir. 1975).
13. W.D.N.Y. No. 97-CV-607(H), decided 3/25/99. Published online 5/21/99.
14. See *Benjamin v. Coughlin,* 69 F.3d 22 (5th Cir. 1995).

CHAPTER 6

MAIL

INTRODUCTION

The First Amendment also protects speech. Speech, in this context, is more than someone making a formal speech to a gathering of citizens. Speech under the Constitution includes communication by the media (television, radio, and newspapers), publishers (books and magazines), and mail. Today, very few of us take the time to sit down and compose a letter to a friend in another part of the state or in a different city; rather, we simply pick up the telephone and call them. We may even fax them a joke or receipt. Additionally, many citizens use the Internet and e-mail to communicate with friends, co-workers, and supervisors. However, prisoners do not have access to many of these methods of communication, so they rely on the mail to send and receive a wide variety of information.

Correctional officials regulate inmate mail for a variety of reasons. The three most common reasons are security, the orderly administration of the institution, and rehabilitation.

Prison Security

Prison security is a wide-ranging area that includes preventing contraband from entering the prison (narcotics and other items being sent into the prison), the detection of escape plans (either information being sent from the prison to a confederate or information coming into the prison from a confederate dealing with escape), and material that might incite the prison population (such as nude photographs).

Orderly Administration

The orderly administration of a correctional institution is very similar to the security rationale, because institutions do not have funds to hire extra help or employees to monitor and/or enforce the restrictions placed on the use of mail. Therefore institutions are justified in restricting the type, amount, and nature of mail that prisoners may send or receive.

Rehabilitation

Rehabilitation of prisoners is frequently cited as a reason for control of mail. The institution may place limits or establish lists of sources that the inmate may correspond with or receive mail from in an effort to avoid contact with gang members on the outside or other sources that might impede the rehabilitation process.

REGULATION OF MAIL

In *Procunier v. Martinez*, the Supreme Court ruled that regulations prohibiting inmate correspondence that contained complaints or grievances about the correctional institution were unconstitutional because they was not related to a legitimate penal or governmental interest.[1] In *Martinez*, the court held that the restrictions on outgoing mail were valid only if they are "generally necessary" to further a valid penal interest. The regulation must further a substantial governmental interest. This was a strict or heavy burden imposed on prison officials to justify censorship of inmate mail. The court indicated that only outgoing mail concerning escape plans, ongoing criminal activity, or threats of blackmail posed threat to prison security sufficient to justify censorship.

Martinez also established the process that correctional officials must follow when censoring mail. The affected inmate must be notified and allowed to object to the censorship. This protest must then be decided by an official other than the one who made the original decision to refuse delivery.

In *Turner v. Safley* (1987) the Supreme Court modified the standard used to determine prisoners' constitutional challenges to prison regulations.[2]

The Court held that an inquiry should be made into whether the regulation was reasonably related to legitimate penological interests. To determine this, the Supreme Court stated that a four-part test should be used:

1. Is there a valid rational connection between the regulation and a legitimate governmental interest?
2. Are there alternative means of exercising the asserted constitutional rights that remain open to prisoners even after the regulation is enforced?
3. What is the impact on correctional staff and resources?
4. Is the regulation an exaggerated response to correctional concerns?

This reasonable relationship test is much less burdensome than the substantial governmental interest test established by *Martinez*.

In *Thornburgh v. Abbott*, the Supreme Court held that mail regulations must be analyzed using the standards established by *Turner*.[3] Thus, mail regulation and censorship is valid if it is reasonably related to a legitimate penological interest. Correctional officials are given considerable deference in regulating prisons. *Martinez*, which used a stricter standard and required mail censorship to be generally necessary to protect a governmental interest, was held to apply only to outgoing correspondence.

Since *Abbott*, other lower courts have addressed the issue of outgoing mail. *Stow v. Grimaldi*, held that a review of outgoing mail was proper as a security measure to decrease opportunities to plot escapes.[4] *Martucci v. Johnson* upheld the withholding of both incoming and outgoing mail when there was reasonable cause to believe the inmate was planning an imminent escape attempt.[5]

In *Gassler v. Woods*, the prison officials delivered a prisoner's outgoing non-legal mail to an investigator who reviewed it. The court upheld such a process because the purpose was to determine if the mail revealed plans to intimidate or murder certain witnesses in the inmate's upcoming trial.[6]

> ### Sexually-Oriented Publications
>
> May an inmate receive publications that espouse consensual sexual relationships between adult and juvenile males? In *Harper v. Wallingford*, 877 F.2d. 728 (9th Cir. 1989), the Court of Appeals approved the prison's decision to prohibit the inmate from receiving such material. The court accepted the prison officials' statements that there were various ways in which the material would promote violence and that the possession of it could be detrimental to the rehabilitation of the inmate as well as other inmates.

In *Thornburgh v. Abbott*, the Supreme Court upheld as constitutional a Federal Bureau of Prisons regulation that provided that publications that may be rejected by a warden include, but are not limited to, publications that meet one of the following criteria:

- Material that depicts or describes procedures for the construction or use of weapons, ammunition, bombs, or incendiary devices
- Material that depicts, encourages, or describes methods of escape from correctional facilities, or contains blueprints, drawings, or similar descriptions of Bureau of Prisons institutions
- Material that depicts or describes procedures for the brewing of alcoholic beverages, or the manufacture of drugs

- Material written in code
- Material that depicts, describes, or encourages activities which may lead to the use of physical violence or group disruption
- Material that encourages or instructs in the commission of criminal activities
- Material that is sexually explicit which by its nature or content poses a threat to the security, good order, or discipline of the institution, or facilitates criminal activity[7]

The regulations in question also placed certain restrictions on a warden's power to limit a prisoner's receipt of publications. For example, the warden could not reject a publication solely because its content is religious, philosophical, political, social, or sexual, or because its content is unpopular or repugnant. In addition, the warden could not set up a "hit list" of publications that were absolutely barred from distribution within the prison. The warden was required to review each issue of a publication to determine whether some portion of that particular issue posed a threat to the institutional security or would facilitate a crime.

OBSCENE MATERIAL

As indicated in other chapters, the First Amendment to the Constitution protects our freedom of expression. This includes the right to make, sell, and view sexually-explicit material so long as it does not cross over the line and become obscene. Although the First Amendment protects free speech and expression, not all such activity is protected. Our courts have determined that certain speech-related activity does not warrant First Amendment protection. This means that the state is free to regulate it and make it a crime. This is the case with obscenity. The United States Supreme Court has defined *obscenity* as requiring a finding of all three of the following elements:

1. The average person, applying contemporary community standards, would find that the work, taken as a whole, appeals to the prurient interest [in sex]; and

2. The work depicts or describes, in a patently offensive way, sexual conduct; and

3. The work, taken as a whole, lacks serious literary, artistic, political, or scientific value.[8]

Thus, the Supreme Court has established the principle that we may regulate obscene movies, pictures or other material. Because we can regulate obscene material outside prison walls, it stands to reason that we can prohibit prisoners from receiving, viewing or possessing obscene material.

Obscene material may cover a wide range of topics, including sex with children. Clearly, a movie that depicts a minor involved in sex acts with another person falls within this realm. Therefore, such activity is not protected under the First Amendment. As a result, state and federal statutes can and have made it a crime to involve a minor in a sexually-explicit movie.

Congress enacted a federal statute prohibiting the use of minors in sexually-explicit films in 1978 and amended it in 1984. This statute is known as the Child Protection Act of 1984. It prohibits any person from enticing a minor to engage in any sexually-explicit conduct for the purpose of producing any visual depiction of that conduct. The act imposes liability on parents, guardians, producers, and distributors of child pornography. The statute has been upheld by the courts as a valid exercise of the police power of the state.[9]

NUDE PHOTOGRAPHS

Pornography is any form of expression that deals with explicit sexual activity that is not considered obscene. The courts have held that adult citizens have a right to possess pornographic material, and many people can go to local video stores and rent such material. Others can find pornographic Websites and view pictures or clips on their home computer. What about prisoners? Do they have the same rights as free citizens in this area?

An argument can be made that these types of photographs might cause prisoners to react violently and, therefore, may be controlled under the *Safley* test. Nevertheless, some institutions allow prisoners to receive publications that contain nude or erotic photographs. However, nude or erotic pictures of a prisoner's wife or friend can be restricted by institutions. In *Pepperling v. Crist*, an appellate court ruled that such photographs might lead to violent confrontations among prisoners.[10] In *Giano v. Senkowski*, the institution allowed prisoners to receive commercially published erotic magazines.[11] However, the faculty banned nude photographs of girlfriends or wives because such photographs could cause violent alterations among prisoners if they were passed around the institution or fell into the possession of the wrong inmate.

CASES ON POINT

Procunier v. Martinez, 416 U.S. 396 (1974)

MR. JUSTICE POWELL delivered the opinion of the Court.

This case concerns the constitutionality of certain regulations promulgated by appellant Procunier in his capacity as Director of the California Department of Corrections. Appellees brought a class action on behalf of themselves and all other prisoners of penal institutions under the Department's jurisdiction to challenge the rules relating to censorship of prisoner mail and the ban against the use of law students and legal paraprofessionals to conduct attorney-client interviews with prisoners. . . .

I

First we consider the constitutionality of the Director's rules restricting the personal correspondence of prison prisoners. Under these regulations, correspondence between prisoners of California penal institutions and persons other than licensed attorneys and holders of public office was censored for nonconformity to certain standards. Rule 2401 stated the Department's general premise that personal correspondence by prisoners is "a privilege, not a right . . . ." More detailed regulations implemented the Department's policy. Rule 1201 directed prisoners not to write letters in which they "unduly complain" or "magnify grievances." Rule 1205 (d) defined as contraband writings "expressing inflammatory political, racial, religious or other views or beliefs . . . ." Finally, Rule 2402 (8) provided that prisoners "may not send or receive letters that pertain to criminal activity; are lewd, obscene, or defamatory; contain foreign matter, or are otherwise inappropriate."

Prison employees screened both incoming and outgoing personal mail for violations of these regulations. No further criteria were provided to help members of the mail room staff decide whether a particular letter contravened any prison rule or policy. When a prison employee found a letter objectionable, he could take one or more of the following actions: (1) refuse to mail or deliver the letter and return it to the author; (2) submit a disciplinary report, which could lead to suspension of mail privileges or other sanctions; or (3) place a copy of the letter or a summary of its contents in the prisoner's file, where it might be a factor in determining the inmate's work and housing assignments and in setting a date for parole eligibility.

The District Court held that the regulations relating to prisoner mail authorized censorship of protected expression without adequate justification in violation of the First Amendment and that they were void for vagueness. The court also noted that the regulations failed to provide minimum procedural safeguards against error and arbitrariness in the censorship of inmate correspondence. Consequently, it enjoined their continued enforcement.

A

Traditionally, federal courts have adopted a broad hands-off attitude toward problems of prison administration. In part this policy is the product of various limitations on the scope of federal review of conditions in state penal institutions. More fundamentally, this attitude springs from complementary perceptions about the nature of the problems and the efficacy of judicial intervention. Prison administrators are responsible for maintaining internal order and discipline, for securing their institutions against unauthorized access or escape, and for rehabilitating, to the extent that human nature and inadequate resources allow, the prisoners placed in their custody.

The Herculean obstacles to effective discharge of these duties are too apparent to warrant explication. Suffice it to say that the problems of prisons in America are complex and intractable, and, more to the point, they are not readily susceptible of resolution by decree. Most require expertise, comprehensive planning, and the commitment of resources, all of which are peculiarly within the province of the legislative and executive branches of government.

For all of those reasons, courts are ill-equipped to deal with the increasingly urgent problems of prison administration and reform. Judicial recognition of that fact reflects no more than a healthy sense of realism. Moreover, where state penal institutions are involved, federal courts have a further reason for deference to the appropriate prison authorities.

But a policy of judicial restraint cannot encompass any failure to take cognizance of valid constitutional claims whether arising in a federal or state institution. When a prison regulation or practice offends a fundamental constitutional guarantee, federal courts will discharge their duty to protect constitutional rights. *Johnson v. Avery*. This is such a case. Although the District Court found the regulations relating to prisoner mail deficient in several respects, the first and principal basis for its decision was the constitutional command of the First Amendment, as applied to the States by the Fourteenth Amendment. . . .

B

We begin our analysis of the proper standard of review for constitutional challenges to censorship of prisoner mail with a somewhat different premise from that taken by the other federal courts that have considered the question. For the most part, these courts have dealt with challenges to censorship of prisoner mail as involving broad questions of "prisoners' rights." This case is no exception. . . In determining the proper standard of review for prison restrictions on inmate correspondence, we have no occasion to consider the extent to which an individual's right to free speech survives incarceration, for a narrower basis of decision is at hand. In the case of direct personal correspondence between prisoners and those who have a particularized interest in communicating with them, mail censorship implicates more than the right of prisoners.

Communication by letter is not accomplished by the act of writing words on paper. Rather, it is effected only when the letter is read by the addressee. Both parties to the correspondence have an interest in securing that result, and censorship of the communication between them necessarily impinges on the interest of each. Whatever the status of a prisoner's claim to uncensored correspondence,with an outsider, it is plain that the latter's interest is grounded in the First Amendment's guarantee of freedom of speech. And this does not depend on whether the nonprisoner correspondent is the author or intended recipient of a particular letter, for the addressee as well as the sender of direct personal correspondence derives from the First and Fourteenth Amendments a protection against unjustified governmental interference with the intended communication. . . .

Accordingly, we reject any attempt to justify censorship of inmate correspondence merely by reference to certain assumptions about the legal status of prisoners. Into this category of argument falls appellants' contention that "an inmate's rights with reference to social correspondence are something fundamentally different than those enjoyed by his free brother." This line of argument and the undemanding standard of review it is intended to support fail to recognize that the First Amendment liberties of free citizens are implicated in censorship of prisoner mail.

The case at hand arises in the context of prisons. One of the primary functions of government is the preservation of societal order through enforcement of the criminal law, and the maintenance of penal institutions is an essential part of that task. The identifiable governmental interests at stake in this task are the preservation of internal order and discipline, the maintenance of institutional security against escape or unauthorized entry, and the rehabilitation of the prisoners.

While the weight of professional opinion seems to be that inmate freedom to correspond with outsiders advances rather than retards the goal of rehabilitation, the legitimate governmental interest in the order and security of penal institutions justifies the imposition of certain restraints on inmate correspondence. Perhaps the most obvious example of justifiable censorship of prisoner mail would be refusal to send or deliver letters concerning escape plans or containing other information concerning proposed criminal activity, whether within or without the prison. Similarly, prison officials may properly refuse to transmit encoded messages. Other less obvious possibilities come to mind, but it is not our purpose to survey the range of circumstances in which particular restrictions on prisoner mail might be warranted by the legitimate demands of prison administration as they exist from time to time in the various kinds of penal institutions found in this country. Our task is to determine the proper standard for deciding whether a particular regulation or practice relating to inmate correspondence constitutes an impermissible restraint of First Amendment liberties.... Thus a restriction on inmate correspondence that furthers an important or substantial interest of penal administration will nevertheless be invalid if its sweep is unnecessarily broad. This does not mean, of course, that prison administrators may be required to show with certainty that adverse consequences would flow from the failure to censor a particular letter. Some latitude in anticipating the probable consequences of allowing certain speech in a prison environment is essential to the proper discharge of an administrator's duty. But any regulation or practice that restricts inmate correspondence must be generally necessary to protect one or more of the legitimate governmental interests identified above. . . .

On the basis of this standard, we affirm the judgment of the District Court. . . .

Case Discussion and Significance. *Martinez* established a strict standard or test that prison officials had to meet to justify censorship of prisoners' mail. This standard required that the regulation further an important or substantial governmental interest and be no greater than is necessary to protect that particular interest.

The Supreme Court held that the censorship of direct personal correspondence involves incidental restrictions on the right to free speech of both prisoners and their correspondents and is justified if the following criteria are met: it must further one or more of the important and substantial governmental interests of security, order, and the rehabilitation of prisoners; and it must be no greater than is necessary to further the legitimate governmental interest involved.

The court went on to state that the decision to censor or withhold delivery of a particular letter must be accompanied by minimum procedural safeguards against arbitrariness or error.

Turner v. Safley,
482 U.S. 78 (1987)

JUSTICE O'CONNOR delivered the opinion of the Court.

Respondents brought this class action for injunctive relief and damages in the United States

District Court for the Western District of Missouri. The regulations challenged in the complaint were in effect at all prisons within the jurisdiction of the Missouri Division of Corrections. This litigation focused, however, on practices at the Renz Correctional Institution (Renz), located in Cedar City, Missouri. The Renz prison population includes both male and female prisoners of varying security levels. Most of the female prisoners at Renz are classified as medium or maximum security prisoners, while most of the male prisoners are classified as minimum security offenders. Renz is used, on occasion, to provide protective custody for prisoners from other prisons in the Missouri system. The facility originally was built as a minimum security prison farm, and it still has a minimum security perimeter without guard towers or walls.

The first of the challenged regulations relates to correspondence between prisoners at different institutions. It permits such correspondence "with immediate family members who are prisoners in other correctional institutions," and it permits correspondence between prisoners "concerning legal matters." Other correspondence between prisoners, however, is permitted only if "the classification/treatment team of each inmate deems it in the best interest of the parties involved." Trial testimony indicated that as a matter of practice, the determination whether to permit prisoners to correspond was based on team members' familiarity with the progress reports, conduct violations, and psychological reports in the prisoners' files, rather than on individual review of each piece of mail. At Renz, the District Court found that the rule "as practiced is that prisoners may not write non-family prisoners."

. . . .We begin, as did the courts below, with our decision in *Procunier v. Martinez*, supra, which described the principles that necessarily frame our analysis of prisoners' constitutional claims. The first of these principles is that federal courts must take cognizance of the valid constitutional claims of prison prisoners. Prison walls do not form a barrier separating prison prisoners from the protections of the Constitution. Hence, for example, prisoners retain the constitutional right to petition the government for the redress of grievances, *Johnson v. Avery*; they are protected against invidious racial discrimination by the Equal Protection Clause of the Fourteenth Amendment, *Lee v. Washington*; and they enjoy the protections of due process, *Wolff v. McDonnell*. Because prisoners retain these rights, "[w]hen a prison regulation or practice offends a fundamental constitutional guarantee, federal courts will discharge their duty to protect constitutional rights." *Procunier v. Martinez.*

A second principle identified in *Martinez*, however, is the recognition that "courts are ill-equipped to deal with the increasingly urgent problems of prison administration and reform." As the *Martinez* Court acknowledged, "the problems of prisons in America are complex and intractable, and, more to the point, they are not readily susceptible of resolution by decree."

Running a prison is an inordinately difficult undertaking that requires expertise, planning, and the commitment of resources, all of which are peculiarly within the province of the legislative and executive branches of government. Prison administration is, moreover, a task that has been committed to the responsibility of those branches, and separation of powers concerns counsel a policy of judicial restraint. Where a state penal system is involved, federal courts have, as we indicated in

Martinez, additional reason to accord deference to the appropriate prison authorities.

Our task, then, as we stated in *Martinez*, is to formulate a standard of review for prisoners' constitutional claims that is responsive both to the "policy of judicial restraint regarding prisoner complaints and [to] the need to protect constitutional rights." As the Court of Appeals acknowledged, *Martinez* did not itself resolve the question that it framed. *Martinez* involved mail censorship regulations proscribing statements that "unduly complain," "magnify grievances," or express "inflammatory political, racial, religious or other views." In that case, the Court determined that the proper standard of review for prison restrictions on correspondence between prisoners and members of the general public could be decided without resolving the "broad questions of `prisoners' rights.'" The *Martinez* Court based its ruling striking down the content-based regulation on the First Amendment rights of those who are not prisoners, stating that "[w]hatever the status of a prisoner's claim to uncensored correspondence with an outsider, it is plain that the latter's interest is grounded in the First Amendment's guarantee of freedom of speech." Our holding therefore turned on the fact that the challenged regulation caused a "consequential restriction on the First and Fourteenth Amendment rights of those who are not prisoners." We expressly reserved the question of the proper standard of review to apply in cases "involving questions of prisoners' rights.'"

In four cases following *Martinez*, this Court has addressed such "questions of prisoners' rights." The first of these, *Pell v. Procunier* ... the Court rejected the prisoners' First Amendment challenge to the ban on media interviews. . . .The next case to consider a claim of prisoners' rights was *Jones v. North Carolina Prisoners' Union.* There the Court considered prison regulations that prohibited meetings of a "prisoners' labor union," inmate solicitation of other prisoners to join the union, and bulk mailings concerning the union from outside sources...the Court determined that the First and Fourteenth Amendment rights of prisoners were "barely implicated" by the prohibition on bulk mailings, and that the regulation was "reasonable" under the circumstances. The prisoners' constitutional challenge to the union meeting and solicitation restrictions was also rejected, because "[t]he ban on inmate solicitation and group meetings . . . was rationally related to the reasonable, indeed to the central, objectives of prison administration."

Bell v. Wolfish concerned a First Amendment challenge to a Bureau of Prisons rule restricting prisoners' receipt of hardback books unless mailed directly from publishers, book clubs, or bookstores. The rule was upheld as a "rational response" to a clear security problem. Because there was "no evidence" that officials had exaggerated their response to the security problem, the Court held that "the considered judgment of these experts must control in the absence of prohibitions far more sweeping than those involved here." And in *Block v. Rutherford,* a ban on contact visits was upheld on the ground that "responsible, experienced administrators have determined, in their sound discretion, that such visits will jeopardize the security of the facility," and the regulation was "reasonably related" to these security concerns.

. . .If *Pell, Jones,* and *Bell* have not already resolved the question posed in *Martinez,* we resolve it now:

when a prison regulation impinges on prisoners' constitutional rights, the regulation is valid if it is reasonably related to legitimate penological interests. In our view, such a standard is necessary if "prison administrators . . ., and not the courts, [are] to make the difficult judgments concerning institutional operations." *Jones v. North Carolina Prisoners' Union.* Subjecting the day-to-day judgments of prison officials to an inflexible strict scrutiny analysis would seriously hamper their ability to anticipate security problems and to adopt innovative solutions to the intractable problems of prison administration. The rule would also distort the decision making process, for every administrative judgment would be subject to the possibility that some court somewhere would conclude that it had a less restrictive way of solving the problem at hand.

. . .The prohibition on correspondence between institutions is logically connected to these legitimate security concerns. Undoubtedly, communication with other felons is a potential spur to criminal behavior. This sort of contact frequently is prohibited even after an inmate has been released on parole. In Missouri prisons, the danger of such coordinated criminal activity is exacerbated by the presence of prison gangs. The Missouri policy of separating and isolating gang members—a strategy that has been frequently used to control gang activity, logically is furthered by the restriction on prisoner-to-prisoner correspondence. Moreover, the correspondence regulation does not deprive prisoners of all means of expression. Rather, it bars communication only with a limited class of other people with whom prison officials have particular cause to be concerned— prisoners at other institutions within the Missouri prison system.

. . .The prohibition on correspondence is reasonably related to valid corrections goals. The rule is content neutral, it logically advances the goals of institutional security and safety identified by Missouri prison officials, and it is not an exaggerated response to those objectives. On that basis, we conclude that the regulation does not unconstitutionally abridge the First Amendment rights of prison prisoners.

It is so ordered.

Case Discussion and Significance. *Safley* is one of the key cases in corrections law. It establishes the present day standard of review of actions taken by correctional officials that infringe on prisoners' constitutional rights. It establishes four factors to be considered when evaluating a constitutional challenge to a prison regulation.

1. Whether there is a "valid, rational connection" between the regulation and a legitimate and neutral governmental interest put forward to justify it, which connection cannot be so remote as to render the regulation arbitrary or irrational.

2. Whether there are alternative means of exercising the asserted constitutional right that remain open to prisoners, which alternatives, if they exist, will require a measure of judicial deference to the corrections officials' expertise.

3. Whether, and the extent to which, accommodation of the asserted right will have an impact on prison staff, on prisoners' liberty, and on the allocation of limited prison resources, which impact, if substantial, will require particular deference to corrections officials.

4. Whether the regulation represents an "exaggerated response" to prison concerns, the existence

of a ready alternative that fully accommodates the prisoner's rights at *de minimis* costs to valid penological interests being evidence of unreasonableness.

If the regulation is reasonably related to a legitimate penological interest, it will be upheld under the *Safley* standard.

CASE SUMMARIES

The refusal to treat prisoner mail to all state agencies and officials as "legal mail" was justified by prison interest in security and prevention of criminal activity, federal appeals court rules. *O'Keefe v. Van Boening*, 82 F.3d 322 (9th Cir. 1996).

Boxes of legal materials, originating from prisoner's attorney and clearly marked legal mail, qualified as legal mail and should have been examined in the prisoner's presence, despite the fact that they were delivered to the prison by an individual, rather than being delivered via the U.S. mail or a private delivery service such as UPS. *Kensu v. Haigh*, 87 F.3d 172 (6th Cir. 1996).

Prison policy prohibiting the receipt of all "free advertising" or bulk rate mail (such as catalogs) by prisoners did not violate inmates' First Amendment rights, federal appeals court rules. *Sheets v. Moore*, 97 F.3d 164 (6th Cir. 1996).

Prison employee entitled to qualified immunity for denying prisoner loan for postage for outgoing legal mail unless he agreed to allow her to briefly inspect it in his presence to make sure it qualified as legal mail. *Bell-Bey v. Williams*, 87 F.3d 832 (6th Cir. 1996).

Prisoner's right to use his legally adopted religious name on outgoing mail together with his committed name was clearly established in 1990, federal appeals court rules, and prison officials were not entitled to qualified immunity for allegedly punishing him for doing so; notary, however, was entitled to qualified immunity for refusing to notarize document when signature presented did not match prison identification shown. *Malik v. Brown,* 71 F.3d 724 (9th Cir. 1995).

Destruction of inmate's beard trimmer, received in the mail, without prior hearing on whether it was contraband, did not violate his due process rights when there were adequate state-law post-deprivation remedies available to seek compensation for his property. *Diaz v. Coughlin,* 909 F. Supp. 146 (S.D.N.Y. 1995).

County jail's complete lack of law library or legally trained personnel to assist prisoners did not violate constitutional rights of prisoner confined there for brief 18-day period, in absence of any showing of prejudice to prisoner's legal claims; federal appeals court also upholds correctional officials' inspection of prisoner's outgoing non-legal mail. *Beville v. Ednie,* 74 F. 3d 210 (10th Cir. 1996).

"Cursory visual inspection" of contents of envelope Nevada inmate wanted to send to state Attorney General did not violate inmate's rights; regulation providing for inspection served legitimate security interest. *Giano v. Senkowski,* 54 F.3d 1050 (2d Cir. 1995).

A Federal appeals court rules that prison policy excluding all newspaper clippings from prisoner's incoming correspondence may violate First Amendment; prison officials were entitled, however, to qualified immunity from personal liability, since right to receive such clippings was not "clearly established." *Allen v. Coughlin,* 64 F.3d 77 (2nd Cir. 1995).

SUMMARY

- Prison officials may regulate inmate mail using one or all of three justifications.
    1. Security
    2. Administration of the institution
    3. Rehabilitation

- *Martinez* required that censorship of mail meet a substantial governmental purpose to be constitutional.
- *Safley* established a more lenient standard that states the regulation will be upheld if it reasonably related to a legitimate penological interest.
- *Abbott* applied the *Safley* standard to incoming mail and held that *Martinez* was overruled in that area and now only applied to outgoing mail.
- Although prisoners may receive nude pictures that are published in commercial magazines, they cannot receive nude photographs of their spouse or friends.

DISCUSSION QUESTIONS

1. How does the control or censorship of mail aid in the rehabilitation of prisoners?
2. Why didn't the court in *Safley* simply overrule *Martinez*?
3. Should prisoners be allowed to receive publications from commercial vendors? Why? Why not?
4. What purpose does it serve to allow inmates to receive nude photographs? What problems do you see in such a procedure?
5. Does a male inmate have a constitutional right to inseminate his wife through artificial means which includes the use of mail? See *Goodwin v. Turner*, 908 F.2d. 1395 (8th Cir. 1990).

ENDNOTES

1. 416 U.S. 346 (1974).
2. 482 U.S. 78 (1987).
3. 490 U.S. 401 (1989).
4. 993 F.2d 1002 (1st Cir. 1993).
5. 944 F.2d 291 (6th Cir. 1991).
6. 14 F.3d 306 (8th Cir. 1994).
7. 490 U.S. 401 (1989).
8. *Miller v. California*, 413 U.S. 15 (1973), reh. den. 414 U.S. 881 (1973).
9. *United States v. Reedy*, 632 F. Supp. 1415 (W.D. Okl. 1986), affirmed 845 F.2d 239 (10th Cir. 1988).
10. 678 F.2d 787 (9th Cir. 1982).
11. 54 F.3rd 1050 (2nd Cir. 1995).

CHAPTER 7

SEARCH AND SEIZURE

The right of the people to be secure in their persons, houses, papers, and effects, against unreasonable searches and seizures, shall not be violated....

Fourth Amendment, U.S. Constitution

In this chapter, we will examine search and seizure issues involving prisoners and the authority to search visitors. The Supreme Court has repeatedly held that prisons are not beyond the reach of the Constitution and that no "iron curtain" separates one from the other.[1] The Court has insisted that prisoners be accorded those rights not fundamentally inconsistent with imprisonment itself or incompatible with the objectives of incarceration. The Court also stated that while prisoners enjoy many protections of the Constitution, it is also clear that imprisonment carries with it the circumscription or loss of many significant rights. Accordingly, the rights of prisoners against searches and seizures are drastically less than those enjoyed by persons outside of institutions.

SEARCHES OF PRISONERS

Under what circumstances may prison inmates be searched? Note that the extract from the amendment printed above does not prohibit all searches and seizures, only those that are unreasonable. Accordingly, for the amendment to apply, there must be a search, and the search must be unreasonable.

The starting point in examining search and seizure issues is determining what constitutes a search. In *Katz v. United States*, the U.S. Supreme Court held that a search is a government intrusion into an area in which a person has a reasonable expectation of privacy.[2] As noted by Justice Harlan, in his concurring opinion in *Katz*, there is a two-fold requirement to constitute a search under the Fourth Amendment:

1. A person must have an actual (subjective) expectation of privacy.
2. The expectation must be one that the society is prepared to recognize as "reasonable."

Regarding the first of the two-fold requirements, most prisoners do not have an actual expectation of privacy while confined in a correctional institution. The Supreme Court held in *Hudson v. Palmer* that prisoners have no expectation of privacy in their cell, and thus the Fourth Amendment does not apply to cell searches.[3] The Court stated that the recognition of privacy rights for prisoners in their individual cells simply cannot be reconciled with the concept of incarceration and the needs and objectives of penal institutions. Prisons, by definition, are places of involuntary confinement of persons who have demonstrated proclivity for antisocial, criminal, and often violent, conduct. Inmates have necessarily shown a lapse in ability to control and conform their behavior to the legitimate standards of society. The Court also noted that because the citizen must have a reasonable expectation of privacy, it is not the place that is protected, but the person occupying or using that place who is protected.

Regarding the second requirement, the public is unlikely to recognize and accept as reasonable that an individual being held in a correctional institution has a right of privacy. In *Wolf*, the Court stated that the administration of a prison was "at best an extraordinarily difficult undertaking," and it would be literally impossible to accomplish prison objectives if inmates retained a right of privacy in their cells. Virtually the only place that inmates can conceal weapons, drugs, and other contraband is in their cells, and unfettered access to the cells by prison officials is imperative. Accordingly, prisoners have traditionally enjoyed only limited protection from searches and seizures. However, a search conducted in a manner that destroys the inmate's property may lead to civil liability on the part of the officer conducting the search.[4] Does the prisoner have a right to be present when his or her cell is searched? In *Block v. Rutherford*, the Supreme Court said no, the inmate had no right to be present during the search.[5]

RANDOM PAT-DOWN SEARCHES

Randomly held pat-down searches are generally upheld by the courts. The courts have refused to require that prison searches be conducted only pursuant to an enunciated general policy or when suspicion is directed at a particular prisoner. Random searches of inmates, individually or collectively, and of their cells and lockers are considered by the courts as necessary to ensure the security of the institution and the safety of inmates and others within its boundaries. As one court noted, "Wholly random searches are essential to the effective security of penal institutions."[6]

If, however, the pat-down searches are being done to harass individual inmates and not for legitimate institutional purposes, the courts have, on several occasions, held them to be unreasonable. As the Court noted, its holding that a respondent does not have a reasonable expectation of privacy enabling him to invoke the protections of the Fourth Amendment does not mean that he is without remedy for calculated harassment unrelated to prison needs. Nor does it mean that prison attendants can ride roughshod over inmates' property rights with impunity. The Eighth Amendment stands as a protection against "cruel and unusual" punishment. In addition, there are tort and common law remedies available to prisoners to redress the alleged destruction of personal property belonging to prisoners.

CROSS-GENDER SEARCHES

In several cases, the courts have criticized cross-gender pat-down searches (male-female).[7] Most of the cases involving cross-gender searches were decided on Eighth Amendment issues rather than on the Fourth Amendment. In *Grummett v. Rushen*, a court of appeals held that the momentary discomfort caused by pat-down searches performed by female guards on male prisoners did not show sufficient evidence of pain to make out a cognizable "cruel and unusual" pain to violate the Eighth Amendment.[8] In *Jordan v. Gardner*, the same court of appeals held that the search of female prisoners by male officers did violate the Eighth Amendment clause prohibiting "cruel and unusual punishment."[9] In *Gardner*, the court noted that the frequency and scope of the searches were more invasive than those in the *Grummet* case. In addition, in *Gardner*, there was evidence that some of the female prisoners had a long history of sexual abuse by men and that they suffered severe distress by the cross-gender clothed body search.

STRIP SEARCHES

Strip searches of inmates have given the courts problems. The Court has used the test of reasonableness by balancing the need for the particular search against the invasion of the personal rights that the search entails. Under this reasonableness test, the courts must consider the scope of the particular intrusion, the manner in which it was conducted, the justification for initiating it and the place in which it was conducted. The Court noted that not all strip search procedures will be reasonable; some could be excessive, vindictive, harassing, or unrelated to any legitimate penological interests.[10] They are generally approved if the strip search was accomplished for a legitimate institutional purpose and in a reasonable manner. *Legitimate institutional purposes* include strip searching inmates following any exposure to the opportunity to obtain contraband, or when inmates are returned to segregation cells.[11] For example, *Michenfeder v. Sumner* upheld the practice of body cavity searches after contact visits as a means of preventing prisoners' possession of weapons and contraband, even absent of probable cause.[12] The court of appeals also stated that the prisoner bears the burden of showing that prison officials intentionally used exaggerated or excessive means to enforce security during a strip search. In addition, the court approved strip searches held in view of other prisoners by stating that having the searches in an entirely separate area would potentially allow prisoners to discard contraband on the way to the separate area.

URINE AND BLOOD TESTS

The Supreme Court has determined that a compelled urinalysis or blood test constitutes a search or seizure within the meaning of the Fourth Amendment. If prison officials have a reasonable suspicion of drug use, they may compel a urinalysis or blood test. The problem situations are those in which the institution officials have no reason to suspect that the prisoner or prisoners are involved in illegal drug use. However, the courts have accorded prison administrators wide-ranging deference in the adoption and execution of policies and practices that in their judgment are needed to preserve internal order and discipline and to maintain institutional security. Many courts have adopted a balancing test in response to challenges to random urinalysis and have concluded that, upon a determination that the procedures for selecting the inmates to be tested are "truly random," such testing is not unreasonable.[13] The requirement of random tests stems from a concern that correctional officials could harass particular inmates by subjecting them to repeated drug tests. One court has noted that where large numbers of prisoners were required to give urinalyses, the danger of a prison harassing particular prisoners is "illusory."[14] The use of K-9 dogs to give alerts and then using the alerts to select which inmates' cells to search and which inmates to test was upheld in the *Jordan* case. In *Jordan*, the drug test was given in a bathroom where the prisoner and the official were the only people present. The floor was damp and the prisoner did not have shoes on. The correctional official stood within eight inches of the prisoner and watched the prisoner urinate into a small plastic bottle. The court of appeals held that this procedure was reasonable to safeguard the integrity of the test and to maintain control over the prisoner. In another case, the selection of all prisoners in one barracks to test was not a violation of the Fourth Amendment.

SEARCH OF VISITORS

May prison officials search visitors? The general rule is that visits may be conditioned on the requirement that visitors submit to reasonable searches of their persons and property. Body cavity and strip searches are an exception to this general rule. The courts have stated that a citizen's right to unfettered visitation of a prisoner does not rise to constitutional dimension. In seeking entry to such a controlled environment, the visitor simultaneously acknowledges a lesser expectation of privacy. Accordingly, prison officials have greater leeway in conducting searches of visitors. Visitors can be subjected to some searches, such as a pat-down or metal detector sweep, merely as a condition of visitation, absent any suspicion. In these situations, the courts have attempted to balance the need for institutional security against the remaining privacy interests of visitors. However, because strip and body cavity searches are the most intrusive searches possible, courts have concluded that prison officials must have at least a reasonable suspicion that the visitor is bearing contraband before conducting a strip or body cavity search. Reasonable suspicion does not mean evidence beyond a reasonable doubt, or by clear and convincing evidence, or even by a preponderance of evidence. Reasonable suspicion is not equal to a finding of probable cause. It requires only specific objective facts upon which a prudent official, in light of his or her experience, would conclude that illicit activity might be in progress.

In *Spear v. Sowders,* prison officials believing that Spear would be bringing drugs into the prison refused to allow her to visit unless she submitted to a strip search.[15] She refused and started to leave. They refused to allow her to leave without a similar search. A female nurse conducted the strip and body cavity search with another female officer present. The officials also searched her car, which was in the prison parking lot. No contraband was found. The court of appeals held that the prison officials had reasonable suspicion to require a search prior to the visit based on information that she could be bringing drugs into the prison. The court held, however, that prison officials must allow a visitor who objects to the search a chance to abort the visit and depart and that she could be detained and searched only with probable cause. The count also held that merely by entering the facility, a person consents to a strip and body cavity search and that the person must be given the opportunity to depart.

Unanswered in the *Spear* case was the question regarding the search of her vehicle. Courts have upheld the search of an automobile parked on prison grounds if there are warning signs that all vehicles entering the premises are subject to being searched.

 CASES ON POINT

Hudson v. Palmer
468 U.S. 517 (1984)

CHIEF JUSTICE BURGER delivered the opinion of the Court.

We granted certiorari in No. 82-1630 to decide whether a prison inmate has a reasonable expectation of privacy in his prison cell entitling him to the protection of the Fourth Amendment against unreasonable searches and seizures. . . . The facts underlying this dispute are relatively simple. Respondent Palmer is an inmate at the Bland Correctional Center in Bland, Va., serving sentences for forgery, uttering, grand larceny, and bank robbery convictions. On September 16, 1981, petitioner Hudson, an officer at the Correctional Center, with a fellow officer, conducted a "shakedown" search of respondent's prison locker and cell for contraband. During the "shakedown," the officers discovered a ripped pillowcase in a trash can near respondent's cell bunk. Charges against Palmer were instituted under the prison disciplinary procedures for destroying state property. . . .

The first question we address is whether respondent has a right of privacy in his prison cell entitling him to the protection of the Fourth Amendment against unreasonable searches. . . .

We have repeatedly held that prisons are not beyond the reach of the Constitution. No "iron curtain" separates one from the other. *Wolff v. McDonnell*, 418 U.S. 539, 555 (1974). Indeed, we have insisted that prisoners be accorded those rights not fundamentally inconsistent with imprisonment itself or incompatible with the objectives of incarceration. For example, we have held that invidious racial discrimination is as intolerable within a prison as outside, except as may be essential to "prison security and discipline." *Lee v. Washington*, 390 U.S. 333 (1968). Like others, prisoners have the constitutional right to petition the Government for redress of their grievances, which includes a reasonable right of access to the courts. *Johnson v. Avery*, 393 U.S. 483 (1969).

. . .However, while persons imprisoned for crime enjoy many protections of the Constitution, it is also clear that imprisonment carries with it the circumscription or loss of many significant rights. See *Bell v. Wolfish*, 441 U.S. at 545. These constraints on inmates, and in some cases the complete withdrawal of certain rights, are "justified by the considerations underlying our penal system.". . .The curtailment of certain rights is necessary, as a practical matter, to accommodate a myriad of "institutional needs and objectives" of prison facilities . . . chief among which is internal security. . . .

. . .Our holding that respondent does not have a reasonable expectation of privacy enabling him to invoke the protections of the Fourth Amendment does not mean that he is without a remedy for calculated harassment unrelated to prison needs. Nor does it mean that prison attendants can ride roughshod over inmates' property rights with impunity. The Eighth Amendment always stands as a protection against "cruel and unusual punishments." By the same token, there are adequate state tort and common law remedies available to respondent to redress the alleged destruction of his personal property....

Case Discussion and Significance. The general rule regarding the searches of prisoners may be taken from this case. That rule is that prisoners have no reasonable expectation of privacy while confined. Accordingly, prisoners may be searched without probable cause or reasonable suspicion. Do you agree with the rule that the Fourth Amendment prohibition against "unreasonable searches" does not apply in a prison cell? Why not simply decide that random searches of prison cells are not "unreasonable" and therefore not in violation of the Fourth Amendment? Although the above case deals with prisoners who have been convicted of a crime and are presently serving sentence in a correctional institution, the courts have followed similar guidelines for cases involving persons being held in jail prior to trial, such as the *Edwards* case set forth below.

UNITED STATES v. EDWARDS
415 U.S. 800 (1974)

MR. JUSTICE WHITE delivered the opinion of the Court.

The question here is whether the Fourth Amendment should be extended to exclude from evidence certain clothing taken from respondent Edwards while he was in custody at the city jail approximately 10 hours after his arrest.

Shortly after 11 p.m. on May 31, 1970, respondent Edwards was lawfully arrested on the streets of Lebanon, Ohio, and charged with attempting to break into that city's Post Office. He was taken to the local jail and placed in a cell. Contemporaneously or shortly thereafter, investigation at the scene revealed that the attempted entry had been made through a wooden window which apparently had been pried up with a pry bar, leaving paint chips on the window sill and wire mesh screen. The next morning, trousers and a T-shirt were purchased for Edwards to substitute for the clothing which he had been wearing at the time of and since his arrest. His clothing was then taken from him and held as evidence. Examination of the clothing revealed paint chips matching the samples that had been taken from the window. This evidence and his clothing were received at trial over Edwards' objection that neither the clothing nor the results of its examination were admissible because the warrantless seizure of his clothing was invalid under the Fourth Amendment.

The prevailing rule under the Fourth Amendment that searches and seizures may not be made without a warrant is subject to various exceptions. One of them permits warrantless searches incident to custodial arrests... and has traditionally been justified by the reasonableness of searching for weapons, instruments of escape, and evidence of crime when a person is taken into official custody and lawfully detained....

It is also plain that searches and seizures that could be made on the spot at the time of arrest may legally be conducted later when the accused arrives at the place of detention. If need be, *Abel v. United States*, 362 U.S. 217 (1960), settled this question. There the defendant was arrested at his hotel, but the belongings taken with him to the place of detention were searched there. In sustaining the search, the Court noted that a valid search of the property could have been made at the place of arrest and perceived little difference "when the accused decides to take the property with him, for the search of it to occur instead at the first place of detention when the accused arrives there, especially as the search of property carried by an accused to the place of detention has additional justifications, similar to those which justify a search of the person of one who is arrested."

. . .[The courts have] long since concluded that once the accused is lawfully arrested and is in custody, the effects in his possession at the place of detention that were subject to search at the time and place of his arrest may lawfully be searched and seized without a warrant even though a substantial period of time has elapsed between the arrest and subsequent administrative processing, on the one hand, and the taking of the property for use as evidence, on the other. This is true where the clothing or effects are immediately seized upon arrival at the jail, held under the defendant's name in the "property room" of the jail, and at a later time searched and taken for use at the subsequent criminal trial.

In upholding this search and seizure, we do not conclude that the Warrant Clause of the Fourth Amendment is never applicable to post-arrest seizures of the effects of an arrestee. . .

The judgment of the Court of Appeals is reversed.
So ordered.

Case Discussion and Significance. What did the Court mean in *Edwards* by the statement, "We do not conclude that the Warrant Clause of the Fourth Amendment is never applicable to post-arrest seizures of the effects of an arrestee"? Would the Court have decided differently if "suitable clothes" had been available when he was first arrested?

CASE SUMMARIES

Strip searches of inmates following contact with visitors did not violate their rights; occasional alleged "degrading" remarks by officers conducting the search and the presence of other prisoners also being searched did not alter the result. *Fernandez v. Rapone*, 926 F. Supp. 255 (D. Mass. 1996).

A roadblock stop of car entering correctional facility, sniffing of vehicle and occupants by narcotics-detecting dog, and strip search of female visitor to whom dog alerted were all reasonable, federal appeals court rules. *Romo v. Champion*, 46 F.3d 1013 (10th Cir. 1995).

A "brief" presence of female correctional officer during strip search of male prisoner being transferred because of information about impending prisoner disturbance did not violate prisoner's privacy rights; decision to strip search him again before placing him in segregation at receiving facility was not unreasonable; transfer and segregation were justified by belief that he was an "instigator" of feared disturbance. *Jones v. Harrison*, 864 F. Supp. 166 (D. Kan. 1994).

Strip searches of male inmate being placed in temporary administrative segregation was not unconstitutional, nor did presence of female officer or alleged racial/sexual remark constitute rights violations. *Merritt-Bey v. Salts*, 747 F. supp. 536 (E.D. Mo. 1990).

An administrative directive providing that cells should be searched prior to placing new occupants in them did not give inmates a constitutionally protected liberty interest in having such searches conducted; inmates were properly found guilty of possession of contraband even though their cells were not searched prior to them being placed in them. *Lasley v. Godinez*, 833 F. Supp. 714 (N.D. Ill. 1993).

Routine random warrantless search of cell, without probable cause or particularized suspicion, did not violate Vermont State Constitution. *State v. Berard*, 576 A.2d 118 (Vt. 1990).

A statute requiring prisons to take and store blood of convicted felons for DNA analysis does not violate the Fourth Amendment or any legitimate expectation of privacy rights. *Jones v. Murray*, 763 F. Supp. 842 (W.D. Va. 1991).

Visual body cavity searches of prisoners before and after contact visits were reasonable regardless of whether there was probable cause, when conducted to prevent possession of weapons and contraband; possible violation of Wisconsin prison regulation in conducting search was not a violation of constitutional rights. *Zunker v. Bertrand*, 798 F. Supp. 1365 (E.D. Wis. 1992).

SUMMARY

- The rights of prisoners against searches and seizures are drastically less than those enjoyed by persons outside of institutions.
- The U.S. Supreme Court defines a search as a government intrusion into an area in which a person has a reasonable expectation of privacy.
- A search conducted in a manner that destroys the inmate's property may lead to liability on the part of the officer conducting the search.
- Randomly held pat-down searches are generally upheld by the courts. If, however, the pat-down searches are being done to harass individual inmates and not for

legitimate institutional purposes, the courts have, on several occasions, held them to be unreasonable.

- In several cases, the courts have criticized cross-gender (male-female) pat-down searches.
- May prison officials search visitors? The general rule is that visits may be conditioned on the requirement that visitors submit to reasonable searches of their persons and property. An exception to this general rule is body cavity or strip searches.

DISCUSSION QUESTIONS

1. What Fourth Amendment rights do prisoners retain while confined?
2. If prisoners have no reasonable expectation of privacy in their prison cells, under what circumstances could cell searches be considered as a violation of their constitutional rights?
3. Under what circumstances may a visitor be searched?
4. What is necessary before an inmate may be required to submit to a body cavity search?

ENDNOTES

1. *Wolf v. McDonnell*, 418 U.S. 539 (1974).
2. *Katz v. United States*, 389 U.S. 347 (1967).
3. 104 S.Ct.3194 (1984).
4. *Brown v. Hilton,* 492 F. Supp. 771 (D N.J.1980).
5. 104 S.Ct. 3227 (1984).
6. *Marrero v. Commonwealth*, 222 Va. 754 (1981).
7. *Jordan v. Gardner*, 986 F.2d 1521 (9th Cir. 1993).
8. 779 F.2d. 491 (9th Cir., 1985).
9. 986 F.2d. 1521 (9th Cir. 1993).
10. *Thompson v. Souza*, No. 96-55662 (9th Cir. 1997).
11. *Goff v. Nixon*, 803 F.2d. 358 (8th Cir. 1986).
12. 860 F.2d. 328 (9th Cir. 1988).
13. *Spence v. Farrier*, 807 F.2d 753 (8th Cir. 1986).
14. *Forbes v. Trigg*, 976 F.2d. 308 (7th Cir. 1992).
15. 1995 FED app. 0366P (6th. Cir.1995).

CHAPTER 8

THE EIGHTH AMENDMENT: CRUEL AND UNUSUAL PUNISHMENT

> *Excessive bail shall not be required, nor excessive fines imposed, nor cruel and unusual punishments inflicted.*
>
> U.S. Constitution, Amendment VIII

> *Those who are to execute the laws of the Union... If they have power to execute their laws in this manner, in what situation are we placed? Your men who go to Congress are not restrained by a bill of rights. They are not restrained from inflicting unusual and severe punishments, though the bill of rights of Virginia forbids it.*
>
> Statement of Delegate Wythe of Virginia during the debates at the Several States Convention on the Adoption of the Federal Constitution,
> June 16, 1788

INTRODUCTION

The quotations above are the complete text of the Eighth Amendment and the comment of Delegate Wythe regarding the amendment. The language of direct concern to corrections is the phrase "nor cruel and unusual punishment inflicted" of the Eighth Amendment. For the amendment to apply, a punishment must be involved. What constitutes punishment? According to one court, "any treatment to which a prisoner is exposed is a form of punishment."[1] In Chapter 9, we will discuss the issue of use of force against an inmate. In Chapter 7, we noted that one court has held that the cross-gender search of a prisoner may violate the cruel and unusual clause. In this chapter, we will look at the other aspects of the protection against cruel and unusual punishment.

DISPROPORTIONATE PUNISHMENT

In non-capital cases, the cruel and unusual punishment claims are generally founded on the alleged gross disproportionality of the penalty to the severity of the crime. The U.S. Supreme Court has used the "cruel and unusual" phrase to evaluate the sentencing process and the manner in which the sentence is carried out. In evaluating sentences, the Court in *Trop v. Dulles* held that a court-martial sentence for desertion during wartime was cruel and unusual when the sentence included the loss of nationality.[2] In another case, the Court also held that a sentence of 12 to 20 years at hard labor, in chains to be worn during the entire service and the perpetual loss of civil rights, as cruel and unusual punishment for being an accessory to falsification of a government document.[3] The Court in that case stated that a sentence was cruel and unusual if it is greatly disproportionate to the offense for which it was imposed, or if it goes far beyond what is necessary to achieve a sentencing aim, even if the aim is justified. However, the Court has demonstrated a reluctance to hold sentences cruel and unusual because they are grossly disproportional punishments, except in death penalty cases.

The Supreme Court stated that three factors should be examined in conducting a proportionality review:

➢ The gravity of the offense and the harshness of the penalty.

➢ The sentences imposed on other criminals in the same jurisdiction.

> The sentences imposed for commission of the same crime in other jurisdictions.

MANDATORY SENTENCES AS CRUEL AND UNUSUAL PUNISHMENT

In *United States v. Kratsas*, the defendant was sentenced to mandatory life imprisonment for distributing more than 5 kilograms of cocaine. He appealed, stating that a life sentence was disproportionate to the offense. The Court, in noting that he had two prior convictions, concluded that mandatory penalties may be cruel, but they are not unusual in the constitutional sense, having been employed in various forms throughout our nation's history. The Court also stated that a sentence that is not otherwise cruel and unusual does not become so simply because it is mandatory.

In *Solem v. Helm,* the U.S. Supreme Court held that a South Dakota statute that imposed a mandatory life imprisonment sentence without parole on the third conviction of a nonviolent felony was cruel and unusual.[4] In this case, the defendant was convicted of attempting to cash a "no account" check for $100 dollars. The Court stated that life imprisonment without possibility of parole was an extremely severe punishment for a bad check offense and that life imprisonment is generally imposed for much more heinous offenses such as manslaughter, treason, arson, or kidnapping. The Court noted that sentences imposed in other jurisdictions for commission of the same crime are much less severe than life incarceration.

DEATH PENALTY AS CRUEL AND UNUSUAL PUNISHMENT

Few areas in corrections have prompted as much debate as the death penalty. Is the death penalty constitutional, and, if so, under what circumstances? The follow-up question is, Assuming that the death penalty is constitutional, should a civilized society ever resort to the execution of a person? The U.S. Supreme Court has held that the death penalty is not inherently cruel and unusual, and may, pursuant to proper procedure, be imposed upon a defendant. The procedure used must be adequate to assure evenhanded determinations of whether the penalty is appropriate in each case. Presently, 35 states authorize the death penalty for murder under special circumstances.

In the 1972 case of *Furman v. Georgia*, the Court had held that the death penalty statutes presently being used provided for arbitrary use of the death penalty, and thus the punishment was cruel and unusual.[5] However, in 1976 the Court upheld the Georgia death penalty statute that provided that a death sentence may be imposed only if one of ten statutory aggravating circumstances is found by the jury to exist beyond a reasonable doubt.[6] The use of aggravating factors is an attempt to reduce arbitrariness and discrimination by requiring that one of a series of factors be present before the death penalty may be imposed. Some states have attempted to reduce the arbitrariness and discrimination by making the death penalty mandatory for certain crimes. Generally, the mandatory schemes in capital cases have been held unconstitutional by the Court. The Court opined that because the jury may make an unguided decision about whether to convict or acquit, the decision is potentially discriminatory, based on whether the jury desires the imposition of the death penalty.

The Electric Chair

In re Kimmler, 136 U.S. 443 [1890]

[This case was filed by the defendant to prevent the use of the electric chair. From the court's opinion.]...We have examined this testimony, and can find but little in it to warrant the belief that this new mode of execution is cruel, within the meaning of the Constitution, though it is certainly unusual. On the contrary, we agree with the court below that it removes every reasonable doubt that the application of electricity to the vital parts of the human body, under such conditions and in the manner contemplated by the statute, must result in instantaneous, and consequently in painless, death.

President Nixon's Comments on the *Furman v. Georgia* Decision

[Public Papers of the Presidents, Nixon, 1972, p.714 - p.715]

Q. Mr. President, do you regard capital punishment as cruel and unusual, and do you think steps should be taken to reinstate it?

THE PRESIDENT. I was expecting that question tonight, but as you know, the Court just handed down its decision and I immediately got hold of Mr. Dean, Counsel to the President, and I said, "Send it over to me." He said, "There are nine opinions."

Now I try to read fast, but I couldn't get through all nine opinions. But I did get through the Chief Justice's. As I understand it, the holding of the Court must not be taken at this time to rule out capital punishment in all kinds of crimes. This has dealt apparently with crimes at the State level and will apply to 35 States in which we do have the situation where capital punishment does apply.

It is my view that as far as cruel and inhuman punishment is concerned, any punishment is cruel and inhuman which takes the life of a man, or woman, for that matter. . . .

I have expressed my views and I will also say, of course, that we will carry out whatever the Court finally determines to be the law of the land. But I would hope that the Court's decision does not go so far as to rule out capital punishment for kidnaping and hijacking.

According to a 1998 study, it costs an average of $365,000 per case to prosecute a death penalty case and approximately $218,112 to defend one. This was up 15 percent from 1994. The average cost to prosecute a murder case not involving the death penalty is approximately $55,772.[7]

Medicate to Execute

Is it constitutional to execute an insane person? In *Ford v. Wainwright*, the Supreme Court decided that executing an insane person would constitute cruel and unusual punishment.[8] The Court noted that the death penalty can not serve its retributive aim when the individual being executed is so mentally deranged that he or she cannot understand why they are being killed. In addition, the Court acknowledged the religious roots of the opposition to the execution of the insane—the belief that people should have a chance to ask God to forgive them for their sins before they are executed.

Consider the case of Michael Owen Perry. He is on death row in the state of Louisiana, and he will probably never be executed. Perry was convicted of killing five members of his family on July 17, 1983. Apparently, Perry went to his grandmother's house and calmly blew the heads off of his two sleeping cousins. He then walked across the backyard to his parents' home, where he killed his mother and two other people. He was found guilty of capital murder and sentenced to death. At his trial, the issue of insanity was never raised.

While on death row, he was found to be insane. The U.S. Supreme Court ruled that the state could not execute him until he regained his sanity and he could therefore understand the nature and gravity of his punishment. In addition, the Louisiana Supreme Court ruled that the statue could not forcibly medicate him in order to assist him in regaining his sanity for the purpose of executing him.

Points to Consider

1. Should it be cruel and unusual punishment, and thus a constitutional violation, to execute a person who does not understand the nature and gravity of his punishment?

2. Does it make sense to wait until an individual is sane before we execute him?
3. What difference does it make if he understands the nature and gravity of the punishment if he is going to die immediately?

Minimum Age for Capital Punishment

Does the imposition of capital punishment on an individual for a crime committed at 16 years of age constitute cruel and unusual punishment? The Supreme Court looked at this issue in *Stanford v. Kentucky*.[9] The Court stated that whether a particular punishment violates the Eighth Amendment depends on whether it constitutes one of those acts of punishment considered cruel and unusual at the time that the Bill of Rights was adopted or is contrary to the evolving standards of decency that mark the progress of a maturing society. The Court then noted that the petitioner has not alleged that the sentence would have been considered cruel and unusual in the eighteenth century and that at least 281 offenders under the age of 18, and 126 under the age of 17, have been executed in this country. The Court then looked at whether the penalty violated the evolving standards of decency. In determining this issue, the Court noted that of the 37 states that permit capital punishment, 15 decline to impose it on 16 year olds and 12 on 17 year olds. The Court held that it was not cruel and unusual to impose the death penalty on individual who was over the age of 16 at the time the crime was committed.

In *Thompson v. Oklahoma*, a plurality of the Court reversed the death penalty in a case in which the offender was 15 years old at the time of the murder.[10] Four justices stated that the death penalty for 15 year olds violated societal standards of decency, because no state that specified the age below which the death penalty could not be imposed authorized the death penalty for defendants who were that young at the time they committed their crimes. The death penalty was overturned in *Thompson*, because Justice O'Connor, who was the fifth vote, wrote a concurring opinion and her ruling was not clear in this regard.

Accordingly, the issue of whether the death penalty is always unconstitutional when imposed on a defendant who was 15 years of age or younger at the time the crime was committed is still in doubt.

The Supreme Court has treated mental age of the defendant somewhat differently than the chronological age. The mental age of the defendant is only one factor that could, and should, be considered in deciding whether the imposition of the death penalty is warranted in a particular case. For example, in the case of *Penry v. Lynaugh*, the Supreme Court looked at the issue of mental age.[11] A psychologist testified that Penry was moderately retarded and had a mental age of a 6½-year-old child. The Court, in holding that a person of low mental intelligence may be executed, returned the case to the Texas courts with the instructions that the jury should be instructed to consider the mitigating evidence of mental retardation and abused background to ensure that the punishment is directly related to the defendant's personal culpability, and that a person with emotional or mental problems may be less culpable than one who has no such excuse.

Delay in Imposition of Death Penalty

Is it cruel and unusual punishment to delay the execution of a person on death row? The U.S. Court of Appeals for the Ninth Circuit looked at this issue in the case of *McKenzie v. Day*.[12] McKenzie had been on death row in Montana for approximately 20 years. He argued that to execute him after the great delay would be cruel and unusual. The appeals court noted that although the defendant should not be penalized for pursuing his constitutional rights, he should not be able to benefit from the ultimately unsuccessful pursuit of those rights, and that it would be a mockery of justice if the delay incurred because of his appeals had accrued into a substantive claim to the very relief that he sought.

PUNISHMENT IMPOSED BECAUSE OF A PERSON'S STATUS

Is it cruel and unusual punishment for a state to make it a crime for a person to be addicted to drugs? To alcohol? This issue was discussed in *Robinson v. California*.[13] A California statute makes it a criminal offense for a person to be addicted to the use of narcotics. The Court noted that the authority of a state to exercise its police power to regulate the administration, sale, prescription and use of dangerous and habit-forming drugs was not questioned, and that it was unnecessary to discuss this firmly established point. It was clear that California could punish Robinson for the illegal use of drugs within the state. In this case, however, he was being punished because of his status or chronic condition of being addicted to the use of drugs. A statute that makes the status of a person a criminal offense is cruel and unusual. The Court noted that the punishment in this case was only 90-days confinement and that 90 days is not, in the abstract, a punishment that is either cruel or unusual. But the punishment can not be considered in the abstract. Even one day in prison would be cruel and unusual punishment for a "crime" of having a common cold.

MEDICAL TREATMENT

Is it cruel and unusual to refuse to provide medical treatment to an inmate? The Supreme Court looked at this issue in *Estelle v. Gamble*.[14] Gamble, an inmate in a Texas prison, sued the director of the Texas Department of Corrections in a civil suit complaining that the failure to provide medical treatment for a back injury he suffered in prison constituted a violation of the Eighth Amendment. Medical personnel saw Gamble on 17 occasions during a 3-month span and treated his injury and other problems. They did not perform an X-ray or use additional diagnostic techniques. The Court held that while the level of treatment may constitute, at most, medical malpractice cognizable in the state courts, it did not constitute cruel and unusual punishment under the Eighth Amendment. The Court held that deliberate indifference by prison personnel to a prisoner's serious illness or injury would constitute cruel and unusual punishment contravening the Eighth Amendment. The Court, however, concluded that Gamble's claims do not suggest such indifference.

 CASES ON POINT

Gregg v. Georgia
428 U.S. 153 (1976)

[Judgment of the Court, and opinion of Justices STEWART, POWELL, and STEVENS were announced by Justice STEWART. Chief Justice BURGER and Justice REHNQUIST filed a statement concurring in the judgment. Justice WHITE filed an opinion concurring in the judgment, in which Chief Justice BURGER and Justice REHNQUIST also joined. Justice BLACKMUN filed a statement concurring in the judgment. Justices BRENNAN and MARSHALL filed dissenting opinions. The excerpts are from the opinion of Stewart only.]

The issue in this case is whether the imposition of the sentence of death for the crime of murder under the law of Georgia violates the Eighth and Fourteenth Amendments.

Troy Gregg was charged with committing armed robbery and murder. In accordance with Georgia procedure in capital cases, the trial was in two stages, a guilt stage and a sentencing stage.... The trial judge submitted the murder charges to the jury on both felony murder and nonfelony murder theories. He also instructed on the issue of self-defense, but declined to instruct on manslaughter. He submitted the robbery case to the jury on both an armed robbery theory and on the lesser-included offense of robbery by intimidation. The jury found the petitioner guilty of two counts of armed robbery and two counts of murder.

At the penalty stage, which took place before the same jury, neither the prosecutor nor the petitioner's lawyer offered any additional evidence. Both counsel, however, made lengthy arguments dealing generally with the propriety of capital punishment under the circumstances and with the weight of the evidence of guilt. The trial judge instructed the jury that it could recommend either a death sentence or a life prison sentence on each count. The judge further charged the jury that, in determining what sentence was appropriate, the jury was free to consider the facts and circumstances, if any, presented by the parties in mitigation or aggravation.

Finally, the judge instructed the jury that it "would not be authorized to consider the penalty of death" unless it first found beyond a reasonable doubt one of these aggravating circumstances:

One—That the offense of murder was committed while the offender was engaged in the commission of two other capital felonies, to-wit the armed robbery....
Two—That the offender committed the offense of murder for the purpose of receiving money and the automobile described in the indictment.
Three—The offense of murder was outrageously and wantonly vile, horrible and inhuman, in that they involved the depravity of the mind of the defendant.

Finding the first and second of these circumstances, the jury returned verdicts of death on each count. The Supreme Court of Georgia affirmed the convictions and the imposition of the death sentences for murder.... After reviewing the trial transcript and the record, including the evidence, and comparing the evidence and sentence in similar cases in accordance with the requirements of Georgia law, the court concluded that, considering the nature of the crime and the defendant, the sentences of death had not resulted from prejudice or any other arbitrary factor and were not excessive or disproportionate to the penalty applied in similar cases. The death sentences imposed for armed robbery, however, were vacated on the grounds that the death penalty had rarely been imposed in Georgia for that offense, and that the jury improperly considered the murders as aggravating circumstances for the robberies after having considered the armed robberies as aggravating circumstances for the murders. We granted the petitioner's application for a writ of certiorari limited to his challenge to the imposition of the death sentences in this case as "cruel and unusual" punishment in violation of the Eighth and the Fourteenth Amendments.

...We address initially the basic contention that the punishment of death for the crime of murder is, under all circumstances, "cruel and unusual" in violation of the Eighth and Fourteenth Amendments of the Constitution....

The Court on a number of occasions has both assumed and asserted the constitutionality of capital punishment. In several cases that assumption provided a necessary foundation for the decision, as the Court was asked to decide whether a particular method of carrying out a capital sentence would be allowed to stand under the Eighth Amendment. But until *Furman v. Georgia*, 408 U.S. 238 (1972), the Court never confronted squarely the fundamental claim that the punishment of death always, regardless of the enormity of the offense or the procedure followed in imposing the sentence, is cruel and unusual punishment in violation of the Constitution. Although this issue was presented and addressed in Furman, it was not resolved by the Court. Four Justices would have held that capital punishment is not unconstitutional per se; two Justices would have reached the opposite conclusion; and three Justices, while agreeing that the statutes then before the Court were invalid as applied, left open the question whether such punishment may ever be imposed. We now hold that the punishment of death does not invariably violate the Constitution.

The history of the prohibition of "cruel and unusual" punishment already has been reviewed at length. The phrase first appeared in the English Bill of Rights of 1689, which was drafted by Parliament at the accession of William and Mary. [See Granucci, "Nor Cruel and Unusual Punishments Inflicted: The Original Meaning," 57 *Calif. L. Rev.* 839, 852-853 (1969)]. The English version appears to have been directed against punishments unauthorized by statute and beyond the jurisdiction of the sentencing court, as well as those disproportionate to the offense involved. Id., at 860. The American draftsmen, who adopted the English phrasing in drafting the Eighth Amendment, were primarily concerned, however, with proscribing "tortures" and other "barbarous" methods of punishment." *Id.*, at 842.

In the earliest cases raising Eighth Amendment claims, the Court focused on particular methods of execution to determine whether they were too cruel to pass constitutional muster. The constitutionality of the sentence of death itself was not at issue, and the criterion used to evaluate the mode of execution was its similarity to "torture" and other "barbarous" methods. See *Wilkerson v. Utah*, 99 U.S. 130, 136 (1879) ("[I]t is safe to affirm that punishments of torture . . . and all others in the same line of unnecessary cruelty, are forbidden by that amendment . . ."); *In re Kemmler*, 136 U.S. 436, 447 (1890) ("Punishments are cruel when they involve torture or a lingering death . . ."). See also Louisiana ex rel. *Francis v. Resweber*, 329 U.S. 459, 464 (1947) (second attempt at electrocution found not to violate Eighth Amendment, since failure of initial execution attempt was "an unforeseeable accident" and "[t]here [was] no purpose to inflict unnecessary pain nor any unnecessary pain involved in the proposed execution").

But the Court has not confined the prohibition embodied in the Eighth Amendment to "barbarous" methods that were generally outlawed in the 18th century. Instead, the Amendment has been interpreted in a flexible and dynamic manner. The Court early recognized that "a principle to be vital must be capable of wider application than the mischief which gave it birth." *Weems v. United States*, 217 U.S. 349, 373 (1910). Thus the Clause forbidding "cruel and unusual" punishments "is not fastened to the obsolete but may acquire meaning as public opinion becomes enlightened by a humane justice." *Id.*, at 378. See also *Furman v. Georgia*, 408 U.S., at 429-430 (POWELL, J., dissenting); *Trop v. Dulles*, 356 U.S. 86, 100-101 (1958) (plurality opinion).

. . .Of course, the requirements of the Eighth Amendment must be applied with an awareness of the limited role to be played by the courts. This does not mean that judges have no role to play, for the Eighth Amendment is a restraint upon the exercise of legislative power.

"Judicial review, by definition, often involves a conflict between judicial and legislative judgment as to what the Constitution means or requires. In this respect, Eighth Amendment cases come to us in no different posture. It seems conceded by all that the Amendment imposes some obligations on the judiciary to judge the constitutionality of punishment and that there are punishments that the Amendment would bar whether legislatively approved or not." *Furman v. Georgia,* 408 U.S., at 313-314.

Case Discussion and Significance. The U.S. Supreme Court in *Gregg v. Georgia* held that the death penalty was not cruel and unusual when used under the Georgia statute. Look at the Court's discussion of the Louisiana ex rel. *Francis v. Resweber* case. Does the discussion mean that a punishment is within the prohibition of cruel and unusual only when there was a "purpose to inflict unnecessary pain?"

Edmund v. Florida
458 U.S. 782 (1982)

The petitioner and a codefendant, at a jury trial in a Florida court, were convicted of first-degree murder and robbery of two elderly persons at their farmhouse, and were sentenced to death. The Florida Supreme Court affirmed. The petitioner challenged the death sentence on the grounds that he did not himself kill and was not present at the killings, and there was no evidence on whether he intended that the victims be killed or anticipated that lethal force might be used to effectuate the robbery or escape. The U.S. Supreme Court held that the imposition of the death penalty upon petitioner in this case was inconsistent with the Eighth and Fourteenth Amendments.

The Court noted that only a small minority of states—eight—allow the death penalty to be imposed solely because the defendant somehow participated in the robbery in the course of which a murder was committed, but did not take or attempt or intend to take life, or intend that lethal force be employed. The evidence is overwhelming that American juries have repudiated imposition of the death penalty for crimes such as petitioner's, the statistics demonstrating that juries—and perhaps prosecutors—consider death a disproportionate penalty for those who fall within petitioner's category.

The Court stated that although robbery is a serious crime deserving serious punishment, it is not a crime "so grievous an affront to humanity that the only adequate response may be the penalty of death." The death penalty, which is "unique in its severity and irrevocability," is an excessive penalty for the robber, who, as such, does not take human life. Here, the focus must be on petitioner's culpability, not on those who committed the robbery and killings. He did not kill or intend to kill, and thus his culpability is different from that of the robbers who killed, and it is impermissible for the state to treat all the parties involved alike and attribute to petitioner the culpability of those who killed the victims. The Court also stated that neither deterrence of capital crimes nor retribution is a sufficient justification for executing petitioner. It is unlikely that the threat of the death penalty for murder will measurably deter one, such as petitioner, who does not kill or intend to kill. As to retribution, this depends on the degree of petitioner's culpability, which must be limited to his participation in the robbery. Putting him to death to avenge two killings that he did not commit or intend to commit or cause would not measurably contribute to the retribution end of ensuring that the criminal gets his just deserts.

Case Discussion and Significance. In the case of *Edmund v. Florida*, the Court examined whether or not the death penalty was cruel and unusual for a defendant who was an aider and an abettor in robbery in which a person is killed. Do you agree with the Court's rationale in this case that the death penalty is an excessive penalty for the robber who did not do the actual killing, and when there was no plot to commit a murder? If, as stated by the Court, neither deterrence of capital threat of the death penalty nor retribution is a sufficient justification for executing the defendant in this case, what would be sufficient justification in any case for executing a defendant? In the above case, an innocent victim was killed. The Court, however, indicated that executing the defendant, an individual who participated in the robbery, "would not measurably contribute to . . .ensuring that the criminal gets his just deserts." Do you agree with the Court on this conclusion? What does the Court mean by "ensuring that the criminal gets his just deserts?"

Wilson v. Seiter
501 U.S. 294 (1991)

The petitioner Wilson, an Ohio prison inmate, filed suit under 42 U.S.C. § 1983 against the respondents, state prison officials, alleging that certain conditions of his confinement constituted cruel and unusual punishment in violation of the Eighth and Fourteenth Amendments. His affidavits described the challenged conditions and charged that the authorities, after notification, had failed to take remedial action.

The U.S. Supreme Court held that a prisoner claiming that the conditions of his confinement violate the Eighth Amendment must show a culpable state of mind on the part of prison officials. . . . An intent requirement is implicit in that Amendment's ban on cruel and unusual punishment. . . . The "deliberate indifference" standard applied in *Estelle v. Gamble,* 429 U.S. 97, to claims involving medical care applies generally to prisoner challenges to conditions of confinement. There is no merit to respondents' contention that that standard should be applied only in cases involving personal, physical injury, and that a malice standard is appropriate in cases challenging conditions. . . .The "wantonness" of conduct depends not on its effect on the prisoner, but on the constraints facing the official.

Case Significance and Discussion. In this case, the U.S. Supreme Court held that a prisoner claiming that the conditions of his confinement violate the Eighth Amendment must show a culpable state of mind on the part of prison officials and that the intent requirement is implicit in that Amendment's ban on cruel and unusual punishment.

Helling v. McKinney
509 U.S. 25 (1993)

The respondent McKinney, a Nevada state prisoner, filed suit against petitioner prison officials, claiming that his involuntary exposure to environmental tobacco smoke (ETS) from his cellmate's and other inmates' cigarettes posed an unreasonable risk to his health, thus subjecting him to cruel and unusual punishment in violation of the Eighth Amendment. A federal magistrate granted petitioners' motion for a directed verdict, but the Court of Appeals reversed in part, holding that McKinney should have been permitted to prove that his ETS exposure was sufficient to constitute an unreasonable danger to his future health.

The U.S. Supreme Court held that it was not improper for the Court of Appeals to decide the question whether McKinney's claim could be based on possible future effects of ETS. From its examination of the record, the court was apparently of the view that the claimed entitlement to a smoke-free environment subsumed the claim that ETS exposure could endanger one's future, not just current, health. By alleging that petitioners have, with deliberate indifference, exposed him to ETS levels that pose an unreasonable risk to his future health, McKinney has stated an Eighth Amendment claim on which relief could be granted. An injunction cannot be denied to inmates who plainly prove an unsafe, life-threatening condition on the ground that nothing yet has happened to them. . . .

On remand, the District Court must give McKinney the opportunity to prove his allegations, which will require that he establish both the subjective and objective elements necessary to prove an Eighth Amendment violation. With respect to the objective factor, he may have difficulty showing that he is being exposed to unreasonably high ETS levels, since he has been moved to a new prison and no longer has a cellmate who smokes, and since a new state prison policy restricts smoking to certain areas and makes reasonable efforts to respect nonsmokers' wishes with regard to double bunking. He must also show that the risk of which he complains is not one that today's society chooses to tolerate. The subjective factor, deliberate indifference, should be determined in light of the prison authorities' current attitudes and conduct, which, as evidenced by the new smoking policy, may have changed considerably since the Court of Appeals' judgment. The inquiry into this factor also would be an appropriate vehicle to consider arguments regarding the realities of prison administration. . . .affirmed and remanded.

Case Significance and Discussion. The Supreme Court held that the District Court must give McKinney the opportunity to prove his allegations, which will require that he establish both the subjective and objective elements necessary to prove an Eighth Amendment violation. What are the subjective and objective elements involved in an Eighth Amendment violation?

CASE SUMMARIES

A doctor's removal of prisoner's toenail without anesthetic did not constitute cruel and unusual punishment. *Snipes v. Detella*, 95 F.3d 586 (7th Cir. 1996).

Prison officials could not be held liable for deliberate indifference to prisoner's serious medical needs if they were not sufficiently informed of the circumstances as to require them to intervene. *Vance v. Peters*, 97 F.3d 987 (7th Cir. 1996).

An inmate's disagreement with medical treatment provided at prison, and belief that medication previously prescribed by a prior physician would be more appropriate, did not show violation of Eighth Amendment; prison officials supplied medications recommended by doctor and approved of by psychiatrist. *Vaughan v. Lacey*, 49 F.3d 1344 (8th Cir. 1995).

Mere one-time failure to review medical records during treatment of prisoner did not constitute deliberate indifference to serious medical problems. *Sanderfer v. Nichols*, 62 F.3d 151 (6th Cir. 1995).

Housing of protective custody inmates and inmates with mental health problems with punitive segregation inmates violated Eighth Amendment. *Inmates of Occoquan v. Barry*, 717 F. Supp. 854 (D.D.C. 1989).

Alleged denial of "adequate exercise" during three days in jail did not state constitutional claim. *Brown v. Copeland*, 780 S.W. 2d 68 (Mo. App. 1989).

Use of "food loaf" as punishment did not require prior hearing; but "food loaf" punishment cannot continue after charges are dismissed. *U.S. v. State of Michigan*, 680 F.Supp. 270 (W.D. Mich. 1988).

Inmates furnished peanut butter sandwiches as sole nourishment during lockdown suffered no denial of constitutional rights. *Gabel v. Estelle*, 677 F. Supp. 514 (S.D. Tex. 1987).

Failure to supply toilet paper, soap, toothbrush or toothpaste was not cruel and unusual punishment. *Harris v. Fleming*, 839 F.2d 1232 (7th Cir. 1988).

A four-day behavior management program, imposed as disciplinary punishment, during which inmates were deprived, for a time, of underwear, mattresses, exercise, and visits, did not constitute "cruel and unusual punishment." *O'Leary v. Iowa State Men's Reformatory*, 79 F.3d 82 (8th Cir. 1996).

SUMMARY

- The U.S. Supreme Court has used the "cruel and unusual" phrase to evaluate the sentencing process and the manner in which the sentence is carried out.

- The Court has held that the death penalty is not inherently cruel and unusual and may, pursuant to proper procedure, be imposed upon a defendant. The procedure used must be adequate to assure evenhanded determinations as to whether the penalty is appropriate in each case.

- Generally, the mandatory schemes in capital cases have been held unconstitutional by the Court. The Court opined that since the jury may make an unguided decision about whether to convict or acquit, the decision is a potentially discriminatory based on whether the jury desires the imposition of the death penalty.

DISCUSSION QUESTIONS

1. Where did the phrase "cruel and unusual punishment" originate?

2. What was the original motive of the American draftsmen in adopting the "cruel and unusual punishment" phrase?

3. When are punishments cruel and unusual? Does the punishment need to be *both* cruel and unusual to be prohibited by the constitution?

4. Rupe, while on death row in the state of Washington, gained weight until he weighed 410 pounds. Under the state of Washington's laws, a person has a choice to death by lethal injection or by hanging. If the person fails to choose, he is to be executed by hanging. Rupe failed to choose and was thus scheduled to be hung. His attorneys presented evidence to the federal district court that hanging Rupe would risk decapitation and that decapitation would be cruel and unusual. Under state law it was too late for him to choose lethal injection. There is an old case that holds that decapitation is cruel and unusual. As judge, how would you rule? [Facts as reported in *The Washington Post*, August 4 and September 21, 1994.]

ENDNOTES

1. *Landman v. Royster*, 333 F.Supp. 621 (E.D. Va. 1971).
2. 356 U.S. 86 (1958).
3. *Weems v. United States*, 217 U.S. 349 (1909).
4. 463 U.S. 277 (1983).
5. 428 U.S. 153 (1972).
6. *Woodson v. North Carolina*, 428 U.S. 280 (1976).
7. As reported in the *Kansas City Star*, September 9, 1998, p 1.
8. 477 U.S. 399 (1986).
9. 492 U.S. 361 (1989).
10. 487 U.S. 815 (1988).
11. 492 U.S. 302 (1989).
12. 57 F.3d 1493 (9th Cir. 1995).
13. 370 U.S. 660 (1962).
14. 429 U.S. 97 (1976).

CHAPTER 9

THE FOURTH AMENDMENT: USE OF FORCE

INTRODUCTION

Correctional officers are legally authorized to use force against an inmate under certain conditions. For example, the use of force is permitted to stop a fight between inmates. The use of force when not appropriate constitutes assault and battery upon the inmate. Any use of force may open the officers who apply the force, and the administration, to a civil lawsuit. As one officer stated, "The best way to prevent inmate lawsuits over use of force is not to use force."

WHEN IS FORCE JUSTIFIED?

As a general rule, the use of reasonable non-deadly force against an inmate is appropriate when there are no other reasonable alternatives and the force is used for one of the following reasons:

- In self-defense or in defense of others
- To protect property of the government or property of others
- To prevent a crime, including an escape
- To enforce prison rules and discipline

It is important that the force be both reasonable and appropriate, and used as the last alternative. In litigation involving a claim of the use of excessive force, the courts generally look at the following issues:

> Was there a legitimate need to use any force?
> If there was a legitimate need to use force, was the amount and type used appropriate?
> If the force used was not appropriate, did it amount to a violation of the state or federal statutes or constitutions?

Special rules govern the use of deadly force, and its proper use is limited because of the serious consequences of its use. Generally, deadly force may be used only in self-defense and in the protection of others from death or serious bodily harm. Deadly force is not authorized to be used for the protection of property. Clearly, deadly force should not used if there is any other reasonable alternative.

Certain weapons, such as batons, tasers, and choke holds, while not classified as deadly force, may carry a potential for serious injury. Accordingly, the courts have held that the failure of a warden to have a policy regarding the use of inherently dangerous instrumentalities, such as firehoses, may be grounds for imposing civil liability when an inmate is injured by their use.[1] In the *Slakan* case, an inmate mouthed-off to a correctional officer about not getting his morning coffee. When the officer turned his back, the inmate pushed the officer. The officer responded by getting a firehose and hosing the inmate. Other officers squirted tear gas on the inmate and then beat him with nightsticks. As the result of the beating, the inmate needed sixty-nine stitches. The inmate was awarded $32,000 in damages by the court.

USE OF RESTRAINTS

The physical restraint of inmates is permitted if justified for good cause and if the manner in which the restraints are used is reasonable. If the restraints are being used for long periods of time or applied in ways that inflict unnecessary pain, civil liability may result. For example "hog-tying" an inmate after a suicide attempt and leaving the inmate that way for a week violated the inmate's rights, and punitive damages were imposed on the official responsible for the operation of a jail.[2] Areas of concern regarding the use of restraints include:

- ➢ The conditions an inmate may be placed in restraints
- ➢ Who makes the decision to place an inmate in restraints
- ➢ The types of restraint that are approved
- ➢ The maximum length of time that an inmate may be placed in restraints
- ➢ The required monitoring of the inmate for health reasons

FAILURE TO PROTECT PRISONERS

The failure to protect prisoners from other prisoners may in some cases constitute a violation of the cruel and unusual punishment clause. In the case of pretrial detainees, it constitutes a violation of the due process clause. In addition, the failure to protect prisoners from themselves may also constitute a constitutional violation if the prison officials act with deliberate indifference to the substantial risk that a prisoner may commit suicide.

CRUEL AND UNUSUAL PUNISHMENT

As discussed in Chapter 8, the use of excessive force against an inmate may also constitute a violation of the Eighth Amendment's protection against cruel and unusual punishment. In the case of *Whitley v. Albers,* the U.S. Supreme Court looked at the question of when force employed to quell a prison riot or disturbance constitutes cruel and unusual punishment.[3] The U.S. Supreme Court, in *Hudson v. McMillian*, rejected the claim that an inmate must have suffered a significant injury in order for force used to be considered as cruel and unusual.[4]

USE OF FORCE TO QUELL A RIOT

The leading case involving the use of force to quell a riot is the *Whitley v. Albers* case.[5] In *Whitley*, the Supreme Court was faced with the question of the employment of force to quell a prison disturbance. Albers, a prisoner, filed a section 1983 civil suit against several correctional officers after he was shot in the leg during a prison disturbance. The disturbance started when a number of prisoners became upset by what they considered as the too forceful treatment of several other prisoners by correctional officers. The officers had discovered the prisoners to be drunk. Lead by a ringleader, the other prisoners refused to return to their cells, broke furniture, and seized a correctional officer as a hostage. The hostage was placed in a cell in the cellblock.

Captain Whitley, the security supervisor, visited the cellblock several times to confirm that the hostage was safe. The prisoners assured Whitley that they would not harm the hostage, but warned him that they would kill the hostage if a riot squad attempted to enter the cellblock. The prisoners also falsely informed Whitley that one of the prisoners had already been killed.

A decision was made to storm the cellblock in an attempt to save the hostage and to protect other prisoners. The plan was that Whitley was to go into the cellblock first and attempt to reach the cell where the hostage was being detained. Other officers with shotguns were to immediately follow Whitley. One of the officers was directed to fire a warning shot and then to shoot low at any prisoners who tried to run up the stairs to the second tier where the hostage was being held.

Whitley entered the cell block. The officer fired a warning shot. The prisoner, Albers, immediately ran up the stairs to the second tier. The officer shot him in the knee, severely injuring him. Albers later claimed that he was trying to get to the safety of his cell, on the second tier, when he was shot. At the trial, there was conflicting testimony as to whether there was a need to use force.

The technical question before the Supreme Court was the issue of whether a directed verdict should have been ordered. To answer this question, the Court needed to clarify when the use of force would constitute cruel and unusual punishment.

The court indicates that force may be used for a number of different reasons. The Court stated that the unnecessary and wanton infliction of pain violates the Eighth Amendment. The Court then noted that when officials are deciding whether or not to use force to quell a disturbance, they are often faced with a Hobson's choice, i.e., the use of force that may lead to some prisoners and/or hostages being harmed, or to refrain from using force, thus leaving hostages and some prisoners vulnerable to injuries and even death at the hands of other prisoners.

The Court indicated that for the prisoner to prevail in this case, he would have to prove that force was used "maliciously and sadistically for the very purpose of causing harm." The Court listed five factors to be considered in determining whether a correctional officer had acted with the malicious intent needed for the use of force to be considered cruel and unusual:

➢ The need to use force
➢ The relationship between that need and the amount of force that was used
➢ The gravity of the ensuing injuries caused by the use of force
➢ The extent to which, based on facts known by officials at the time, prisoners and staff faced harm if force was employed
➢ The steps, if any, taken by the officials to limit the force employed

Albers also claimed that his substantive due process rights were violated by the shooting. The Supreme Court summarily rejected this claim indicating that the due process clause affords a prisoner no greater protection than the Eighth Amendment when the prisoner is contesting the constitutionality of the force used against him.

MINOR AND NON-PHYSICAL INJURIES

In *Hudson v. McMillian,* the Supreme Court stated that the standards enunciated in *Whitley* were to be applied, not just in the case of prison riots, but whenever a prisoner claims that excessive force was used against him or her.[6] In *Hudson*, the Court held that a prisoner need not suffer a "significant" injury in order for the force to be considered cruel and unusual. The Court indicated that to hold otherwise would leave prisoners vulnerable to forms of torture that cause no physical injuries or leave any lasting physical marks. However, the Court indicated that not every "malevolent touch" by a correctional officer gives rise to a constitutional violation.

The Prison Litigation Reform Act of 1996 prohibits prisoners from bringing civil suits in federal courts for mental or emotional injuries suffered during confinement unless they can first establish that they also suffered physical injury.[7] The constitutionality of the physical-injury requirement will probably be tested in future cases. For example, prior to the passage of the act, a federal district court held that an inmate was subjected to cruel and unusual punishment when the prisoner was forced at gunpoint to kiss the correctional officer's wife's shoes.[8]

CORPORAL PUNISHMENT

Can prison officials use corporal punishment to enforce prison discipline? A 1952 federal district court judge stated:

> From time immemorial prison officials were vested with the power and authority of imposing corporal punishment upon prisoners as part of the discipline and restraint...For centuries, whipping or corporal punishment has been a recognized method of discipline of convicts.[9]

In 1968, the U.S. Court of Appeals for the Eighth Circuit in the case of *Jackson v. Bishop* held that whipping as a means of enforcing prison discipline violated the Eighth and Fourteenth amendments.[10] During the *Jackson* trial, the former Director of Federal Prisons, James V. Bennett, testified that whipping and other forms of corporal punishment were "brutal and did no real good." The decision in the *Jackson* case was written by Judge Blackmun, who later became a U.S. Supreme Court justice. Judge Blackmun stated in his opinion that regulations are easily circumvented. . . and that corporal punishment is easily subject to abuse in the hands of the sadistic and unscrupulous. After *Jackson*, the courts have authorized the use of reasonable force in situations discussed earlier, but not as a form of punishment. [Note, prison officials may still use reasonable force to ensure that a prisoner is brought under control, but not as punishment.]

SUICIDE

Despite the best efforts of correctional officials, some inmates commit suicide. The suicide problem is particularly significant in jails, where nearly half of all prisoner deaths are suicides. This compares to only about 10 percent of the prisoner deaths in prisons and similar correctional institutions. Frequently, civil suits are filed by the estate of the deceased and/or by the surviving family. As one expert stated, "There will be suicides, and there will be lawsuits about them."

Under basic tort law, a custodian has the duty to take reasonable steps to protect those in his or her custody. In most states, liability for a suicide attaches only if the officials acted with deliberate indifference in not preventing the suicide. Simple negligence on the part of prison or jail officials generally is insufficient in most states to make them liable. For example, in the case of *Freedman v. City of Allentown*, the Freedman was booked into the jail.[11] At the time he was locked up, he had prominent scars on his wrists, inside his elbows, and on the back of his neck. The scars were shown to an officer. The officer failed to recognize these scars as indications of previous suicide attempts and failed to take suicide prevention steps. Freedman's probation officer, who knew of the previous attempts, visited the him in jail and failed to warn the jail staff. Freedman committed suicide while in jail. The court ruled that only negligence was shown, not deliberate indifference, and therefore the constitutional rights of the deceased had not been violated.

Civil suits over in-custody suicides usually involve one of three issues:

- ➢ The failure to recognize a potential suicide and take proper steps to prevent it
- ➢ The failure to monitor an identified potential suicide prisoner
- ➢ The failure to properly respond to a suicide attempt once the attempt has been discovered

 CASES ON POINT

DAVID L. PELFREY v. SEAN CHAMBERS et al.
ELECTRONIC CITATION: 1995 FED App. 0002P (6th Cir.)

Before: JONES and BATCHELDER, Circuit Judges; and GILMORE, District Judge. GILMORE, D. J., delivered the opinion of the court, in which JONES, J., joined. BATCHELDER, J., delivered a separate dissenting opinion.

This case presents the question of whether the isolated and unauthorized use of force by a prison guard on an inmate constitutes "punishment" within the meaning of the Eighth Amendment. The district court concluded that a spontaneous assault does not state a cognizable claim under the Eighth Amendment. . . .

Appellant David L. Pelfrey filed this action under 42 U.S.C. § 1983. In his complaint, Mr. Pelfrey alleged that on January 2, 1992, while incarcerated at the London Correctional Institution (LCI), he was assaulted by correctional officers Sean Chambers and Larry Closser. Pelfrey's complaint set forth the following facts in support of his request for damages and injunctive relief:

On January 2, 1992, after returning from my job assignment, I went to the Upstairs Office at the London Correctional Camp . . . to obtain my mail. Correction Officers (and Defendants) Chambers and Closser were in the office. I asked Officer Closser for my mail. I was responding to a question from Officer Closser when he started walking around from where he had been standing behind the desk. He (Officer Closser) pulled out his knife as he walked toward me. When he got within reach of me, Officer Closser put one hand on my shoulder and the other one on top of my head. I instinctively put my hands on top of my head, and at that time, Officer Chambers pulled his knife out and grabbed my hands, forcing them down to my side. Officer Closser then proceeded to cut my hair with his knife. After cutting off a great portion of my hair, Officer Chambers then let me go, and he (Officer Chambers) stood there grinning and smiling, while Officer Closser was laughing and dropping my hair on the floor. These officers had me scared, intimidated, and threatened.

. . . . The defendants asserted that Mr. Pelfrey's complaint did not state a cognizable claim because, even accepting his factual allegations as true, the complaint stated, at most, a claim for common law assault rather than a violation of the Eighth Amendment's proscription against cruel and unusual punishment. The defendants argued that, even if they had cut off Mr. Pelfrey's hair without provocation or justification, their actions did not constitute "punishment" because it was not administered for penological or disciplinary purposes.

. . . . In 1989, the Supreme Court, in an often cited footnote, suggested that all post-conviction excessive force claims were to be raised under the Eighth Amendment rather than the Fourteenth Amendment:

[T]he Due Process Clause protects a pretrial detainee from the use of excessive force that amounts to punishment. After conviction, the Eighth Amendment "serves as the primary source of substantive protection . . . in cases . . . where the deliberate use of force is challenged as excessive and unjustified." Any protection that "substantive due process" affords convicted prisoners against excessive force is, we have held, at best redundant of that provided by the Eighth Amendment.
Graham v. Connor, 490 U.S. 386, 395, n.10 (1989), (quoting *Whitley v. Albers*, 475 U.S. 312, 327 (1979)).

. . . .In *Hudson v. McMillian*, ___ U.S. ___, 112 S. Ct. 995, 117 L.Ed.2d 156 (1992), the Supreme Court clarified the standard to be used in analyzing "excessive force" claims under the Eighth Amendment:

[W]henever prison officials stand accused of using excessive physical force in violation of the Cruel and Unusual Punishments Clause, the core judicial inquiry is that set out in *Whitley v. Albers*, 475 U.S. 312 (1986)]: whether force was applied in a good-faith effort to maintain or restore discipline, or maliciously and sadistically to cause harm.
Id. at 999, 117 L.Ed.2d at 165-66

Although the maintenance of prison security and discipline may often require that prisoners be subjected to physical contact which at common law would be actionable as an assault . . . . , a violation of the Eighth Amendment will nevertheless occur if "the offending conduct reflects an unnecessary and wanton infliction of pain."

In this case, defendants have not asserted that the assault on Pelfrey occurred as a result of a "good-faith effort to maintain or restore discipline." Nor can it be said that defendants' conduct furthered any other legitimate penological or institutional objective. Instead, it would certainly appear that defendants' actions. . .were designed to frighten and degrade Pelfrey by reinforcing the fact that his continued well-being was entirely dependent on the good humor of his armed guards. To us, given the closed nature of the prison environment, this constitutes a totally unwarranted, malicious and sadistic use of force to cause harm. . . .

We categorically reject defendants' argument that "an unprovoked attack is not punishment." To hold otherwise would ignore the power arrangements that exist within the prison environment and lead to the anomalous result in which a prisoner who is assaulted after having provoked a guard can state a cognizable claim for a constitutional violation while his cellmate who is assaulted *for absolutely no reason* is afforded only that relief permitted by state law. Such a result is devoid of all logic and flies in the face of this Court's previous statement that "the motivation of an assault" is relevant to the question of "whether the measure taken inflicted unnecessary and wanton pain."

. . . .we believe that Plaintiff Pelfrey has stated a cognizable claim under § 1983 for a violation of the Eighth Amendment.

Case Discussion and Significance. The *Pelfrey* case holds that the isolated and unauthorized use of force by a prison guard on an inmate constitutes "punishment" within the meaning of the Eighth Amendment. Accordingly, the district court's conclusion that a spontaneous assault did not state a cognizable claim under the Eighth Amendment was reversed. In this case, defendants did not asserted that the assault on Pelfrey occurred as a result of a "good-faith effort to maintain or restore discipline." Nor did they contend that the defendants' conduct furthered any other legitimate penological or institutional objective. The Court concluded that the alleged actions of the defendants were designed to frighten and degrade Pelfrey by reinforcing the fact that his continued well-being was entirely dependent on the good humor of his armed guards. In deciding this issue, the court accepted that the contentions of the plaintiff were true. The case was returned to the district court for a trial to see if the plaintiffs could prove their allegations.

Hudson v. McMillian
503 U.S. 1 (1992)

The petitioner Hudson, a Louisiana prison inmate, testified that minor bruises, facial swelling, loosened teeth, and a cracked dental plate he had suffered resulted from a beating by respondent prison guards McMillian and Woods while he was handcuffed and shackled following an argument with McMillian, and that respondent Mezo, a supervisor on duty, watched the beating, but merely told the officers "not to have too much fun." The Magistrate. . .found that the officers used force when there was no need to do so, and that Mezo expressly condoned their actions, ruled that respondents had violated the Eighth Amendment's prohibition on cruel and unusual punishments, and awarded Hudson damages. The Court of Appeals reversed, holding, *inter alia*, that inmates alleging use of excessive force in violation of the Amendment must prove "significant injury," and that Hudson could not prevail because his injuries were "minor," and required no medical attention.

The U.S. Supreme Court held that the use of excessive physical force against a prisoner may constitute cruel and unusual punishment even though the inmate does not suffer serious injury. Whenever prison officials stand accused of using excessive physical force constituting "the unnecessary and wanton infliction of pain" violative of the Cruel and Unusual Punishments Clause, the core judicial inquiry is ... whether force was applied in a good faith effort to maintain or restore discipline, or maliciously and sadistically to cause harm. Extending *Whitley's* application of the "unnecessary and wanton infliction of pain" standard to all allegations of force, whether the prison disturbance is a riot or a lesser disruption, works no innovation. . . .Since, under the *Whitley* approach, the extent of injury suffered by an inmate is one of the factors to be considered in determining whether the use of force is wanton and unnecessary, the absence of serious injury is relevant to, but does not end, the Eighth Amendment inquiry. There is no merit to respondents' assertion that a significant injury requirement is mandated by what this Court termed, in *Wilson v. Seiter,* . . . the "objective component" of Eighth Amendment analysis: whether the alleged wrongdoing is objectively "harmful enough" to establish a constitutional violation... That component is contextual, and responsive to "contemporary standards of decency." *Estelle v. Gamble*, 429 U.S. 97. In the excessive force context, such standards always are violated when prison officials maliciously and sadistically use force to cause harm, whether or not significant injury is evident. Moreover, although the Amendment does not reach *de minimis* uses of physical force, provided that such use is not of a sort repugnant to the conscience of mankind, *Ibid.*, the blows directed at Hudson are not *de minimis,* and the extent of his injuries thus provides no basis for dismissal of his § 1983 claim.

CASE SUMMARIES

An officer was not liable for use of excessive force against prisoner when he "maliciously" attempted to kick prisoner in the head after prisoner spit on him, because his kick missed prisoner's head, resulting in no injury. *Warren v. Humphrey*, 875 F. Supp. 378 (E.D. Tex. 1995).

A jury awarded $1.18 million to intoxicated arrestee who was allegedly kicked by correctional officers at county jail, shackled to bench, and denied use of a toilet while in custody. *Sosa v. Jefferson County*, C-95-229 (W.D.Ky., March 1, 1996),

An officer's striking of a prisoner solely to harm him rather than for any legitimate penological reason violated the prisoner's Eighth Amendment rights; prisoner was entitled to judgment in federal civil rights suit despite suffering only pain and not permanent injury. *McLaurin v. Prater*, 30 F.3d 982 (8th Cir. 1994).

A sheriff could not be held liable for officer's alleged use of excessive force against a prisoner when he did not personally participate in the incident, and there was not evidence showing that he approved or encouraged the officers' actions, failed to provide adequate training, or failed to conduct an investigation of what occurred. *O'Banion v. Bowman*, 824 F. Supp. 743 (S.D. Ohio 1993).

The use of black box restraint device over handcuffs while transporting prisoner to and from hospital was not itself cruel and unusual punishment; officers who had no discretion as to whether to use the restraint device could not be held liable for prisoner's wrist injuries. *Moody v. Proctor*, 986 F. 2d 239 (8th Cir. 1993).

SUMMARY

- The use of force when not appropriate constitutes assault and battery upon the inmate.
- Any use of force may open the officers who apply the force, and the administration, to a civil lawsuit.

- As a general rule, the use of reasonable non-deadly force against an inmate is appropriate when there are no other reasonable alternatives and the force is used in self-defense or in defense of others; to protect property of the government or property of others; to prevent a crime including an escape; and to enforce prison rules and discipline.
- There are special rules involving the use of deadly force. Generally, deadly force may be used only in self-defense and in the protection of others from death or serious bodily harm.
- Deadly force is not authorized to be used for the protection of property.
- Deadly force should not used if there is any other reasonable alternative.
- The physical restraint of inmates is permitted if justified for good cause and if the manner in which the restraints are used is reasonable. If the restraints are being used for long periods of time or applied in ways that inflict unnecessary pain, civil liability may result.

DISCUSSION QUESTIONS

1. Under what circumstances may deadly force be used on a prisoner?
2. When may a warden use non-deadly force to control a prisoner?
3. Explain the steps that may be used to reduce civil liability.
4. A warden is developing standard rules to be used when placing an inmate in restraints. What items should he/she include?

ENDNOTES

1. *Slakan v. Porter*, 737 F.2d. 368 (4th Cir., 1984).
2. *Jones v. Thompson*, 818 F.Supp 1263 (S.D. Ind., 1993).
3. 475 U.S. 312, (1986).
4. 503 U.S. 1 (1992).
5. 475 U.S. 312 (1986).
6. 503 U.S. 1 (1992).
7. 42 U.S.C. 1997e(e).
8. *Oses v. Fair*, 739 F.Supp. 707 (D.Mass. 1990).
9. *United States v. Jones*, 108 F.Supp. 266 (S.D.Fla. 1952).
10. 404 F.2d. 571 (8th Cir. 1968).
11. 853 F.2d. 1111 (3rd. Cir. 1988).

CHAPTER 10

CIVIL ACTIONS

INTRODUCTION

If a correctional officer commits a crime, such as battery against an inmate, that officer may be criminally prosecuted in state court, federal court, or both systems. Inmates may also file civil actions against institutions and their employees in either system depending on the theories of liability pleaded in the complaint. This chapter discusses the various theories used to hold correctional officers, their supervisors, and institutions liable for their actions.

HABEAS CORPUS

Habeas corpus is a Latin term that means "you have the body." It is also known as the "Great Writ" and is considered the highest remedy for any person who is imprisoned. It is one of the oldest civil actions in the law, and dates back to the Magna Carta of 1215.

> Article 1, Section 9 of the U.S. Constitution states:
>
> The Privilege of the Writ of Habeas Corpus shall not be suspended, unless when in Cases of Rebellion or Invasion the public safety may require it.

Habeas corpus writs were originally authorized in the U.S. Constitution. They were also included in the Judiciary Act of

1789. The Judiciary Act now provides that the federal courts shall have the power to grant Writs of Habeas Corpus in all cases in which the person is restrained in violation of his or her constitutional rights or any law of the United States and under the authority of the United States.[1]

The Judiciary Act only authorized federal courts to hear writs filed by federal prisoners. However, other statutes authorize state prisoners to file writs after they have exhausted all remedies available to them at the state level.

The Writ of Habeas Corpus is a formal court action brought by a person in prison that challenges the legality of the confinement. The relief or prayer in the writ is the release of the person from the illegal confinement. Because it deals with the legality of confinement, it takes precedence over other civil actions.

The writ allows federal and state inmates to file petitions (Writs of Habeas Corpus) in federal courts challenging the constitutionality of their imprisonment. The basic principle of the habeas corpus writ is that the government is accountable to the courts for a person's imprisonment. If the government cannot show that the inmate is lawfully incarcerated, the person is entitled to immediate release from captivity.[2]

Prisoner petitions filed in U.S. district courts, 1980-96

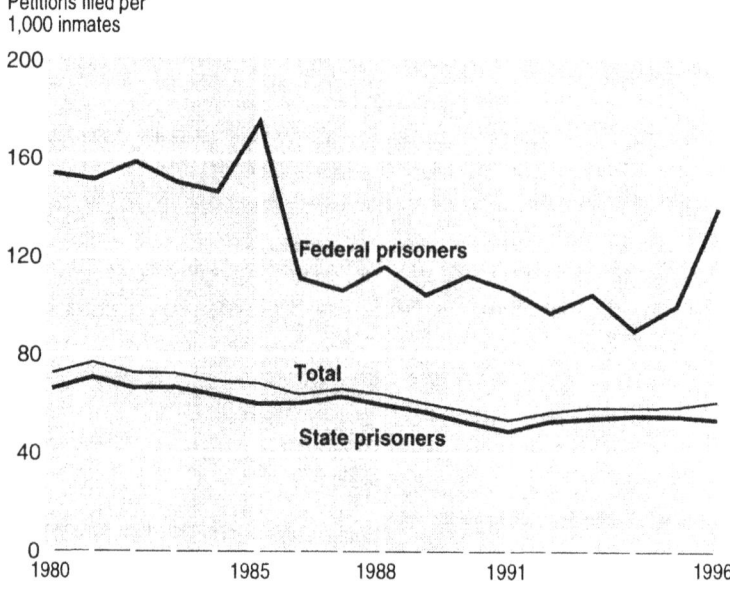

U.S. DOJ, Bureau of Justice Statistics, October 1997, p.6.

Procedurally, what occurs is that the prisoner, or his or her attorney, files the writ in the court that has jurisdiction over the custodian holding the prisoner. The custodian must then appear in court, usually within ten days from the service of the writ, and justify the continued confinement of the inmate.

MANDAMUS

Mandamus is another form of action that may be filed by inmates, and although it does not directly impose civil liability on correctional officials, it is important to understand its function and purpose.

The *writ of mandamus* is a judicial remedy used to compel a lower court or government official to perform a duty owed to the plaintiff. Similar to *habeas corpus*, mandamus is an extraordinary civil action, based in common law, that is only used when the plaintiff has no other means to obtain relief. *Mandamus* can only be used to compel a government official to perform a ministerial or nondiscretionary act. Compared to other remedies, it is used infrequently. However, courts have granted *mandamus* to compel prison official to permit inmates to file petitions *in forma pauperis* or *pre se* or to allow inmates to vote in elections in absentee and to compel payment of federal witness fees to inmates.[3]

CRIMINAL LIABILITY

If a correctional officer commits a criminal act against an inmate, that officer may be criminally prosecuted just like any other citizen. What is distinct about a criminal prosecution against a correctional officer is the status of the victim. The victim will be a person who is confined in prison after conviction of a felony, a person who is confined in a county jail after conviction of either a felony or a misdemeanor, or a person in county jail awaiting charges on either a felony or a misdemeanor. Thus the victim's credibility will always be an issue during any investigation of alleged criminal acts. This is not to say that correctional officers have never committed criminal acts against inmates. Unfortunately, there are those few individuals within the correctional officers' ranks who should not be given the special trust and confidence that go with guarding some of society's most violent individuals. These officers may resort to using excessive force, discriminating against inmates because of their race, or committing other actions that are prohibited by law. When any of these occur, the officer may be charged criminally in state court, federal court, or both.

If the act is a violation of a state criminal statute, the officer may be charged and prosecuted in state court. If the act violated an inmate's federal civil rights, the officer may also be charged and prosecuted for the same act in federal court. There is no double jeopardy in such cases because each case is tried in a different jurisdiction—the criminal case in state court and the civil rights case in federal court. Federal civil rights are discussed in more detail later in this chapter. Additionally, the officer may be sued civilly by the inmate under several different civil law theories that are discussed later in this section.

TORT

A *tort* is another form of lawsuit that may be filed against correctional officers or officials. There is no simple definition of a tort.

TORT

Black's Law Dictionary defines a *tort* as:

A private or civil wrong or injury, including action for bad faith breach of contract, for which the court will provide a remedy in the form of an action for damages.[4]

Two broad categories of torts are of interest to correctional officials:

- **Intentional torts**: Those in which the actor desires a particular result. The major intentional torts are battery, assault, false imprisonment, and infliction of emotional distress.
- **Negligence**: Those injuries that occur where the actor did not intend to harm another, but merely acted carelessly.

There are three elements in any tort action:

- A legal duty owed by the defendant to the plaintiff
- A breach of that duty
- An injury as a result of that breach

For example, leaving someone in a jail past his or her release time might be the civil tort of false imprisonment if the actor (defendant) intended such a result, or it might be negligence if the actor simply forgot to release the inmate. All the elements of a tort are met in this example: (1) there was a legal duty to release the inmate (plaintiff) on a certain date, (2) there was a breach of that duty in that the inmate was not released, and (3) the inmate was illegally confined against his or her will, which is an injury as a result of the breach of duty.

If a tort is committed, the plaintiff can request monetary damages from the correctional officer and the officer's agency. There are two forms of monetary damages: compensatory and punitive. *Compensatory damages* are awarded to compensate the plaintiff for any injuries. *Punitive damages* are awarded to punish the defendant for outrageous conduct.

Some attorneys say that compensatory damages are to make the plaintiff whole or return him to the place he was before the injury. For example, if the plaintiff suffered an injury that required hospitalization and extended medical treatment, compensatory damages would include payment of all the medical expenses. If the plaintiff could no longer work as a result of the injury, compensatory damages would include loss of future earnings. Compensatory damages also include money for pain and suffering. How much a plaintiff may be awarded for pain and suffering depends on the facts of the case, the skill of the attorney, and the receptiveness of the jury.

As indicated above, punitive damages are awarded to punish the defendant. Such damages may be substantial (in the hundreds of thousands of dollars), even though little or no compensatory damages were awarded to the plaintiff. Punitive damages are not awarded in every case; rather, juries tend to award them for outrageous or unlawful conduct by the defendant.

CIVIL LIABILITY (SECTION 1983)

Federal and state inmates may file suits in federal courts alleging violations of their civil rights. The foundation or authority for these suits originates in section 1 of the Fourteenth Amendment.

> *No State shall make or enforce any law which shall abridge the privileges or immunities of citizens of the United States, nor shall any State deprive any person of life, liberty, or property without due process of law.*
>
> *U.S. Constitution, Fourteenth Amendment, Section 1*

There is a great deal of confusion surrounding the historical evolution of the present-day civil rights acts.[5] This is not a history text; however, understanding the background and evolution of these laws assists correctional officials in performing their duties. The first law passed by Congress was the Civil Rights Act of 1866.[6] This law declared that all persons born in the United States were citizens regardless of race or prior conditions of servitude. It made it a crime for any person under color of law to deprive a person of any right secured or protected by the Constitution or the laws of the United States. This law failed to stop the continuing racial strife in the southern states and after race riots in Memphis and New Orleans, Congress enacted the Enforcement Act of 1870.[7] This law was intended to guarantee the right to vote without regard to color, race, or previous conditions of servitude. The Enforcement Act made it a crime for a state official to deny a person the right to vote. The historical roots of the present-day federal civil rights criminal codes are found in the Civil Rights Act of 1866 (18 U.S.C. 242) and in the Enforcement Act of 1870 (18 U.S.C. 241). In response to continuing violence against Blacks, Congress enacted the Ku Klux Klan Act of 1871.[8] This act is best known for its primary civil enforcement mechanism: the ability to file a federal lawsuit for acts under color of law that violate a person's federal civil rights. In addition, it was the forerunner of the present day law allowing such suits (42 U.S.C. 1983). However, when originally enacted, it was viewed as a federal criminal sanction for those who engaged in violence against blacks, specifically members of the Ku Klux Klan.

Title 18 of the United States Code Section 241 prohibits conspiracies to deprive a person of his or her civil rights.[9] Section 242 prohibits civil rights violations by persons acting under color of law. The government must prove four elements to establish a violation of section 242: the victim was an inhabitant of a state, district, or territory of the United States; the defendant acted under color of law; the conduct deprived the victim of a right guaranteed by the United States Constitution; and the defendant acted with a specific intent to violate the protected right.[10]

In addition to the criminal sanctions facing those who violate a person's federal civil rights, Congress has provided an additional remedy in the form of civil damages or the issuance of an injunction to prevent further action. Title 42 of the United States Code Section 1983 provides in part:

> Every person who, under color of any statute, ordinance, regulation, custom, or usage of any State or Territory, subjects, or causes to be subjected, any citizen of the United States or any other person within the jurisdiction thereof to the deprivation of any rights,

privileges, or immunities secured by the Constitution and laws, shall be liable to the party injured in an action at law, suit in equity, or other proper proceedings for redress . . . .[11]

The above quoted language has been the basis for thousands of lawsuits against those employed in the criminal justice system.

Requirement of State Action

The United States Supreme Court addressed the scope of the Civil Rights Act of 1871 when it interpreted the phase "under color of state law" in its decision of *United States v. Classic.*[12] The Court reversed the dismissal of criminal charges brought against election officials who had engaged in fraudulent activities during a primary election. The Court stated that "misuse of power, possessed by virtue of state law and made possible only because the wrongdoer is clothed with the authority of the state, is action taken 'under color of state law.'"[13]

The Supreme Court further expanded this definition four years later in 1945 when it decided *Screws v. United States.* The court held that a sheriff's fatal beating of a black prisoner was conduct "under color of law."[14] Therefore, in criminal cases, conduct *under color of law* involves unauthorized, unlawful conduct of an official where the pretense of authority under which the officer acted furthered or assisted that officer in violating a person's constitutional rights in any way. *Screws* and *Classic* established the availability of criminal actions by persons who were victims of law enforcement misconduct. However, from 1945 until 1961, Section 1983 was virtually ignored by those who were wronged by illegal conduct by agents of the government.

Scope of Liability

The gradual expansion of the due process clause incorporating the Bill of Rights and the growth of the equal protection and due process concepts allowed victims of official misconduct greater latitude in the filing of lawsuits. In 1961, the Supreme Court decided *Monroe v. Pape* and established the framework for future use of Section 1983 by those who were victims of illegal governmental activity.[15] In *Monroe*, the plaintiff and his family filed a civil lawsuit, instead of criminal action, using section 1983 against 13 Chicago police officers and the City of Chicago, alleging that the officers broke into their home without a warrant, forced them out of bed, and made them stand naked while the officers searched the house. The police then took the plaintiff to the police station and held him incommunicado for 10 hours before releasing him without filing any charges. The plaintiff claimed that the police acted "under color of law" and deprived him of his constitutional protection against unreasonable searches and seizures. The Supreme Court held that color of law had the same meaning in a civil case as it did in a criminal case and concluded that because Section 1983 provided for a civil action, that the plaintiffs need not prove that the defendants acted with a specific intent to deprive a person of a federal right. However, the court dismissed the City of Chicago holding that municipalities were immune from liability under the statute.

In 1978, the law surrounding civil rights violations expanded even further with the Supreme Court decision in *Monell v. Department of Social Services*.[16] In *Monell*, the plaintiffs were a class of female employees who alleged that the Board of Education of the City of New York and its Department of Social Services were forcing pregnant employees to take unpaid leaves of absence before those leaves were medically necessary. The lawsuit sought injunctive relief and back pay for the unlawful forced leave. The defendants included the Mayor, the City of New York, the Commissioner of the Board of Education and the Board itself, and the Department of Social Services and its Chancellor. In allowing the lawsuit to go forward, the court held that section 1983 was violated whenever

1. A person was deprived of a right, privilege, or immunity guaranteed under the Constitution and federal laws, and
2. Such a deprivation resulted from the official policy or custom of a local governmental entity.

The Supreme Court decision was to have a tremendous impact on the desirability of suing individuals employed by municipalities. Victims of illegal action by agents of municipalities now had a deep pocket that they could reach. It must be stressed that *Monell* addressed the liability of local governmental agencies and not individual states.

Monell also overruled *Monroe* by holding that municipalities were *persons* and therefore not completely immune from suit under Section 1983. However, *Monell* did not address whether local governments, while not entitled to absolute immunity, could claim limited immunity in some situations. This question was answered in *Owens v. City of Independence,* which held that the city was entitled to limited immunity from lawsuit based upon the good faith of its officials.[17]

Although the act did not address violations by federal officials, in *Bivens v. Six Unknown Narcotic Agents*, the Supreme Court ruled that the Civil Rights Act extended to violations by federal officials.[18]

As indicated in previous chapters, although prison inmates are denied certain constitutional rights, such as freedom of movement and freedom from unreasonable search and seizure, they do retain certain civil rights, and others are merely diminished instead of extinguished. If these rights are violated, they may file a Section 1983 lawsuit.

Unlike the Writ of Habeas Corpus, inmates do not have to exhaust their administrative remedies prior to filing a Section 1983 action. In *McCarthy v. Maddigan*, a federal inmate filed a Section 1983 action for damages without exhausting the Bureau of Prisons' administrative remedies. The U.S. Supreme Court held that unless a federal statute required the exhaustion of remedies before filing an action, federal courts must balance the inmate's rights against the institutions policies favoring use of administrative remedies instead of, or prior to, the filing of lawsuits.[19]

There are a number of acts that may constitute a violation of an inmate's civil rights. Intentional torts may be the basis of a 1983 lawsuit. Additionally, supervisors and employees in correctional institutions need to understand that there is potential liability for acts other than intentional torts. Two of the most common ways of establishing a violation of an inmate's civil rights involve proof of a custom or habit of acting in a certain way and lack of training on the part of the agency. The next two sections examine these issues in more detail.

Custom

Local agencies, such as the sheriff's department and jail operation, may be liable for a violation of an inmate's civil rights not only because of established formal policies, but because of certain customs that have been informally established. In *Thompson v. City of Los Angeles*, the Ninth Circuit Court of Appeals stated that the rationale for imposing liability based on custom was:

> The existence of custom as a basis of liability under Section 1983 thus serves a critical role in ensuring that local government entities are held responsible for widespread abuses or practices that cannot be affirmatively attributed to the decisions or ratifications of an official government policy maker but are so pervasive as to have the force of law.[20]

There are several ways that an inmate may show or prove the existence of a custom in a civil rights lawsuit: the local agency may act in a certain way, even though it has not adopted a formal policy in the area, a high ranking official, such as the sheriff, may customarily act in a certain way and because that official is a policy maker, he or she may bind the local agency without a formal declaration of policy; and low-level employees may engage in an activity so often that it is presumed that the local agency or high ranking officials know of these acts and are reckless with regard to their existence.

Failure to Train

The other common method of establishing liability on the part of an official or local agency involves allegations of failure to train employees. *Monell* established the principle that government liability does not automatically attach simply because of unconstitutional acts by lower-level employees. However, when there are allegations of failure to train or supervise, the U.S. Supreme Court has held that local entities may be liable if the conduct rises to the level of deliberate indifference.[21]

Deliberate indifference is a difficult term to define and it may vary depending on the circumstances. In a prison setting, the U.S. Supreme Court discussed deliberate indifference and the Eighth Amendment in *Whitley v. Albers*.[22] In that case, prison officials were responding to a riot and injured the plaintiff. He sued, alleging a violation of his Eighth Amendment rights, and the court held:

> [I]n making and carrying out decisions involving the use of force to restore order in the face of a prison disturbance, prison officials undoubtedly must take into account the very real threats the unrest presents to inmates and prison officials alike, in addition to the possible harms to inmates against who force might be used... In this setting, a deliberate indifference standard does not adequately capture the importance of such competing obligations or convey the appropriate hesitancy to critique in hindsight decisions necessarily made in haste, under pressure, and frequently without the luxury of a second chance.[23]

The Court went on to state that in those circumstances, liability should be determined by examining whether force was applied in a good faith effort to restore discipline, or maliciously and sadistically for the very purpose of causing harm.[24]

Deliberate indifference is not simply failing to train an officer, even properly trained officers make mistakes that do not amount to a violation of another's civil rights. Rather, it is a reckless disregard for the rights of another. Thus, correctional officers and their supervisors may be liable under Section 1983 if they act in complete or wanton disregard for the rights of the inmates under their control.

 CASES ON POINT

McCleskey v. Zant
499 U.S. 467 (1991)

JUSTICE KENNEDY delivered the opinion of the Court.

The doctrine of abuse of the writ defines the circumstances in which federal courts decline to entertain a claim presented for the first time in a second or subsequent petition for a writ of habeas corpus. Petitioner Warren McCleskey, in a second federal habeas petition, presented a claim under *Massiah v. United States*, that he failed to include in his first federal petition. The Court of Appeals for the Eleventh Circuit held that assertion of the *Massiah* claim in this manner abused the writ.

In December 1978, the jury convicted McCleskey of murder and sentenced him to death. Since his conviction, McCleskey has pursued direct and collateral remedies for more than a decade. We describe this procedural history, both for a proper understanding of the case and as an illustration of the context in which allegations of abuse of the writ arise. . . .

On direct appeal to the Supreme Court of Georgia, McCleskey raised six grounds of error. The court rejected McCleskey's other contentions, and affirmed his conviction and sentence. We denied certiorari.

In December 1981, McCleskey filed his first federal habeas corpus petition in the United States District Court for the Northern District of Georgia, asserting 18 grounds for relief. We granted certiorari limited to the question whether Georgia's capital sentencing procedures were constitutional, and denied relief.

McCleskey continued his postconviction attacks by filing a second state habeas corpus action in 1987 which, as amended, contained five claims for relief. The Supreme Court of Georgia denied McCleskey's application for a certificate of probable cause.

In July 1987, McCleskey filed a second federal habeas action, the one we now review....

The Judiciary Act of 1789 empowered federal courts to issue writs of habeas corpus to prisoners "in custody, under or by color of the authority of the United States." In the early decades of our new federal system, English common law defined the substantive scope of the writ. Federal prisoners could use the writ to challenge confinement imposed by a court that lacked jurisdiction, or detention by the executive without proper legal process.

The common law limitations on the scope of the writ were subject to various expansive forces, both statutory and judicial. The major statutory expansion of the writ occurred in 1867, when Congress extended federal habeas corpus to prisoners held in state custody. For the most part, however, expansion of the writ has come through judicial decision making. As explained in *Wainwright v. Sykes*, the Court began by interpreting the concept of jurisdictional defect with generosity to include sentences imposed without statutory authorization, and convictions obtained under an unconstitutional statute. Later, we allowed habeas relief for confinement under a state conviction obtained without adequate procedural protections for the defendant.

. . .A petitioner may abuse the writ by failing to raise a claim through inexcusable neglect. Our recent decisions confirm that a petitioner can abuse the writ by raising a claim in a subsequent petition that he could have raised in his first, regardless of whether the failure to raise it earlier stemmed from a deliberate choice.

. . .Habeas review extracts further costs. Federal collateral litigation places a heavy burden on scarce federal judicial resources, and threatens the capacity of the system to resolve primary disputes. Finally, habeas corpus review may give litigants incentives to withhold claims for manipulative purposes and may establish disincentives to present claims when evidence is fresh.

Far more severe are the disruptions when a claim is presented for the first time in a second or subsequent federal habeas petition. Perpetual disrespect for the finality of convictions disparages the entire criminal justice system.

If reexamination of a conviction in the first round of federal habeas stretches resources, examination of new claims raised in a second or subsequent petition spreads them thinner still. These later petitions deplete the resources needed for federal litigants in the first instance, including litigants commencing their first federal habeas action. And if reexamination of convictions in the first round of habeas offends federalism and comity, the offense increases when a State must defend its conviction in a second or subsequent habeas proceeding on grounds not even raised in the first petition.

The federal writ of habeas corpus overrides all these considerations, essential as they are to the rule of law, when a petitioner raises a meritorious constitutional claim in a proper manner in a habeas petition. Our procedural default jurisprudence and abuse-of-the-writ jurisprudence help define this dimension of procedural regularity. Both doctrines impose on petitioners a burden of reasonable compliance with procedures designed to discourage baseless claims and to keep the system open for valid ones; both recognize the law's interest in finality; and both invoke equitable principles to define the court's discretion to excuse pleading and procedural requirements for petitioners who could not comply with them in the exercise of reasonable care and diligence. . . .

. . . The history of the proceedings in this case, and the burden upon the State in defending against allegations made for the first time in federal court some 9 years after the trial, reveal the necessity for the abuse of the writ doctrine. The cause and prejudice standard we adopt today leaves ample room for consideration of constitutional errors in a first federal habeas petition and in a later petition under appropriate circumstances. Petitioner has not satisfied this standard for excusing the omission of the *Massiah* claim from his first petition. The judgment of the Court of Appeals is Affirmed.

Case Discussion and Significance. *McCleskey* discusses the proper standard for applying the abuse of the Writ of Habeas Corpus doctrine, which refers to a complex and evolving body of equitable principles informed and controlled by historical usage, statutory developments, and judicial decisions. A claim need not have been deliberately abandoned in an earlier petition in order to establish that its inclusion in a subsequent petition constitutes abuse of the writ. Thus, when a prisoner files a second or subsequent habeas petition, the government bears the burden of pleading abuse of the writ. This burden is satisfied if the government clearly establishes the petitioner's prior writ history, identifies the claims that appear for the first time, and alleges that petitioner has abused the writ. The burden to disprove abuse then shifts to petitioner. To excuse his failure to raise the claim earlier, the petitioner must then establish that he was impeded by some objective factor external to the defense, such as governmental interference or the reasonable unavailability of the factual basis for the claim—as well as actual prejudice resulting from the errors of which he complains. However, the failure to earlier raise a claim may be excused if the petitioner can show that a fundamental miscarriage of justice, the conviction of an innocent person, would result from a failure to entertain the claim.

Canton v. Harris
489 U.S. 378 (1989)

JUSTICE WHITE delivered the opinion of the Court.

In this case, we are asked to determine if a municipality can ever be liable under 42 U.S.C. 1983 for constitutional violations resulting from its failure to train municipal employees. We hold that, under certain circumstances, such liability is permitted by the statute.

...In April 1978, respondent Geraldine Harris was arrested by officers of the Canton Police Department. Mrs. Harris was brought to the police station in a patrol wagon. When she arrived at the station, Mrs. Harris was found sitting on the floor of the wagon.

She was asked if she needed medical attention, and responded with an incoherent remark. After she was brought inside the station for processing, Mrs. Harris slumped to the floor on two occasions. Eventually, the police officers left Mrs. Harris lying on the floor to prevent her from falling again. No medical attention was ever summoned for Mrs. Harris. After about an hour, Mrs. Harris was released from custody, and taken by an ambulance (provided by her family) to a nearby hospital. There, Mrs. Harris was diagnosed as suffering from several emotional ailments; she was hospitalized for one week and received subsequent outpatient treatment for an additional year.

Some time later, Mrs. Harris commenced this action alleging many state-law and constitutional claims against the city of Canton and its officials. Among these claims was one seeking to hold the city liable under 42 U.S.C. 1983 for its violation of Mrs. Harris' right, under the Due Process Clause of the Fourteenth Amendment, to receive necessary medical attention while in police custody.

...In *Monell v. New York City Dept. of Social Services*, we decided that a municipality can be found liable under 1983 only where the municipality itself causes the constitutional violation at issue....

...We agree with the court below that a city can be liable under 1983 for inadequate training of its employees... We hold today that the inadequacy of police training may serve as the basis for 1983 liability only where the failure to train amounts to deliberate indifference to the rights of persons with whom the police come into contact. This rule is most consistent with our admonition that a municipality can be liable under 1983 only where its policies are the "moving force [behind] the constitutional violation." Only where a municipality's failure to train its employees in a relevant respect evidences a "deliberate indifference" to the rights of its inhabitants can such a shortcoming be properly thought of as a city "policy or custom" that is actionable under 1983. Only where a failure to train reflects a "deliberate" or "conscious" choice by a municipality—a "policy" as defined by our prior cases—can a city be liable for such a failure under 1983.

. . .To adopt lesser standards of fault and causation would open municipalities to unprecedented liability under 1983. In virtually every instance where a person has had his or her constitutional rights violated by a city employee, a 1983 plaintiff will be able to point to something the city "could have done" to prevent the unfortunate incident. Thus, permitting cases against cities for their "failure to train" employees to go forward under 1983 on a lesser standard of fault would result in de facto respondeat superior liability on municipalities—a result we rejected in *Monell*. It would also engage the federal courts in an endless exercise of second-guessing municipal employee-training programs. This is an exercise we believe the federal courts are ill-suited to undertake, as well as one that would implicate serious questions of federalism.

. . .Consequently, for the reasons given above, we vacate the judgment of the Court of Appeals and remand this case for further proceedings consistent with this opinion. It is so ordered.

Case Discussion and Significance. *Canton* held that a municipality may, in certain circumstances, be held liable under Section 1983 for constitutional violations resulting from its failure to train its employees. There are limited circumstances in which a "failure to train" allegation can be the basis for liability. This lack of training may serve as the basis for 1983 liability only where the failure to train in a relevant respect amounts to deliberate indifference to the constitutional rights of persons with whom the police come into contact. Only where a failure to train reflects a "deliberate" or "conscious" choice by the municipality can the failure be properly thought of as an actionable city "policy."

Smith v. Wade
461 U.S. 30 (1983)

JUSTICE BRENNAN delivered the opinion of the Court.

We granted certiorari in this case to decide whether the District Court for the Western District of Missouri applied the correct legal standard in instructing the jury that it might award punitive damages under 42 U.S.C. 1983....

...The District Judge also charged the jury that it could award punitive damages on a proper showing:

"In addition to actual damages, the law permits the jury, under certain circumstances, to award the injured person punitive and exemplary damages, in order to punish the wrongdoer for some extraordinary misconduct, and to serve as an example or warning to others not to engage in such conduct."

"If you find the issues in favor of the plaintiff, and if the conduct of one or more of the defendants is shown to be a reckless or callous disregard of, or indifference to, the rights or safety of others, then you may assess punitive or exemplary damages in addition to any award of actual damages. ". . .The amount of punitive or exemplary damages assessed against any defendant may be such sum as you believe will serve to punish that defendant and to deter him and others from like conduct."

The jury returned defense verdicts for two of the three remaining defendants. It found Smith liable, however, and awarded $25,000 in compensatory damages and $5,000 in punitive damages. The District Court entered judgment on the verdict, and the Court of Appeals affirmed.

In this Court, Smith attacks only the award of punitive damages. He does not challenge the correctness of the instructions on liability or qualified immunity, nor does he question the adequacy of the evidence to support the verdict of liability for compensatory damages.

. . .Smith does not argue that the common law, either in 1871 or now, required or requires a showing of actual malicious intent for recovery of punitive damages.

Perhaps not surprisingly, there was significant variation (both terminological and substantive) among American jurisdictions in the latter 19th century on the precise standard to be applied in awarding punitive damages—variation that was exacerbated by the ambiguity and slipperiness of such common terms as *malice* and *gross negligence*. Most of the confusion, however, seems to have been over the degree of negligence, recklessness, carelessness, or culpable indifference that should be required—not over whether actual intent was essential.

This Court further explained the standard for punitive damages, "The tort is aggravated by the evil motive, and on this rests the rule of exemplary damages. To [assess punitive damages], there must have been some wilful misconduct, or that entire want of care which would raise the presumption of a conscious indifference to consequences."

The same rule applies today. . . .

The remaining question is whether the policies and purposes of 1983 itself require a departure from the rules of tort common law. As a general matter, we discern no reason why a person whose federally guaranteed rights have been violated should be granted a more restrictive remedy than a person asserting an ordinary tort cause of action....

...We hold that a jury may be permitted to assess punitive damages in an action under 1983 when the defendant's conduct is shown to be motivated by evil motive or intent, or when it involves reckless or callous indifference to the federally protected rights of others. We further hold that this threshold applies even when the underlying standard of liability for compensatory damages is one of recklessness. Because the jury instructions in this case are in accord with this rule, the judgment of the Court of Appeals is Affirmed.

Case Discussion and Significance. *Wade* held that punitive damages are available in a 1983 action. A jury may be permitted to assess punitive damages when the defendant's conduct involves reckless or callous indifference to the plaintiff's federally protected rights, as well as when it is motivated by evil motive or intent. The common law allows recovery of punitive damages in tort cases not only for actual malicious intent, but also for reckless indifference to the rights of others. Neither the policies nor the purposes of 1983 require a departure from the common-law rule.

CASE SUMMARIES

A Michigan corrections department was not liable for escaped prisoner's murder of man at home he broke into; prisoner's own criminal actions, rather than allegedly "insecure prison system" was the cause of the death. *Peters v. Dept. of Corrections*, 546 N.W.2d 668 (Mich. App. 1996).

State officials may be sued for damages in their individual capacities in federal civil rights cases, even if they were acting "in their official capacities" during the complained of conduct, U.S. Supreme Court rules. *Hafter v. Melo,* 60 U.S.L.W. 4001 (U.S. Nov. 5, 1991).

Prison officials cannot be held liable, in federal civil rights suits, for inadequate prison conditions absent a showing of "deliberate indifference" as a mental state; U.S. Supreme Court adopts tougher standard for inmate suits. *Wilson v. Seiter*, 111 S. Ct. 2321 (1991).

Civil rights suit dismissed when plaintiff-inmates did not clearly state that they were suing state corrections officials in their individual capacities; Eleventh Amendment immunity applied to their official capacities. *Wells v. Brown*, 891 F. 2d 591 (6th Cir. 1989).

A policy directive on use of chemical agents, such as mace, against resisting prisoners did not create constitutionally protected liberty interest for violation of which Michigan state prisoner could sue correctional officer. *McLaurin v. Morton*, 48 F.3d 944 (6th Cir. 1995).

An overflowed toilet in prisoner's cell which was allegedly not cleaned up for four days did not amount to a constitutional violation for "exposure to raw sewage." *Smith v. Copeland*, 87 F.3d 265 (8th Cir. 1996).

A prisoner who weighed 330 pounds did not suffer cruel and unusual punishment when prison was unable to furnish him with two pairs of pants which fit him, and as a result he sometimes had to wear ill-fitting, dirty, or torn clothing. *Young v. Berks County Prison*, 940 F. Supp. 121 (E.D. Pa. 1996).

A lack of hot water, constantly "running" toilet, and failure of toilet to properly flush for 20 day period did not constitute cruel and unusual punishment of prisoner in segregation unit cell. *Neal v. Clark*, 938 F. Supp. 484 (N.D. Ill. 1996).

SUMMARY

- *Habeas corpus* is the process by which an inmate may challenge the legality of his or her confinement.
- *Mandamus* is a judicial remedy that is used to compel a lower court or a governmental entity to perform a duty or do a certain act.
- Torts are civil remedies for violation of duties owed others. They are private, rather than public, wrongs.
- Correctional officers may be held criminally liable for their acts against inmates.
- Section 1983 actions allow inmates to sue correctional officers if their federal civil rights have been violated.

DISCUSSION QUESTIONS

1. Distinguish between a *Writ of Habeas Corpus* and a *Writ of Mandate*.
2. List the type of crimes a correctional officer might be charged with if he shot an inmate without any justification.
3. Distinguish between custom and lack of training.
4. Define *deliberate indifference*.

ENDNOTES

1. Portions of this chapter have been adapted from *Prisoner Petitions in the Federal Courts. 1980-96*, Bureau of Justice Statistics, U.S. Department of Justice, Washington D.C., October 1997.
2. *Id.*
3. See *Prisoner Petitions in the Federal Courts. 1980-96*, Bureau of Justice Statistics, U.S. Department of Justice, Washington D.C., October 1997. p. 15.
4. *Black's Law Dictionary*, 6th Edition, (West Publishing 1990) p. 1489.
5. Portions of this section have been adapted from Harvey Wallace, *Victimology: Legal, Psychological, and Social Perspectives*, (Allyn & Bacon, 1998) used with permission of author.
6. Civil Rights Act (Enforcement Act) of 1866, ch. 31, 14 Stat. 27.
7. Enforcement Act of 1870 (Act of May 31, 1870), ch. 114, 16 Stat. 140, amended by Act of Feb. 28, 1871, ch. 99, 16 Stat. 433.
8. Ku Klux Klan (Anti-lynching) Act, ch. 22, 17 Stat. 13 (1971).
9. 18 U.S.C. section 241 (1988).
10. 18 U.S.C. section 242 (1988).
11. 42 U.S.C. Section 1983 (1981, West Supp. 1985).
12. 313 U.S. 299 (1941).
13. 313 U.S. at 326.
14. 325 U.S. 91 (1945).
15. 365 U.S. 167 (1961).
16. 436 U.S. 658(1978).
17. 455 U.S. 622 (1980).
18. 403 U.S. 388 (1971).
19. 503 U.S. 140 (1992).
20. 885 F.2d 1439, 1444 (9th Cir. 1989).
21. *City of Canton v. Harris*, 489 U.S. 378 (1989).
22. 475 U.S. 312 (1986).
23. *Id.* at 320.
24. *Id.* at 320.

CHAPTER 11

CIVIL LIABILITY DEFENSES

IMMUNITY

Immunity provides a shield against lawsuits and liability. Three basic types of immunity arise in correctional cases:

- Sovereign immunity
- Absolute immunity
- Qualified immunity

It is important to understand each type of immunity and their relationship to each other.

Doctrine of Sovereign Immunity

The doctrine is based upon the ancient principle that "the king can do no wrong," and therefore his subjects cannot question his decisions. The doctrine has been passed down from medieval times to the present day, and now shields the government from civil liability. Therefore, absent an exception, no one can sue the government. For example, in *Alabama v. Pugh*, inmates sued the state of Alabama alleging that its prison conditions constituted cruel and unusual punishment.[1] The U.S. Supreme Court dismissed the state of Alabama and the State Board of Corrections from the lawsuit because the Eleventh Amendment to the Constitution prohibits federal courts from proceeding with lawsuits against states without the states' permission. The Court allowed the lawsuit to remain against individuals, reasoning that when an individual violates the constitutional rights of another, he or she is not acting as an authorized agent of the state and, therefore, sovereign immunity does not apply.

Doctrine of Absolute Immunity

The philosophy behind sovereign immunity was used to establish absolute immunity. Certain government officials should be free to carry out their duties without fear of being sued. If an official has absolute immunity, no one can maintain a civil lawsuit against that person. This doctrine applies even if there was extensive damages or injuries and the person shielded by absolute immunity acted with an evil heart or maliciously.

Because this type of immunity prevents all civil lawsuits, legislatures and courts have limited its application to only a few officials. Traditionally, the only persons protected by absolute immunity are judges.[2] Early case law has extended this immunity to witnesses and attorneys while in court.[3] Even if the official is not protected by absolute immunity, he or she may be shielded from liability if qualified immunity is available.

Doctrine of Qualified Immunity

Qualified immunity is also known as good faith immunity. If it applies, the official is immune from any civil action. However, qualified immunity is not always available to governmental officials. It is a complex doctrine that relies upon various factors in determining whether an official is immune from civil action.

The principles governing the application of qualified immunity were clarified in the U.S. Supreme Court case of *Wood v. Strickland*.[4] In *Wood*, the Court established a two-prong test to determine whether an official was protected by qualified immunity:

1. The official did not know nor should have known that the action violated the constitutional rights of the person, nor did he act with malicious intent to injure the other person.

2. The official acted with good faith and a belief that what he was doing was constitutional.

Thus, the *Wood* case requires officials to have a basic knowledge of constitutional rights afforded those for whom he or she is responsible. Therefore, there is no qualified immunity available if the official knew, or should have known, that his actions violated the constitutional rights of another person, or if the official acted with malicious intent to violate another's constitutional rights. The principles established in *Wood* were applied to correctional officials in *Procunier v. Navarette*.[5] The court held that qualified immunity was not available to prison officials if they violated the *Wood* standard.

What happens if a correctional official acts according to a good faith belief in the law and the courts or the legislature subsequently change that law so that the official's acts now violate an inmate's constitutional rights? Is the official liable or can the defense of qualified immunity apply in these situations? In *Harlow v. Fitzgerald*, the U.S. Supreme Court stated:

> If the law [at the time of the act] was not clearly established, an official could not reasonably be expected to anticipate subsequent legal developments, nor could he fairly be said to 'know' that the law forbade conduct not previously identified as unlawful.[6]

However, if the official knew that he or she was violating an inmate's constitutional rights or the law was clearly established, qualified immunity is not available.[7]

Procedurally, the burden of proof shifts from one party to the other when dealing with qualified immunity. The plaintiff (inmate) files an action alleging injury based on tort or the violation of certain constitutional rights. The defendant (correctional officer or official) then files an answer or other motion to dismiss the case raising the issue or defense of qualified immunity.

DOUBLE JEOPARDY

Similar to other procedural defenses, the prohibition against double jeopardy is covered in more detail in criminal and/or constitutional law texts. This is included only as a brief overview of another form of defense. The Fifth Amendment states that

"No person . . . shall. . . be subject for the same offense to be twice put in jeopardy of life or limb. . . ."

This amendment protects individuals from governmental efforts to repeatedly attempt to convict them of the same crime. The right attaches as soon as the defendant is put to trial. This normally occurs with the impaneling and swearing of the jury.

The prohibition against double jeopardy prohibits the government from prosecuting the defendant for the same crime after a conviction or an acquittal. It also prohibits multiple punishments for the same offense. However, it does not prevent the government from retrying the case if the jury cannot agree on the guilt or innocence of the defendant. This is called a hung jury and the case is set for a new trial.

Practicum

Officer Jones was hired by the state. The state had limited background checks and did not conduct any psychological evaluations of its correctional officers. After working three months on the job, Officer Jones raped and physically beat inmate Jane Smith.

The Federal Bureau of Investigation conducted an investigation and filed criminal charges against Officer Jones claiming he violated Smith's constitutional rights. He was convicted in federal court and sentenced to 10 years in prison.

After the federal conviction, the local District Attorney, who was running for reelection, decided to file rape and assault charges against Jones. Jones' attorney filed a motion to dismiss, claiming the second

> prosecution was barred by the Fifth Amendment. Is this a violation of the double jeopardy clause?
> No. The bar does not apply to different jurisdictions, and therefore the local prosecution can go forward.

STATUTE OF LIMITATIONS

The statute of limitations requires that criminal prosecutions commence within a certain period of time after the crime occurred. It is a jurisdictional requirement. Accordingly, failure to commence prosecution within the required time period bars the state or federal government from prosecuting the accused. The statute is designed to ensure that an individual is not accountable indefinitely for the commission of an offense. For example, in some states most felonies have a four-year statute of limitations, which means that the state must imitate criminal proceedings against the defendant within four years from the date the offense was discovered or should have been discovered. Serious offenses, such as murder, rape and kidnapping, generally do not have a statute of limitations. The statute does not toll (run or expire) while the accused is outside the jurisdiction of the state or federal government in cases of federal crimes. For example, the crime of forgery has a four-year statute of limitations. Defendant commits forgery and then leaves the state for two years. In determining whether the statute of limitations has run (expired), the two years that the defendant was beyond the jurisdiction of the court would be excluded in computing the time period.

The statute of limitations is an affirmative defense and must be raised by the accused. This is normally accomplished at pretrial hearings. Once it has been raised by the defendant, the prosecution must then establish that the statute has not run. The statute of limitations differs from a speedy-trial problem. The statute of limitations starts running when the crime is discovered, or should have been discovered, and stops when prosecution is initiated, which in most cases is the filing of the formal complaint. Time is computed by excluding the first day (date crime was committed or should have been discovered) and including the last day (when the prosecution starts). Speedy trial starts when the accused is charged or arrested.

SELF-DEFENSE

In understanding the concept of self-defense it is important to distinguish between deadly force and nondeadly force. Normally, a person is justified in using deadly force only to protect himself or others from what he reasonably believes is necessary to combat imminent, unlawful deadly force. The self-defense contains the components of proportionality and necessity. *Proportionality* requires that the force used must not be out of proportion to the force necessary to protect. A person is not privileged to use force that is disproportional to the threat that the actor reasonably believes he is facing.

There must also be a necessity to use the force to prevent imminent, unlawful deadly force. For example, if an inmate threatened to attack a correctional officer at some future date, the officer has alternatives other than the use of force to protect him or herself. Deadly force is generally defined as force likely to cause death or grievous bodily injury. In most cases, the identification of force as deadly is based on the objective likelihood of the outcome.

The use of force is based on what appears to be reasonably necessary. Accordingly, self-defense is permitted if the actor makes a reasonable mistake of fact regarding the need to use deadly force.

> An inmate points a weapon at a correctional officer. The officer can reasonably assume that the weapon is loaded and act accordingly to protect himself. It would not matter if later it was determined that the inmate's weapon was unloaded.

Generally the use of deadly force in self-defense is limited to those situations where the actor is not the aggressor. In most jurisdictions, a person may not start a fight and then use deadly force to protect himself. There are exceptions to this general rule.

Example 1:

Two correctional officers are having a drink in a bar after their shift and D mildly insults A. A becomes unreasonably outraged and attempts to kill D. In this case, D probably could use self-defense to protect himself.

In most jurisdictions, if an aggressor starts a fight and then tries clearly to retreat, deadly force may be justified if retreat is unsuccessful. An *aggressor* is one whose affirmative unlawful conduct was reasonably calculated to produce an affray foreboding injurious or fatal consequences. [Note: in determining whether a person is an aggressor the courts look only at the conduct at the time that he used the deadly force.]

Example 2:

An inmate starts a fight with a correctional officer. The fight is broken up. The next day, without warning, the officer attacks the inmate. In this situation, the officer would be considered as the aggressor.

The general rule is that a non-aggressor has no duty to retreat prior to using deadly force. However, a significant number of jurisdictions reject this rule and hold that if the actor can safely retreat, then he must prior to resorting to deadly force.

The rules regarding the use of nondeadly force are similar to those for the use of deadly force. The actor must reasonably believe that the force used is necessary to prevent an imminent unlawful force. However, there is no duty for a non-aggressor actor to retreat prior to using nondeadly force.

DEFENSE OF OTHERS

As a general rule, a person is justified in using force to prevent an unlawful attack upon another person when the one using force reasonably believes that the one under attack is in imminent danger of harm, and the use of force is necessary to avoid the danger. Some early English and American cases required the one being defended to be related to the defender. However, the modern view does not retain this requirement, and a person can use force to defend a stranger. In most jurisdictions, the actor has the same rights to use force as the person being attacked. It is often stated that when you use force to save a third person, you step into the shoes of the third person with whatever rights that third person had to defend himself. However, some jurisdictions allow a person to defend a third person based on reasonable appearances, i.e., what a reasonable person would believe was appropriate.

CASE ON POINT

Cleavinger v. Saxner
474 U.S. 193 (1985)

Respondent federal prison inmates were found guilty by the prison's discipline committee, composed of petitioner prison officials, of encouraging other inmates to engage in a work stoppage and of other charges, and were ordered to be placed in administrative detention and to forfeit a specified number of days of "good time." On appeals to the Warden and the Regional Director of the Bureau of Prisons, respondents were ordered released from administrative detention and all material relevant to the incident in question was ordered expunged from their records. They were later paroled and released. But in the meantime, they brought suit in Federal

District Court against petitioners, alleging a violation of various federal constitutional rights and seeking declaratory and injunctive relief and damages. After initially dismissing the complaint on the ground that petitioners were entitled to absolute immunity from liability, the District Court, on reconsideration, reinstated the suit. The case was tried to a jury, which found that petitioners [prison officials] had violated respondents' Fifth Amendment due process rights, and awarded damages. The Court of Appeals affirmed, rejecting petitioners' claim for absolute immunity.

JUSTICE BLACKMUN delivered the opinion of the Court.

This case presents the issue whether members of a federal prison's Institution Discipline Committee, who hear cases in which inmates are charged with rules infractions, are entitled to absolute, as distinguished from qualified, immunity from personal damages liability for actions violative of the United States Constitution.

I

Respondents David Saxner and Alfred Cain, Jr., in January 1975 were inmates at the Federal Correctional Institution at Terre Haute, Ind. They were serving 4- and 5-year sentences, respectively, and each was within 18 months of a possible release date. Each was soon to appear before the parole board. The prison-conduct record of each was good.

On January 6, 1975, William Lowe, a black inmate at Terre Haute died in the prison hospital. He was the first of four black inmates to die there within the ensuing 7-month period. A work stoppage to protest Lowe's death took place at the prison on January 7 and 8. Respondent Saxner, a white inmate who had served as a "jailhouse lawyer," and respondent Cain, a black inmate who was the librarian for the African and New World Cultural Society, assert that neither of them participated in the stoppage. . . .Each, however, was active in gathering information about Lowe's death and about conditions at the prison hospital, and in passing that information to the press, Members of Congress, prison officials, and Saxner's attorney. On February 14, respondents were cited in separate Incident Reports for encouraging other inmates to engage in work stoppage. Each was immediately placed in administrative segregation, that is, removed from the general inmate population, and assigned to a separate cell in an unused part of the hospital.

On the following day, each respondent was given a copy of the Bureau of Prisons Policy Statement 7400.5c (subject: Inmate Discipline) (Oct. 4, 1974). Saxner signed a written notice which explained his rights at a hearing to be held before an Institution Discipline Committee. Among these were the right to have a written copy of the charge; the right to have a member of the prison staff represent him; the rights, except where institutional safety would be jeopardized, to be present at the hearing, to call witnesses, and to submit documentary evidence; and the right to receive a written explanation of the committee's decision. Although the record does not so disclose, we assume that respondent Cain received a similar notice at that time.

Respondents were brought before the Institution Discipline Committee on February 21. The committee was composed of petitioners Theodore Cleavinger, Associate Warden, as chairman; Marvin Marcadis, correctional supervisor; and Tom P.

Lockett, chief of case management. Respondent Saxner was accompanied at the hearing by Ralph Smith, staff counselor, whom Saxner had selected to represent him. After reading the charge and reviewing Saxner's rights, the committee introduced Saxner's Incident Report and three documents found in his cell. These were, respectively, a "press release" Saxner had sent to 50 newspapers; a four-page document which detailed interviews with inmates about their medical treatment at the prison hospital; and a letter from Saxner to an American Civil Liberties Union lawyer, Saunders, which enclosed the other two documents and which discussed medical conditions, possible litigation on behalf of the Lowe family and other inmates, communications with the press, and the obtaining of local counsel. The press release, among other things, advocated administrative approval of a prisoners' union and amnesty for those who had participated in the work stoppage. Neither the investigating officer nor the charging officer nor any guard was called as a witness. Saxner, however, testified and introduced affidavits of several inmates. His request that he be permitted to call inmates to confirm that he did not encourage any work stoppage was denied on the ground that such testimony would be cumulative. While admitting that he had written the press release and had mailed it to persons outside the prison without authorization, Saxner asserted his innocence on the specific charge referred.

The committee found respondent Saxner guilty of encouraging a work stoppage. Also, although not specifically so charged, he was found guilty of unauthorized use of the mail and of possession of contraband, that is, material advocating an illegal prisoners' union. The committee ordered that Saxner be placed in administrative detention and forfeit 84 days of "good time." His transfer to another institution was recommended.

Respondent Cain's hearing took place the same day before the same committee and immediately prior to Saxner's hearing. He was accompanied by J. R. Alvarado, a staff representative. He was advised of his rights. His Incident Report was produced. Two documents found in his cell (Saxner's letter to Saunders and a manuscript concerning "Ideals and Proposals of the Prisoner Labor Union") were introduced. Cain testified and denied that he had encouraged inmates not to work. He requested the right to cross-examine his accusers, but no other witness was called.

At the conclusion of Cain's hearing, the committee found him guilty of encouraging a work stoppage and, although not specifically so charged, of possessing contraband, that is, "inflammatory material . . . supporting disruptive conduct in the institution." The committee ordered that Cain be placed in administrative detention and forfeit 96 days of "good time." His transfer to another institution also was recommended.

Respondents appealed to the Warden of the institution. The Warden ordered their release from administrative detention, restored the good time, and directed that each respondent's record carry a notation that "the incident not reflect unfavorably" upon consideration for parole.

The Warden refused, however, to expunge respondents' records. *Ibid.* Saxner and Cain were released into the general prison population on March 21.

Respondents next appealed to the Regional Director of the Bureau of Prisons. The Regional Director ruled that the disciplinary report, the action by the committee on the incident, and material relevant thereto were to be expunged from each respondent's record. Thus, in the end, after these appeals, respondents obtained all the administrative relief they sought. But in the meantime, for a definite interval, each had been condemned (improperly as it turned out) to "administrative detention."

Respondent Saxner was paroled and released in April 1975. Respondent Cain was granted parole in June and released in December.

Meanwhile, in March 1975, respondents brought suit in the United States District Court for the Southern District of Indiana against petitioners, the Terre Haute Warden, and the institution's administrative supervisor. Their third amended complaint alleged that the defendants had violated their rights under the First, Fourth, Fifth, Sixth, and Eighth Amendments. *Id.*, at 12. See *Bivens v. Six Unknown Fed. Narcotics Agents*, 403 U.S. 388 (1971). Respondents sought declaratory and injunctive relief and compensatory damages.

The District Court granted petitioners' motion to dismiss the complaint on the ground that their functioning as hearing officers entitled them to absolute immunity. Nearly two years later, however, in April 1981, the District Court, on reconsideration, reinstated the suit in light of its controlling court's decision in *Mary v. Ramsden*, 635 F.2d 590 (CA7 1980), where the Court of Appeals held that members of a disciplinary committee at a Wisconsin juvenile facility were entitled to only qualified immunity.

The case then was tried to a jury. In response to special interrogatories, the jury found that petitioners had violated respondents' Fifth Amendment due process rights. The jury awarded each respondent $1,500 compensatory damages against each petitioner, or a total of $4,500; each petitioner was thus subjected to liability totaling $3,000.

Petitioners' subsequent motion for judgment notwithstanding the verdict was denied. They appealed, contending, among other things, that, as members of the discipline committee, they were entitled to absolute immunity.

The United States Court of Appeals for the Seventh Circuit, by a divided vote, affirmed. *Saxner v. Benson*, 727 F.2d 669 (1984). It held that petitioners' claim for absolute immunity was foreclosed by Seventh Circuit precedent denying such immunity to state correctional officers serving in a similar capacity.

Because of the importance of the issue, and because the Seventh Circuit rulings, although consistent with *Jihaad v. O'Brien*, 645 F.2d 556, 561 (CA6 1981), were claimed to be in some conflict with the en banc decision of the Fourth Circuit in *Ward v. Johnson*, 690 F.2d 1098 (1982), we granted certiorari..

II
A. This Court has observed: "Few doctrines were more solidly established at common law than the immunity of judges from liability for damages for acts committed within their judicial jurisdiction." *Pierson v. Ray*, 386 U.S. 547, 553-554 (1967). The Court specifically has pronounced and followed this doctrine of the common law for more than a century. In *Bradley v. Fisher*, 13 Wall. 335 (1872), it ruled

that a federal judge may not be held accountable in damages for a judicial act taken within his court's jurisdiction. Such immunity applies "however erroneous the act may have been, and however injurious in its consequences it may have proved to the plaintiff." "Nor can this exemption of the judges from civil liability be affected by the motives with which their judicial acts are performed." In *Pierson v. Ray,* supra, the Court held that absolute immunity shielded a municipal judge who was sued for damages under 42 U.S.C. 1983 by clergymen who alleged that he had convicted them unconstitutionally for a peaceful protest against racial segregation. The Court stressed that such immunity was essential to protect the integrity of the judicial process. . .The Court once again enunciated this principle, despite any "informality with which [the judge] proceeded," and despite any ex parte feature of the proceeding.

With this judicial immunity firmly established, the Court has extended absolute immunity to certain others who perform functions closely associated with the judicial process. The federal hearing examiner and administrative law judge have been afforded absolute immunity. "There can be little doubt that the role of the modern federal hearing examiner or administrative law judge . . . is `functionally comparable' to that of a judge." *Butz v. Economou,* 438 U.S. 478, 513 (1978). Full immunity also has been given to federal and state prosecutors. The same is true for witnesses, including police officers, who testify in judicial proceedings. Witnesses are "integral parts of the judicial process" and, accordingly, are shielded by absolute immunity. *Briscoe v. LaHue,* 460 U.S. 325, 335 (1983). And the Court has noted the adoption in this country of the principle of immunity for grand jurors.

Although this Court has not decided whether state parole officials enjoy absolute immunity as a matter of federal law, see *Martinez v. California*, 444 U.S. 277, 284 (1980), federal appellate courts have so held.

B. The Court has extended absolute immunity to the President when damages liability is predicated on his official act. *Nixon v. Fitzgerald*, 457 U.S. 731, 744-758 (1982)." For executive officials in general, however, our cases make plain that qualified immunity represents the norm.". . . Absolute immunity flows not from rank or title or "location within the Government," *Butz v. Economou*, 438 U.S., at 511, but from the nature of the responsibilities of the individual official. And in Butz the Court mentioned the following factors, among others, as characteristic of the judicial process and to be considered in determining absolute as contrasted with qualified immunity: (a) the need to assure that the individual can perform his functions without harassment or intimidation; (b) the presence of safeguards that reduce the need for private damages actions as a means of controlling unconstitutional conduct; (c) insulation from political influence; (d) the importance of precedent; (e) the adversary nature of the process; and (f) the correctability of error on appeal.

III

We turn to the application of these principles to the facts of the present case. Judge Cudahy of the Court of Appeals, in his separate concurring opinion, 727 F.2d, at 673, stressed the Butz factors and was persuaded by what he felt were the absence of procedural safeguards, the rare and exceptional character of absolute immunity, and the need for such immunity only when public policy requires it.

Petitioners, in response, and seemingly in order to negate the significance of certain of the specified factors, point out that grand jury proceedings possess few procedural safeguards that are associated with court proceedings, and are largely immune from any type of judicial review. . . . Petitioners also observe that prosecutorial decision-making is not subject to the formalities of trials; instead, the prosecutor exercises broad and generally unreviewable discretion. Yet grand jurors and prosecutors enjoy absolute immunity. Petitioners finally argue that the Court's cases teach that absolute immunity shields an official if (a) the official performs an adjudicatory function comparable to that of a judge, (b) the function is of sufficient public importance, and (c) the proper performance of that function would be subverted if the official were subjected to individual suit for damages.

When we evaluate the claim of immunity for the committee members, we bear in mind that immunity status is for the benefit of the public as well as for the individual concerned. *Pierson v. Ray*, 386 U.S., at 554. The committee members, in a sense, do perform an adjudicatory function in that they determine whether the accused inmate is guilty or innocent of the charge leveled against him; in that they hear testimony and receive documentary evidence; in that they evaluate credibility and weigh evidence; and in that they render a decision. We recognize, too, the presence of some societal importance in this dispute-resolution function. The administration of a prison is a difficult undertaking at best, for it concerns persons many of whom have demonstrated a proclivity for antisocial, criminal, and violent conduct. See *Hudson v. Palmer*, 468 U.S. 517, 526-527 (1984). We also acknowledge that many inmates do not refrain from harassment and intimidation. The number of nonmeritorious prisoners' cases that come to this court's notice is evidence of this. Tension between prison officials and inmates has been described as "unremitting." *Wolff v. McDonnell*, 418 U.S. 539, 562 (1974). "Retaliation is much more than a theoretical possibility." *Ibid*. And we do not underestimate the fact, stressed by petitioners, that committee members usually are persons of modest means and, if they are sue-able and unprotected, perhaps would be disinclined to serve on a discipline committee. See *Ward v. Johnson*, 690 F.2d, at 1108.

We conclude, nonetheless, that these concerns, to the extent they are well grounded, are overstated in the context of constitutional violations. We do not perceive the discipline committee's function as a "classic" adjudicatory one, as petitioners would describe it. Surely, the members of the committee, unlike a federal or state judge, are not "independent"; to say that they are is to ignore reality. They are not professional hearing officers, as are administrative law judges. They are, instead, prison officials, albeit no longer of the rank and file, temporarily diverted from their usual duties. They are employees of the Bureau of Prisons, and they are the direct subordinates of the warden who reviews their decision. They work with the fellow employee who lodges the charge against the inmate upon whom they sit in judgment. The credibility determination they make often is one between a co-worker and an inmate. They thus are under obvious pressure to resolve a disciplinary dispute in favor of the institution and their fellow employee. It is the old situational problem of the relationship between the keeper and the kept, a relationship that hardly is conducive to a truly adjudicatory performance.

. . .We are not persuaded. To be sure, the line between absolute immunity and qualified immunity often is not an easy one to perceive and structure.

That determination in this case, however, is not difficult, and we readily conclude that these committee members fall on the qualified-immunity side of the line.

Under the Bureau's disciplinary policy in effect at the time of respondents' hearings, few of the procedural safeguards contained in the Administrative Procedure Act under consideration in *Butz* were present. The prisoner was to be afforded neither a lawyer nor an independent nonstaff representative. There was no right to compel the attendance of witnesses or to cross-examine. There was no right to discovery. There was no cognizable burden of proof. No verbatim transcript was afforded. Information presented often was hearsay or self-serving. The committee members were not truly independent. In sum, the members had no identification with the judicial process of the kind and depth that has occasioned absolute immunity.

Qualified immunity, however, is available to these committee members. That, we conclude, is the proper point at which to effect the balance between the opposing considerations. This less-than-absolute protection is not of small consequence. As the Court noted in *Butz*, 438 U.S., at 507-508, insubstantial lawsuits can be recognized and be quickly disposed of, and firm application of the Federal Rules of Civil Procedure "will ensure that federal officials are not harassed by frivolous lawsuits." *Id.*, at 508. All the committee members need to do is to follow the clear and simple constitutional requirements of *Wolff v. McDonnell*, supra; they then should have no reason to fear substantial harassment and liability. Qualified immunity has been widely imposed on executive officials who possess greater responsibilities.

CASE SUMMARIES

The U.S. Supreme Court reviewed the issue of whether correctional officers working for privately run state prison may assert qualified immunity defense in federal civil rights lawsuit; federal appeals court held that this defense was not available to such defendants in prisoner's lawsuit. *McKnight v. Rees*, 88 F.3d 417 (6th Cir.), cert. granted, sub nom., *Richardson v. McKnight*, 117 S. Ct. 504, 1996 U.S. LEXIS 7155 (U.S. Nov. 27, 1996). The Supreme Court ruled that qualified immunity defense in federal civil rights lawsuits is not available to correctional officers working for privately run state prisons. *Richardson v. McKnight*, 117 S. Ct. 2100, 1997 U.S. LEXIS 3866 (June 23, 1997).

Prison officials could have reasonably believed that it did not violate the Eighth Amendment to fail to repair a defective oven door; defendant officials were entitled to qualified immunity in suit brought by prisoner burned when door fell off. *Osolinski v. Kane*, 92 F.3d 934 (9th Cir. 1996).

Psychiatrist was entitled to qualified immunity for ordering single dose of anti-psychotic drug to prisoner suffering seizure when it was feared that prisoner would injure himself; no prior case law "clearly established" need to hold a prior hearing in such an emergency situation. *Hogan v. Carter*, 85 F.3d 1113 (4th Cir. 1996).

Prison employee entitled to qualified immunity for denying prisoner loan for postage for outgoing legal mail unless he agreed to allow her to briefly inspect it in his presence to make sure it qualified as legal mail. *Bell-Bey v. Williams*, 87 F.3d 832 (6th Cir. 1996).

Prison officials were entitled to qualified immunity on prisoner's suit claiming that his segregation with other HIV-positive prisoners violated his constitutional right of freedom of association with prisoners in the general prison population. *Camarillo v. McCarthy*, 998 F.2d 638 (9th Cir. 1993).

SUMMARY

- Immunity is a shield against lawsuits and liability. There are two basic types of immunity: absolute and qualified.

- The double jeopardy prohibitions protect individuals from repeated prosecutions, but do not bar separate state and federal prosecutions for the same offense.

- The statute of limitations prevents the government from filing prosecutions after a certain period of time.

- Self-defense and defense of others are common defenses used by correctional officers who have used force on inmates.

DISCUSSION QUESTIONS

1. Explain the difference between absolute and qualified immunity. Should absolute immunity be available to correctional officers who staff towers with weapons? Why? Why not?

2. Should double jeopardy bar state and federal prosecution for the same act?

3. When should deadly force be used in a correctional setting? During an escape? During a riot? During an assault on another inmate? During an assault on a correctional officer?

ENDNOTES

1. 438 U.S. 781 (1978).
2. *Pierson v. Roy,* 386 U.S. 547 (1967)
3. *Yaselli v. Goff,* 275 U.S. 503 (1927).
4. 420 U.S. 308 (1975).
5. 434 U.S. 555 (1978).
6. 457 U.S. 800 (1982).
7. See *Bennett v. Williams,* 689 F.2nd 1370 (11th Cir. 1983) holding Alabama prison officials liable for living conditions that were considered cruel and unusual punishment since there was prior litigation putting them on notice of the continuing nature of the violations.

INDEX

A

absolute immunity   268
aggressor   273
allocution   104
American Bar Association's
    Canons of Professional
    Conduct   59
Antiterrorism and Effective Death
    Penalty Act   29
appearance   79
appellate judge   70
appellate jurisdiction   55
appointed counsel   68
arraignment   80
attorney
  defense   66
  retained   66

B

bail   77
Bill of Rights   58
blind plea   91
blood feuds   2
burden of proof   269

C

chain gangs   31
challenge for cause   83
charging the jury   84
Child Protection Act of 1984
    166
citation release   77
civil death   3

Civil Rights Act of 1866   246, 247
Civil Rights Act of 1871   248
Civil Rights Act, Section 1983   27
Code of Draco   4
collective bargaining   122
collective incapacitation   9
color of law   249
compensatory damages   246
conditional release   77
conservative ideology   5
contract system   66
courts
  appellate jurisdiction   55
  general jurisdiciton   54
  geographic organization   52
  limited jurisdiction   53
  structure of   53
  trial   53
courts of appeals   55
courts of last resort   55
criminal sanctions
  goals of   6
cross-gender searches   188

D

deadly force   272
defendant   58
defense attorney
  role of   66
deference period   26
deferred adjudication   15
deliberate indifference   252
determinate sentencing   11
deterrence   8
discharge   22
double jeopardy   270

Due Process Clause 28, 129, 227

E

Eighth Amendment 213, 217, 232, 233, 234, 235
Enforcement Act of 1870 247
equity 54
evidence
  insufficient 77

F

factual basis 102
federal circuit courts of appeals 56
federal court judges 73
federal court system
  establishment of 51
federal district courts 56
federal magistrates 74
Federal Magistrates Act of 1968 74
federal prisoners
  educational grants 31
Federal Sentencing Guidelines 13
federalism 51
Fifth Amendment 270, 275, 280
First Amendment 165
  rights 121
force
  justification of 225
  use of 225
forced labor 3
Fourteenth Amendment 217
Fourth Amendment 189, 194, 196
friedensgeld 2

G

general deterrence 8, 35
general jurisdiction 54
geographic organization of courts 52
good faith immunity 268
good-time guidelines 12
grand jury 79–80
Great Writ 28
grievance procedures 18

H

habeas actions 29
habeas corpus 241
Hammurabic Code 3
hands-off period 26
hung jury 84

I

ideology 5
  classifications of 5–6
immunity
  absolute 268
  qualified 268
  types of 267
impeachment 72
incapacitation 9
indictment 79
information 80
intensive supervision probation 22
intentional torts 245

J

judges
  appellate 70
  impeachment 72
  recall 72
  selection of 71

Judicial Conduct Commission 72
judicial districts 52
Judiciary Act of 1789 56, 241
jurisdiction 52
jury
  hung 84
just deserts 7

K

Ku Klux Klan 247
Ku Klux Klan Act of 1871 247

L

legitimate institutional purposes 188
liberal ideology 5
limited jurisdiction 53

M

Magna Carta 241
mandamus 243
mandatory supervision 21
mark of slavery 3
Middle Ages 4-5
misdemeanants 14
misdemeanors 14
Missouri Plan 71
Model Penal Code 15
mutilation 3

N

negligence 245
negotiated pleas 91
nolo contendere 89
nolo contendere plea 15
non-aggressor 273
noncontact visits 125
nullification 84

O

obscenity 165
opening statement 83
outlaws 3

P

parole 21
parole guidelines 12
pat-down searches 187
penal servitude 3
personal retaliation 3
plea bargaining 89
pleas
  types of 81-88
pornography 166
presentence report (PSI) 12
pretrial confinement facilities 28
pretrial detainees 129
pretrial diversion 16
Prison Litigation Reform Act 30
Prison Litigation Reform Act of 1996 230
prison terms
  mandatory 12
prisoners
  right to privacy 130
  right to visitation 131
Prisoners' Labor Union 122
privacy
  expectation of 186
privileged communication 68
proportionality 272
prosecutor 59
public defender 64
punishment 1, 10
punitive damages 245

Q

qualified immunity 268

R

radical ideology 6
recidivism 8
rehabilitation 9
release on recognizance 77
release order 30
request for proposals 66
retained counsel 68
retaliation 2
retribution 6
revenge 6
rights period 26
riot 228
rules of conduct 20

S

searches
  cross-gender 188
  pat-down 187
  strip 188
  visitor 190
selective incapacitation 9
self-defense 272
  deadly force 272
sentencing guidelines 12
Sixth Amendment 74
sovereign immunity 267
specialization
  of courts 52
specific deterrence 8
statute of limitations 271–272
strip searches 188
Sumerian Code 3
supreme courts 55

T

The Inquisition 4
third-party custody 77
tort 27, 244
traditional bail system 77
trial courts 53
trial judge 69
trials by ordeal 4

U

U.S. attorney 59, 62
U.S. Sentencing Reform Act of 1984 13
U.S. Supreme Court 56
  creation of 56

V

values 5
vendettas 2
verdict
  guilty 84
victim 57–58
Violent Crime Control and Law Enforcement Act of 1994 10
voir dire 82

W

wergeld 2
whipping 3, 5
writ of certiorari 57
writs of habeas corpus 28

Made in the USA
Monee, IL
06 January 2021